Lecture Notes in Computer Science   11145

Commenced Publication in 1973
Founding and Former Series Editors:
Gerhard Goos, Juris Hartmanis, and Jan van Leeuwen

More information about this series at http://www.springer.com/series/7407

David Doty · Hendrik Dietz (Eds.)

DNA Computing and Molecular Programming

24th International Conference, DNA 24
Jinan, China, October 8–12, 2018
Proceedings

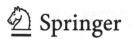

Editors
David Doty 🆔
University of California
Davis, CA
USA

Hendrik Dietz
Technical University Munich
Garching
Germany

ISSN 0302-9743   ISSN 1611-3349   (electronic)
Lecture Notes in Computer Science
ISBN 978-3-030-00029-5   ISBN 978-3-030-00030-1   (eBook)
https://doi.org/10.1007/978-3-030-00030-1

Library of Congress Control Number: 2018952644

LNCS Sublibrary: SL1 – Theoretical Computer Science and General Issues

This Springer imprint is published by the registered company Springer Nature Switzerland AG
The registered company address is: Gewerbestrasse 11, 6330 Cham, Switzerland

Preface

This volume contains the papers presented at DNA 24: the 24th International Conference on DNA Computing and Molecular Programming. The conference was held at Shandong Normal University in Jinan, China during October 8–12, 2018, and was organized under the auspices of the International Society for Nanoscale Science, Computation, and Engineering (ISNSCE). The DNA conference series aims to draw together researchers from the fields of mathematics, computer science, physics, chemistry, biology, and nanotechnology to address the analysis, design, and synthesis of information-based molecular systems.

Papers and presentations were sought in all areas that relate to biomolecular computing, including, but not restricted to: algorithms and models for computation on biomolecular systems; computational processes in vitro and in vivo; molecular switches, gates, devices, and circuits; molecular folding and self-assembly of nanostructures; analysis and theoretical models of laboratory techniques; molecular motors and molecular robotics; information storage; studies of fault-tolerance and error correction; software tools for analysis, simulation, and design; synthetic biology and in vitro evolution; and applications in engineering, physics, chemistry, biology, and medicine.

Authors who wished to orally present their work were asked to select one of two submission tracks: Track A (full paper) or Track B (one-page abstract with supplementary document). Track B is primarily for authors submitting experimental results who plan to submit to a journal rather than publish in the conference proceedings. We received 25 submissions for oral presentations: 14 submissions to Track A and 11 submissions to Track B. Each submission was reviewed by at least four reviewers, with an average of five reviewers per paper. The Program Committee accepted 12 papers for Track A and 8 papers for Track B.

This volume contains the papers accepted for Track A, as well as an obituary authored by Natasha Jonoska, Gheorghe Păun, and Grzegorz Rozenberg, in tribute to Tom Head, one of the founders of the field of DNA Computing, who sadly passed away last year.

We express our sincere appreciation to our invited speakers, Ho-Lin Chen, Chunhai Fan, Laura Na Lui, Arvind Murugan, William Shih, and Ricard Sole, and invited tutorial speakers, Dongsheng Liu, Chris Thachuk, and Diming Wei. We especially thank all of the authors who contributed papers to these proceedings, and who presented papers and posters during the conference. Last but not least, the editors thank the members of the Program Committee and the additional invited reviewers for their hard work in reviewing the papers and providing constructive comments to authors.

October 2018

David Doty
Hendrik Dietz

Organization

Steering Committee

Anne Condon (Chair)	University of British Columbia, Canada
Luca Cardelli	Microsoft Research, Cambridge, UK
Masami Hagiya	University of Tokyo, Japan
Natasha Jonoska	University of South Florida, USA
Lila Kari	University of Western Ontario, Canada
Satoshi Kobayashi	University of Electro-Communication, Chofu, Japan
Chengde Mao	Purdue University, USA
Satoshi Murata	Tohoku University, Japan
John Reif	Duke University, USA
Grzegorz Rozenberg	University of Leiden, The Netherlands
Nadrian Seeman	New York University, USA
Friedrich Simmel	Technical University of Munich, Germany
Andrew Turberfield	Oxford University, UK
Hao Yan	Arizona State University, USA
Erik Winfree	California Institute of Technology, USA

Program Committee for DNA 24

David Doty (Co-chair)	University of California, Davis, USA
Hendrik Dietz (Co-chair)	Technical University of Munich, Germany
Ebbe Andersen	Aarhus University, Denmark
Robert Brijder	Hasselt University, Belgium
Yuan-Jyue Chen	Microsoft Research, Redmond, USA
Anne Condon	University of British Columbia, Canada
Mingjie Dai	Wyss Institute at Harvard, USA
Andre Estevez-Torres	CNRS, France
Elisa Franco	University of California, Riverside, USA
Deborah Fygenson	University of California, Santa Barbara, USA
Anthony Genot	CNRS, France
Manoj Gopalkrishnan	Electrical Engineering, Indian Institute of Technology, Bombay, India
Rizal Hariadi	Arizona State University, USA
Natasha Jonoska	University of South Florida, USA
Ralf Jungmann	Max Planck Institute of Biochemistry, Germany
Ibuki Kawamata	Tohoku University, Japan
Yonggang Ke	Georgia Institute of Technology, USA
Matthew Lakin	University of New Mexico, USA
Chenxiang Lin	Yale University, USA

Yan Liu	Arizona State University, USA
Olgica Milenkovic	University of Illinois, Urbana-Champaign, USA
Satoshi Murata	Tohoku University, Japan
Pekka Orponen	Aalto University, Finland
Tom Ouldridge	Imperial College London, UK
Matthew Patitz	University of Arkansas, Fayetteville, USA
Lulu Qian	California Institute of Technology, USA
John Reif	Duke University, USA
Andrea Richa	Arizona State University, USA
Yannick Rondolez	CNRS, France
Joseph Schaeffer	Autodesk Research, USA
Rebecca Schulman	Johns Hopkins University, USA
Robert Schweller	University of Texas, Rio Grande Valley, USA
William Shih	Wyss Institute at Harvard, USA
David Soloveichik	University of Texas, Austin, USA
Darko Stefanovic	University of New Mexico, USA
Chris Thachuk	California Institute of Technology, USA
Andrew Turberfield	University of Oxford, UK
Bryan Wei	Tsinghua University, China
Shelley Wickham	University of Sydney, Australia
Erik Winfree	California Institute of Technology, USA
Andrew Winslow	University of Texas, Rio Grande Valley, USA
Damien Woods	Inria, France
Bernard Yurke	Boise State University, USA

Additional Reviewers

Kasra Tabatabaei	Ryan Gabrys
Grigory Tikhomirov	Reinhard Heckel
Farzad Farnoud Hassanzadeh	Dina Zielinski

Local Organizing Committee for DNA 24

Bo Tang (Chair)	Shandong Normal University, China
Dongsheng Liu (Co-chair)	Tsinghua University, China
Chunhai Fan (Co-chair)	Shanghai Institute of Applied Physics, Chinese Academy of Sciences, China
Peiyong Duan	Shandong Normal University, China
Qian Li	Shanghai Institute of Applied Physics, Chinese Academy of Sciences, China
Lihua Wang	Shanghai Institute of Applied Physics, Chinese Academy of Sciences, China
Shu Wang	Institute of Chemistry, Chinese Academy of Sciences, China

Chunyang Zhang   Shandong Normal University, China
Wenxin Zhang   Shandong Normal University, China

Committee Affairs Group for DNA 24 at Shandong Normal University

Zhenzhen Chen   Jinkai Liu
Guanwei Cui   Yu Ma
Wen Gao   Jinshan Wang
Xiaonan Gao   Huaxiang Zhang
Lu Li   Wei Zhang
Na Li   Lianyong Zhou
Ping Li

Sponsors

Shandong Normal University, China
2018 Taishan Academic Forum, China
National Science Foundation of China
National Science Foundation, USA

Transdisciplinarity, Creativity, Elegance
(Obituary for Tom Head)

Natasha Jonoska[1], Gheorghe Păun[2], and Grzegorz Rozenberg[3]

[1] Department of Mathematics, University of South Florida,
4202 e. Fowler Av. CMC345, Tampa, FL, USA
[2] Romanian Academy, Calea Victoriei 125, Bucharest, Romania
[3] Leiden University, LIACS, Niels Bohrweg 1, 2333 CA Leiden,
The Netherlands

Thomas J. Head, known by friends and collaborators as Tom, passed away on November 10, 2017, at the age of 83 (he was born in Tonkawa, Oklahoma, on January 6, 1934). His undergraduate and graduate studies were in pure mathematics, at University of Oklahoma and University of Kansas. He received a PhD in 1962, at the University of Kansas, and held professorships at Iowa State University, University of Alaska, and Binghamton University. Tom was a professor at Binghamton University from 1988 until retirement – and remained professor emeritus of this university until his last days.

Tom's initial area of scientific interest was algebra focused on abelian groups and modules, with the first published paper being "Dense submodules", *Proc. Amer. Math. Soc.*, 13 (1962), 197–199. In 1974 he published a book on algebra, *Modules. A Primer of Structure Theorems*, Brooks/Cole, 1974 whose extended second edition *Modules and the Structure of Rings* was published by Marcel Dekker Inc, New York, NY in 1991.

Around the middle of 1970s he expanded his interest to theoretical computer science, with the first papers written in cooperation with M. Blattner. Two of them were published in 1977 ("Single valued a-transducers" and "Automata that recognize intersections of free monoids").

This was also the time when people started to recognize the informational character of biomolecules, in particular DNA, which prompted speculations about the usefulness of DNA and other (bio)molecules in performing computation (M. Conrad, R. Feynman, Ch. Bennet, etc.). More generally, it was hypothesized that mathematical linguistics, in particular, formal language theory, could be applied in the study of DNA structure and biochemistry. It is worth mentioning here a paper published in 1974 by "the patriarch of the Romanian theoretical computer science", Solomon Marcus (1925–2016), a close friend of Tom Head, with the title "Linguistics structures and generative devices in molecular genetics".

These developments did not escape Tom's curiosity and by the end of the seventies he was studying Lindenmayer systems (L systems), bio-inspired generative devices which model the development of multicellular structures. Although Tom published a series of papers in the L systems area, his history making paper came in 1987: "Formal language theory and DNA: an analysis of the generative capacity of specific recombinant behaviors", published in *Bulletin of Mathematical Biology*, 49 (1987), 737–759.

In this paper, Tom Head introduced what he called *the splicing operation*, a cut-and-paste operation with strings modeling the recombination of DNA molecules under the influence of restriction enzymes. Soon, this operation was used as the basic ingredient of *splicing systems*, language generating devices, referred to as *H systems*, with "H" standing for "Head" in honor of Tom. The bibliography of H systems is impressive, with hundreds of papers written by researchers from all over the world.

Thus, 1987 can be considered as the beginning of DNA computing, at least at the theoretical level. In 1994, when L. Adleman reported in *Science* the first lab experiment of computing with DNA ("Molecular computation of solutions to combinatorial problems"), Tom became enthusiastic about the possibility of using biomolecules for computing and got very interested in, and dedicated to, experimental research in molecular computing. He designed several innovative experimental protocols of what he used to call *aqueous computations*, at the same time attracting his students as well as students in other institutions to this fascinating and promising research field. This is an important point to mention: Tom Head was a dedicated mentor, careful as a father, and always very proud of all of his seven PhD students with a visible love–E. Rutter, J. Delaney, J. Harrison, N. Jonoska, A. Weinberger, E. Goode, J. Loftus.

For his achievements, in 2002 Tom received "The Tulip Award" (now renamed "The Rozenberg Tulip Award") an annual award recognizing a DNA Computing Scientist of the Year awarded by the International Society of Science Computing and Engineering. In 2004 the scientific community recognized his work with the volume *Aspects of Molecular Computing. Essays Dedicated to Tom Head on the Occasion of His 70th Birthday* (LNCS 2950, Springer-Verlag, Berlin, 2004, edited by the authors of this obituary).

Tom was a deeply intellectual person with a broad spectrum of interests extending far beyond science, e.g., arts, philosophy, world religions, "end-of-the-century" culture of Vienna, and music. Music was very important to Tom and he was fascinated by Gustav Mahler. He wrote to one of us (about nine months before he passed away): "I feel like shouting to the World: *You must keep identified with Mahler after I'm gone! Don't forget!*".

On the Binghamton University website, Tom Head had humbly listed for his scientific interests algebra, computing with biomolecules, and also *formal representations of communication*. Still this list is way shorter than it should be. Tom's scientific interests were broad, which naturally led him to creation of original bridges between seemingly unrelated areas. Several of his recent publications deal with "computing with light". Tom's most recent paper listed by the DBLP (http://dblp.uni-trier.de/pers/hd/h/Head:Tom) has a rather instructive title: "Computing with light: toward parallel Boolean algebra", *Int. J. Found. Comput. Sci.* 22(7) (2011), 1625–1637. Back to algebra, through computing by light, after many years of molecular computing and L systems–the paper is a testimony of the transdisciplinarity of Tom's journey in science, as we mentioned in the title. We point out yet another intriguing title, significant for Tom's wide and deeply original preoccupations: "Does light direct life toward cosmic awareness?"; it was published in *Fundamenta Informaticae*, 64 (1–4) (2005), 185–189, in a volume edited in honor of S. Marcus.

Two great scientists, Tom Head and Solomon Marcus, meet now in "the world of light", while their ideas remain with us, to be continued, to be developed...

Contents

CRN++: Molecular Programming Language

Marko Vasic$^{(\boxtimes)}$, David Soloveichik, and Sarfraz Khurshid

The University of Texas at Austin, Austin, USA
{vasic,david.soloveichik,khurshid}@utexas.edu

Abstract. Synthetic biology is a rapidly emerging research area, with expected wide-ranging impact in biology, nanofabrication, and medicine. A key technical challenge lies in embedding computation in molecular contexts where electronic micro-controllers cannot be inserted. This necessitates effective representation of computation using molecular components. While previous work established the Turing-completeness of chemical reactions, defining representations that are faithful, efficient, and practical remains challenging. This paper introduces CRN++, a new language for programming deterministic (mass-action) chemical kinetics to perform computation. We present its syntax and semantics, and build a compiler translating CRN++ programs into chemical reactions, thereby laying the foundation of a comprehensive framework for molecular programming. Our language addresses the key challenge of embedding familiar imperative constructs into a set of chemical reactions happening simultaneously and manipulating real-valued concentrations. Although some deviation from ideal output value cannot be avoided, we develop methods to minimize the error, and implement error analysis tools. We demonstrate the feasibility of using CRN++ on a suite of well-known algorithms for discrete and real-valued computation. CRN++ can be easily extended to support new commands or chemical reaction implementations, and thus provides a foundation for developing more robust and practical molecular programs.

1 Introduction

A highly desired goal of synthetic biology is realizing a programmable chemical controller that can operate in molecular contexts incompatible with traditional electronics. In the same way that programming electronic computers is more convenient at a higher level of abstraction than that of individual flip-flops and logic circuits, we similarly expect molecular computation to admit specification via programming languages sufficiently abstracted from the hardware. This paper focuses on developing a compiler for a natural imperative programming language to a deterministic (mass-action) chemical reaction network implementing the desired algorithm. We do not directly make assumptions on how the resulting reactions would be implemented in chemistry. This could in principle be achieved by DNA strand displacement cascades [15], or other programmable chemical technologies such as the PEN toolbox [3].

© Springer Nature Switzerland AG 2018
D. Doty and H. Dietz (Eds.): DNA 2018, LNCS 11145, pp. 1–18, 2018.
https://doi.org/10.1007/978-3-030-00030-1_1

Deterministic (mass-action) chemical kinetics is Turing universal [9], thus in principle allowing the implementation of arbitrary programs in chemistry. Turing universality was demonstrated by showing that arbitrary computation can be embedded in a class of polynomial ODEs [4], and then implementing these polynomial ODEs with mass-action chemical kinetics. While these results establish a sound theoretical foundation and show the power of chemistry for handling computation tasks in general, translating and performing specific computational tasks can lead to infeasibly large and complex sets of chemical reactions.

In this work we develop a programming paradigm for chemistry, based on the familiar imperative programming languages, with the aim of making molecular programming more intuitive, and efficient. Most commonly used programming languages such as C, Java and Python, are imperative in that they use statements that change a program's state, with typical branching constructs such as if/else, loops, etc. Note that although CRNs are sometimes talked about as a programming language [7], they are difficult to program directly (it is even unfair to equate them with assembly language). In contrast, *CRN++* operates at a much higher level.

A mapping of imperative program logic to chemical reactions manipulating continuous concentrations poses various challenges that we must address. All reactions happen concurrently, making it difficult to represent sequential computation where, for example, the result of one operation is first computed and then used in another operation. Similarly, all branches of the program execution (i.e., if / else) are followed simultaneously to some degree.

We introduce the syntax and semantics of *CRN++*, which is, to our knowledge, the first imperative programming language which compiles to deterministic (mass-action) chemical reaction networks. *CRN++* has an extensible toolset including error analysis, as well as simulation framework [8]. We thus provide an automatic environment for simulating experiments based on *CRN++* programs.

A user specifies a *sequence* of statements, termed commands, to execute. Assignment, comparison, loops, conditional execution, and arithmetic operations are supported. The generated reactions are logically grouped into modules performing the corresponding command. Each module transforms initial species concentrations to their steady-state values which are the output of the module. We ensure that such modules are composable by preserving the input concentrations at the steady-state. Note that in mass-action chemistry all species occur with non-zero concentrations, and thus all reactions happen in parallel to some extent. To mimic sequential execution, we ensure that the reaction corresponding to the current command happens quickly, while other reactions are slow. For this we rely on a chemical oscillator in which the *clock* species oscillate between low and high concentrations, and sequential execution is achieved by catalyzing reactions with different clock species. To achieve conditional execution, we further need to ensure that the reactions corresponding to the correct execution branch readily occur, while those corresponding to other branches are inhibited. Our *cmp* module sets *flag* species to reflect the result of comparison, and these species catalyze the correct branch reactions.

Sequential execution as well as conditional branching leads to errors. Error is present because instructions (reactions) that should not execute, still do (at a smaller rate, of course). Moreover, the set of basic modules, such as addition, converge to the correct value only in the limit, thus computing approximately in finite time. To mitigate the error, we choose the set of modules to exhibit exponential (fast) convergence, and we provide a toolkit for error analysis and detection. Our tool quantifies the error, which can help a user identify the source of error, and guide the design of more accurate CRN++ programs.

We demonstrate the expressiveness of our language by implementing and simulating common discrete algorithms such as greatest common divisor, integer division, finding integer square root, as well as real-valued (analog) algorithms such as computing Euler's number and computing π, shown in the full version of this paper. We implement the CRN++ compiler to reactions in Mathematica, and use the CRNSimulator package [8] to manipulate and simulate chemical reactions. CRN++ is an extensible programming language allowing for easy addition of new modules; we release the open-source version [1] of the tool to enable others make use of it, and extend it further.

2 Examples

In this section we discuss the characteristics of chemical reaction networks (CRNs) through examples. First, the overall idea of computation in CRNs is presented, followed by example programs in CRN++. The focus is to give a high level idea of our technique, while later sections discuss internal details.

Although historically the focus of the study of CRNs was on understanding the behavior of naturally occurring biological reaction networks, recent advancements in DNA synthesis coupled with general methods for realizing arbitrary CRNs with DNA strand displacement cascades [15] opened the path to engineering with chemical reactions. In this work we are not interested in a way to engineer the molecules implementing a reaction but focus on reaction behavior and dynamics. We abstract away molecule implementation information and denote molecular species with letters (e.g. A).

Molecular systems exhibit complex behaviors governed by chemical reactions. To give a formal notation of chemical reaction networks, consider the CRN 1:

CRN 1 Example chemical reaction network

$$A + B \xrightarrow{1} A + B + C \tag{1}$$

$$C \xrightarrow{1} \emptyset \tag{2}$$

The CRN 1 consists of two reactions. A chemical reaction is defined with *reactants* (left side), *products* (right side), and *rate constant* which quantifies the rate at which reactants interact to produce products. To illustrate this, reaction 1 is composed of $reactants = \{A, B\}$, $products = \{A, B, C\}$, and rate constant

$k = 1$. Since most reactions in CRN++ have the rate constant equal to 1, from now on we drop the rate constant when writing reactions, unless it is different than 1. Note that multiple molecules of same species can be in a list of reactants (analogously for products); to support this we use the multiset notation. As an example, to describe reaction: $A + A \rightarrow B$ we write $reactants = \{A^2\}$, where the upper index (2) represents multiplicity (number of occurrences).

It may seem that a molecule of C is produced out of nothing in reaction 1, since the multiset of reactants is a submultiset of the products. This represents a level of abstraction where $fuel$ species that drive the reaction are abstracted away (i.e., the first reaction corresponds to $F + A + B \rightarrow A + B + C$). Making this assumption allows us to focus on the computationally relevant species. The choice to use general (non-mass/energy preserving) CRNs is an established convention for DNA strand displacement cascades [15].

When the molecular counts of all species are large, and the solution is "well-mixed", the dynamics of the system can be described by ordinary differential equations (mass-action kinetics). Molecular concentrations are quantified by a system of ODEs, where concentration of each species is characterized by an ODE:

$$\frac{d[S]}{dt} = \sum_{\forall rxn \in CRN} k(rxn) \cdot netChange(S, rxn) \cdot \prod_{\forall R \in reactants(rxn)} [R]^{m_{rxn}(R)}(t)$$

This ODE characterizes concentration of species S ($[S]$), in a given CRN. The right side is a sum over reactions in the CRN, where $k(rxn)$ is a rate of reaction rxn, and $netChange(S, rxn)$ is a net change of molecules of S upon triggering of rxn (can be negative). Concentration of a reactant R in time is written $[R](t)$, while $m_{rxn}(R)$ is the multiplicity of reactant R in reaction rxn. To illustrate the general formula, the set of ODEs characterizing CRN 1 is:

$$\frac{d[A]}{dt} = 0, \frac{d[B]}{dt} = 0, \frac{d[C]}{dt} = [A](t) \cdot [B](t) - [C](t)$$

The $[A]$ and $[B]$ are constant (derivatives zero); thus $\frac{d[C]}{dt} = [A](0) \cdot [B](0) - [C](t)$. From this equality follows that $[C](t)$ is increasing when smaller than $[A](0) \cdot [B](0)$, decreasing in the opposite case, and does not change when $[C](t) = [A](0) \cdot [B](0)$. Thus this system has a global stable steady-state $[C] = [A](0) \cdot [B](0)$. We say that this module computes multiplication, due to the relation between initial concentrations and concentrations at the steady state.

We simulate and plot the dynamics of the multiplication CRN, as shown in Fig. 1. Initial

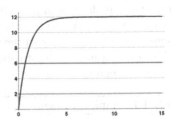

Fig. 1. Multiplication CRN. $[A]$ shown in orange, $[B]$ in green, and $[C]$ in red. (Color figure online)

concentrations of A and B are 6 and 2, respectively, while the concentration of C approaches value 12. Note that the exact value defined by the steady state ($[C](t) = 12$) is reached only at the limit of time going to infinity. Since the computation has to be done in finite time, the presence of error is unavoidable. This error raises challenging issues with programming in chemistry, and necessitates techniques for controlling it. One crucial property that determines the error is the convergence speed of the module. The multiplication command in CRN++ is implemented through the above module, following the design principles of *convergence speed* and *composability* described in Sect. 3. Chemical reactions are abstracted away from a user who can simply write $mul[a, b, c]$ to multiply.

CRN++ is an imperative language, and as such supports sequential execution. Note that even a simple operation of multiplying and storing into the same variable, e.g. $A := A * B$, requires support for sequential execution. We use operator ":=" to relate input and output concentrations; $A := A * B$ denotes that $[A](t)$ converges to $[A](0) * [B](0)$. The above implementation of the *mul* module necessarily assumes that the output species is different from the input species. Otherwise, $mul[a, b, a]$ goes to infinity or 0 depending on the value of B. To implement $A := A * B$, we split the computation into two sequential steps: (1) $C := A * B$, (2) $A := C$. To multiply we use the *mul* module described above. For the assignment we use the load module (*ld*). To ensure the assignment executes after the multiplication, we catalyze the two modules with the clock species that reach their high values in different phases of the oscillator. Importantly, the chemical oscillator and clock species are abstracted away from a user, who simply uses the *step* construct to order reactions: $step[\{mul[a,b,c]\}]$, $step[\{ld[c,a]\}]$.

One of the basic blocks of programming languages are conditional branches, executing upon success of a precondition. Similarly to implementing sequential operations, we implement conditional execution by activating (through catalysis) some reactions and deactivating others, depending on a result of condition. Since no species can be driven to 0 in finite time[1], all branches of condition will be active to some extent, which makes this an interesting source of errors without direct analogy in digital electronics. In contrast to sequential computation catalyzed by clock species, conditional blocks are catalyzed by *flag* species. The flag species have high and low values that reflect the result of the comparison. Our *cmp* module sets the flag species to reflect the result of the comparison. In the following example we demonstrate the usage of *cmp* module and conditional execution.

```
1: procedure GCD(a, b)
2:     while a ≠ b do
3:         if a > b then
4:             a ← a − b
5:         else
6:             b ← b − a
7:         end if
8:     end while
9:     return a
10: end procedure
```

Fig. 2. Euclid's algorithm for computing GCD.

---

[1] Although certain pathological CRNs can drive concentrations to infinity in finite time (e.g., $2A \rightarrow 3A$), and thereby drive certain other species to 0 in finite time (e.g., with an additional $B + A \rightarrow A$), these cases cannot be implemented with any reasonable chemistry.

To demonstrate the expressiveness of our language we showcase the implementation of Euclid's algorithm (Fig. 2) to compute the greatest common divisor (GCD) of a two numbers. The GCD is computed by subtracting the smaller of the values from the larger one until they become equal.

Figure 3a shows the implementation of Euclid's algorithm in *CRN++*. Lines 2–3 define the initial concentrations of species a, b; $a0$ and $b0$ represent the values for which GCD is computed. To order the execution, the *step* construct is used. Multiple instructions that do not conflict with each other can be part of the same step and they are executed in parallel. In the first step a and b are stored into temporary variables and compared, setting the flag species to reflect the result of the comparison. The second step uses the result of the previous comparison, and effectively stores $a - b$ into a if $a > b$, and vice versa. Since the same species cannot be used as both input and output to *sub* module, temporary variables are used (*atmp* and *btmp*). Steps repeatedly execute due to the oscillatory behavior of the clock species, thus implementing looping behavior by default; the steps can be viewed as being inside of the 'forever' loop. *CRN++*, in addition to the language and compiler to chemical reactions, is connected to the simulation backend that enables convenient testing for correctness. We show simulation of the GCD program in Fig. 3b where GCD(32,12) is computed. Steps repeatedly trigger causing a and b to converge to the correct result after a couple iterations.

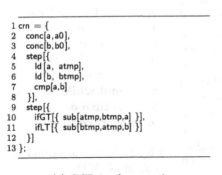

```
1 crn = {
2   conc[a,a0],
3   conc[b,b0],
4   step[{
5     ld [a, atmp],
6     ld [b, btmp],
7     cmp[a,b]
8   }],
9   step[{
10    ifGT[{ sub[atmp,btmp,a] }],
11    ifLT[{ sub[btmp,atmp,b] }]
12  }]
13 };
```

(a) GCD implementation

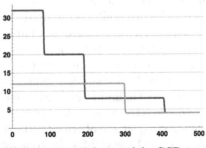

(b) Dynamic simulation of the GCD program for $a0 = 32$, $b0 = 12$. Concentrations of a (green), and b (orange) are shown in function of time.

Fig. 3. Implementation of Euclid's algorithm for computing GCD in *CRN++* (left), simulation results of the implementation (right).

In addition, we implement a set of algorithms in (a) discrete space—counter, integer division, integer square root, as well as in (b) continuous space, by implementing *CRN++* programs that approximate value of *Euler's* constant and π. These examples are shown in the full version of this paper.

3 Technique

This section explains *CRN++*, both the underlying constructs used to build it, as well as high level primitives that represent the language itself. We start by presenting high-level modules that are at the core of *CRN++* (Sect. 3.1), followed by explanation of how the sequential behavior is achieved (Sect. 3.2), after which we give an overview of *CRN++* grammar (Sect. 3.3), and finally we discuss the error detection and analysis tools we provide (Sect. 3.4).

3.1 Modules

Modules represent the core of *CRN++*, and in their form are somewhat analogous to the instruction set architecture (ISA) in machine languages. Modules implement basic operations such as load, add, subtract, multiply, compare. We provide the exhaustive list of modules in Table 1 in Appendix A. Importantly, *CRN++* is extensible, and supports easy addition of new modules.

There are multiple ways of computing addition and other operations in chemistry. As mentioned in the previous section, our implementation choice is led by two basic principles: (a) convergence speed, (b) composability.

3.1.1 Convergence Speed Consider CRN implementing addition:

CRN 2 Addition CRN (inputs preserved). Inputs: A and B, output: C.

$$A \longrightarrow A + C$$
$$B \longrightarrow B + C$$
$$C \longrightarrow \emptyset$$

By solving the system of ODEs that characterize the concentration of C we get the following equation: $[C](t) = [A] + [B] + ([C](0) - [A] - [B]) \cdot e^{-t}$.

$[C](t)$ is concentration of species C at time t; accordingly $[C](0)$ is initial concentration. Since $[A](t)$ and $[B](t)$ are constant we simply write $[A]$ and $[B]$. From the equation above it follows that $[C]$ converges to the value $[A] + [B]$, and thus we say the CRN performs addition. To consider the convergence speed we look at the non-constant part of the equation. Due to the factor e^{-t} the decrease of the non-constant part is exponential, thus we say that the CRN exhibits *exponential* convergence speed. The convergence speed is of great importance, since it directly affects computation error; the sooner reaction converges the sooner it approaches the correct value.

3.1.2 Composability There are alternative ways to implement addition and have exponential convergence speed:

CRN 3 Addition CRN (destructs inputs). Inputs: A and B, output: C.

$$A \longrightarrow C$$
$$B \longrightarrow C$$

For easier discussion, let us call the initial addition module $CRN Add_1$ (CRN 2), and the one above $CRN Add_2$ (CRN 3). To compute $E := (A * B) + D$ we combine the *mul* module (CRN 1), computing $C := A * B$, with an addition module, computing $E := C + D$. If $CRN Add_1$ is used, multiplication converges to the correct value, after which $CRN Add_1$ has correct values at its inputs and converges to the correct value of E. Before the multiplication converges and C becomes equal to $A * B$, reactions of $CRN Add_1$ trigger, but since the module is input-preserving they do not affect steady state of the multiplication module. However, $CRN Add_2$ consumes its inputs, and the composition will give an incorrect result. The *mul* CRN constantly drives C to value $A * B$, and will keep refilling inputs to the $CRN Add_2$, causing the wrong result. This is the reason $CRN Add_1$ is preferred over $CRN Add_2$. Moreover, the composed CRN of the *mul* module and $CRN Add_1$ exhibits the exponential convergence speed, and has a unique stable steady state, the formal proof can be found in work by Buisman et al. [5].

We have set up the two main design criteria (convergence speed and composability) for the modules, and we next describe the core modules of *CRN++*.

3.1.3 *Ld* Module Loads the value from source (first argument) into a destination (second argument). The CRN used for load operation is following:

CRN 4 Load CRN

$$A \longrightarrow A + B$$
$$B \longrightarrow \emptyset$$

A is the input and B is the output species. This module, similar to *add*, has exponential convergence speed [5]. In addition, the concentration of input species is constant, thus ensuring composability.

3.1.4 *Add* Module Adds two values (first and second argument) and stores the result into destination (third argument). The Add CRN is shown in CRN 2; its convergence speed and composability are already discussed.

3.1.5   *Sub* Module Subtracts the second input value from the first and stores into the destination (third argument).

CRN 5 Subtraction CRN

$$A \longrightarrow A + C$$
$$B \longrightarrow B + H$$
$$C \longrightarrow \emptyset$$
$$C + H \longrightarrow \emptyset$$

The above CRN was generated via evolutionary algorithms [5]; by analyzing its system of ODEs, the network computes subtraction. Input species A and B are not affected and the property of composability is satisfied. Neither we nor Buisman et al. found the analytical solution; however, our simulation results show that the module converges exponentially quickly unless $A = B$ (see the Alternative Design subsection of the *cmp* module below for an analogous, easy to analyze case). In a case inputs, A and B, are close to each other the computation error is higher. The error evaluation tools (Sect. 3.4) help in detecting and analyzing problematic cases (e.g., where A and B are close), thus enabling a user to redesign the CRN. In our examples, A and B usually differ by at least 1. Runtime assertions in the simulation package that automatically notify a user about these kind of problems would help identify the source of the error. Note that many algorithms can be refactored to reduce the error (see Sect. 5).

3.1.6   *Mul* Module Multiplies inputs (first and second argument) and stores into destination (third argument). The multiplication CRN is shown in Sect. 2. This CRN does not affect inputs and has exponential convergence speed [5].

We have presented modules for performing arithmetic operations (*ld*, *add*, *sub*, *mul*). These modules are implemented within a single *step*. Multiple modules can be executed in parallel within a single *step* as long as there is no cyclic dependence between species: for example *mul*[a,b,c] and *add*[c,d,a] forms a cycle, the output of the *mul* is input to the *add*, and vice versa. Also, the CRN implementation imposes the restriction that same species cannot be used as both input and output to the same module. We now introduce the *cmp* module providing for conditional execution, which is executed in two *steps*.

3.1.7   *Cmp* Module Compares the two values, and produces signals (flag species) informing which value is greater or if they are equal.

Alternative Designs. Before explaining our implementation of comparison we discuss alternative implementations, and point out design decisions that lead to the current implementation. One of more obvious ways to implement comparison is using the reaction: $A + B \to \emptyset$.

If initially $[A] > [B]$, than at the equilibrium all molecules of B interact with A leaving only A; case $[B] > [A]$ is analogous. The proposed reaction can be used for conditional execution, by using A and B catalytically in reactions that should execute when $[A] > [B]$ and $[B] > [A]$, respectively. The comparison reaction should execute before conditional execution is plausible, thus the comparison is done in a step before the conditionally executed reactions.

The comparison module proposed above does not preserve inputs, and thus it is not composable. This imposes the restriction that in the step in which comparison is used no other module uses the compared values. Our *cmp* module does not have this restriction.

We analyze the ODE describing this CRN to evaluate the convergence speed. Since the amount of B decreases with the same speed as A, we can express $[B](t) = [A](t) + D_0$, where $D_0 = [B](0) - [A](0)$. The following holds:

$$\frac{d[A]}{dt} = -[A](t) * ([A](t) + D_0) \implies [A](t) = \frac{[A](0)D_0}{-[A](0) + [A](0)e^{D_0 t} + D_0 e^{D_0 t}}$$

If $D_0 > 0$ ($[B](0) > [A](0)$) terms with exponential factors tend to infinity, and $[A]$ to zero. Conversely, when $D_0 < 0$, exponential factors converge to zero, and $[A]$ to $-D_0$. A converges exponentially, unless A and B are equal at the beginning ($D_0 = 0$); then the dynamics of A is described with: $[A](t) = \frac{[A](0)}{1+[A](0)t}$.

In conclusion, the module converges fast (exponential speed) when operands are different, while the module converges slow (linear speed) when operands are equal (or close to each other). The linear convergence speed is yet another problem that lead to sub-optimal performance of this module. Recall that the comparison module drives the flag species which then catalyze branches that should execute, thus having a chained effect. It is of great importance to have a reliable comparison module.

Lastly, to detect equality with the above proposed module, absence of a species needs to be detected, since both values are driven to zero in a case of equality. Detecting the absence of species in chemistry is itself non-trivial and error-prone. There are several approaches based on so-called *absence indicators*. Generally speaking, the absence indicator for A is produced at a constant rate and gets degraded by A. The absence indicator has to be produced slowly, or else it will be present in non-negligible concentration even if A is present. The absence indicators in the literature rely on a difference between rate constants of several orders of magnitude. The relatively slow dynamics of the production of the absence indicator lead to a fair amount of error affecting the computation, and necessitate slowing down the clock (i.e., the whole computation) to work properly.

Our Design. The *cmp* module is implemented using two sequentially executed sets of reactions, which trigger in consecutive clock phases. In the first phase, the inputs (X and Y) are mapped to flag species $XGTY$ and $XLTY$. Values are mapped to the range $[0–1]$, by setting the initial concentrations of $XGTY$ and $XLTY$ to 0.5. If, for example, $[X] = 80$ and $[Y] = 20$, signal species $XGTY$ and $XLTY$ converge to 0.8 and 0.2, respectively. The mapping is done in order to preserve original values of the inputs, since the next phase of comparison consumes the compared values (flags), thus mapping allows the inputs to be used freely in other instructions. The mapping CRN is shown in CRN 6, and exhibits exponential convergence speed according to our analysis.

CRN 6 CRN for mapping compared values

$$XGTY + Y \longrightarrow XLTY + Y$$
$$XLTY + X \longrightarrow XGTY + X$$

The goal of the second phase of comparison is to detect which value is greater. We use a chemical *Approximate Majority* (AM) algorithm [6] to detect if $XGTY$ or $XLTY$ is in the majority. All molecules of the less populous species convert to the more populous species. AM reactions are:

CRN 7 Approximate Majority CRN

$$XGTY + XLTY \longrightarrow XLTY + B$$
$$B + XLTY \longrightarrow XLTY + XLTY$$
$$XLTY + XGTY \longrightarrow XGTY + B$$
$$B + XGTY \longrightarrow XGTY + XGTY$$

The majority algorithm causes convergence of $XGTY$ to 1 and $XLTY$ to 0 when $X > Y$, and vice versa. The species $XGTY$ are used as a catalysts in reactions that execute when $X > Y$, and the species $XLTY$ for the opposite case. The AM network has been studied in the stochastic context (stochastic CRNs) and is known to converge quickly, even when inputs are close [2].

Equality Checking. Due to the always present error in chemical computation, checking for equality is actually approximate-equality checking. Consider having a chemical program with real values, then if the values are close to each other it is impossible to tell if they are actually equal but affected with error, or they represent different real valued signals. Due to this issue, while comparing for equality is impossible, we compare for ϵ-range equality, where ϵ can be arbitrarily small. For discrete algorithms we use equality checking with $\epsilon = 0.5$, allowing easy comparison of the integer values (e.g., values in range $(2.5, 3.5)$ are considered to be equal to 2). To support equality checking we compare $x + \epsilon$ with y (generating signals $XGTY$ and $XLTY$), and at the same time compare $y + \epsilon$ with x (generating signals $YGTX$ and $YLTX$). Combining the signals of the two comparisons gives the desired result: If $X = Y$, signal $XGTY$ is high ($XLTY$ low) and $YGTX$ is high ($YLTX$ low) due to the added offset. To execute a reaction upon equality both $XGTY$ and $YGTX$ are used catalytically. If $X > Y$, signal $XGTY$ is high ($XLTY$ low) and $YLTX$ is high ($YGTX$ low), so both $XGTY$ and $YLTX$ should be used catalytically. Symmetrically for $X < Y$, both $XLTY$ and $YGTX$ are used catalytically. Note that unlike in the previously proposed comparison module, this module does not use absence checks and absence indicators, and as such is more reliable in time-constrained environment. After calling cmp in a step, programmer can use $ifGT$, $ifGE$, $ifEQ$, $ifLT$, $ifLE$ in subsequent steps to conditionally execute reactions. Note that the flags are active until the next call to the cmp module.

3.2 Sequential Execution

CRN++ allows programming in a sequential manner, despite the intrinsically parallel nature of CRNs. To model sequential execution in CRNs there is a need to isolate two reactions from co-occurring, and control the order in which they happen. The key construct we rely on to achieve these goals is a chemical oscillator.

A chemical oscillator is a CRN in which the concentrations of species oscillate between low and high values. The oscillatory CRN [12] we use is described with a following set of reactions:

CRN 8 Oscillator CRN

$$i = 1, ..., n - 1 : X_i + X_{i+1} \longrightarrow 2X_{i+1}$$
$$X_n + X_1 \longrightarrow 2X_1$$

Concentrations of the clock species (X_i) oscillate (see Fig. 4). Different clock species have different oscillation phase and reach minimum and maximum at different times. To control the rate at which a reaction fires, clock species are added as both reactant and product (catalyst), in that way preventing reactions from co-occuring and ordering them (see CRN 9). While overlap between the clock species exists, it is small and thus enables sequential execution. To ensure the small overlap, in CRN++ we use every third clock species, i.e. X_3, X_6, X_9, etc., to catalyze the reactions that execute at different time moments.

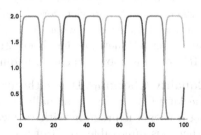

Fig. 4. Chemical oscillator containing 3 species: X_1 (red), X_2 (green), and X_3 (blue). (Color figure online)

CRN 9 Ordering reactions: original reactions (left), ordered (right).

$A \longrightarrow B$	$A + X_3 \longrightarrow B + X_3$
$B \longrightarrow C$	$B + X_6 \longrightarrow C + X_6$

The chemical oscillator is abstracted from a *CRN++* user, who can order reactions using the *step* construct. Reactions in different steps are isolated from each other through clock species acting catalytically.

Non-conflicting instructions can be part of the same step. Splitting instructions across multiple steps is needed in a case of (a) conditional execution—comparison needs to be done before conditional execution is possible; (b) reading and writing to a same species—this is not possible within the step (as discussed earlier), and requires temporal ordering. The number of clock species used is determined by the number of **step** instructions. Each step requires three clock species, with the exception of steps in which *cmp* module is used, for which six clock species are used. The oscillatory behavior of the clock species causes steps to get repeated eventually, causing the loop-like behavior.

3.3   Grammar

Listing 1.1 is an overview of the *CRN++* grammar. At its root the CRN contains a list of *RootS*s, where *RootS* can be either *ConcS* – defines initial concentration of species, *RxnS* – defines a reaction, *ArithmeticS* – performs arithmetic operation, and *StepS* – orders execution. Furthermore, *StepS* is divided into a list of *NestedS*s, where each *NestedS* is either *RxnS*, *ArithmeticS*, *CmpS* – performs comparison, or *ConditionalS*. *ConditionalS* conditionally executes a block based on the result of a previous comparison. Note that the comparison should be done in a step prior to the conditional execution. Based on the result of the comparison, if the first operand is *greater than, greater or equal, equal, less or equal, less than* the second operand, conditional block *ifGT, ifGE, ifEQ, ifLT, ifLE* is executed.

The grammar can be easily extended; e.g., new arithmetic modules can be added to the list of *ArithmeticS* nonterminals. Also, the *CRN++* grammar allows for easy addition of *ifAbsent* conditional statements that can be used to implement the asynchronous programs, in that way enabling comparison between the asynchronous and synchronous programming paradigms.

3.4   Error Evaluation

Programming chemistry is inherently error-prone. We identify three specific sources of error in *CRN++*. First, CRNs converge asymptotically—only in the limit is the correct value reached—thus leaving certain amount of error in a finite time. Second, we cannot completely turn off modules which are not supposed to be currently executing, whether they belong to another sequential step, or to another branch of execution. In addition, comparison has to take into account possible error in the compared values.

Our design decisions were based on minimizing the error; however since error cannot be avoided altogether, we provide a toolkit that helps in error analysis and guiding the CRN (program) design. Using the tool, users can, for any species of interest, track the difference between the correct value, and the (simulated) value in chemistry. For example, if operation $add[a,b,c]$ is executed in a step, than $c = a + b$ is expected in the following step. $CRN\text{++}$ allows measuring the difference between the expected $c = a+b$, and actual simulation value. This helps users analyze the error, and detect if the error builds up over time.

We analyze the value of operand a from GCD example Fig. 3, and plot the error in Fig. 5. In Fig. 5, the x-axis represents time, while the y-axis shows the difference between expected and actual value of a. Note that the error is sufficiently small that the algorithm executes correctly throughout the analyzed time. The error is not constant, which opens interesting questions of correlating the error with instructions in the program. To correlate error with program instructions we examine the GCD simulation (Fig. 3b). By looking at the time axis, it is easy to connect the first two spikes of the error with the subtraction of a.

We provide the error evaluation framework with the vision of it being a guiding element for programming in $CRN\text{++}$. We found this technique particularly useful for validation of programs, analyzing the error, understanding the sources of error, and redesigning the CRN for correctness.

```
⟨Crn⟩ ::= 'crn={' ⟨RootSList⟩ '}'

⟨RootSList⟩ ::= ⟨RootS⟩
  | ⟨RootS⟩ ',' ⟨RootSList⟩

⟨RootS⟩ ::= ⟨ConcS⟩
  | ⟨RxnS⟩
  | ⟨ArithmeticS⟩
  | ⟨StepS⟩

⟨ConcS⟩ ::= 'conc['⟨species⟩', '⟨number⟩']'

⟨RxnS⟩ ::=
    'rxn['⟨Expr⟩','⟨Expr⟩','⟨number⟩']'

⟨ArithmeticS⟩ ::=
    'ld ['⟨species⟩','⟨species⟩]
  | 'add ['⟨species⟩','⟨species⟩','⟨species⟩]
  | 'sub ['⟨species⟩','⟨species⟩','⟨species⟩]
  | 'mul ['⟨species⟩','⟨species⟩','⟨species⟩]

⟨CmpS⟩ ::= 'cmp ['⟨species⟩','⟨species⟩]

⟨StepS⟩ ::= 'step[' NestedSList']'

⟨NestedSList⟩ ::= ⟨NestedS⟩
  | ⟨NestedS⟩ ',' ⟨NestedSList⟩

⟨NestedS⟩ ::= ⟨RxnS⟩
  | ⟨ArithmeticS⟩
  | ⟨CmpS⟩
  | ⟨ConditionalS⟩

⟨ConditionalS⟩ ::= 'ifGT['⟨NestedSList⟩']'
  | 'ifGE['⟨NestedSList⟩']'
  | 'ifEQ['⟨NestedSList⟩']'
  | 'ifLT['⟨NestedSList⟩']'
  | 'ifLE['⟨NestedSList⟩']'

⟨Expr⟩ ::= ⟨species⟩ { '+' ⟨species⟩ }
```

Listing 1.1: $CRN\text{++}$ Grammar

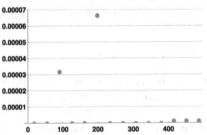

Fig. 5. Error evaluation of species a from GCD program.

4   Related Work

Computational Power of Chemical Reaction Networks. Previous research demonstrated techniques of achieving complex behaviors in chemistry, such as: computing algebraic functions [5], polynomials [14], implementing logic gates [13]. Moreover, the Turing completeness of chemistry has been proven, using the strategy of implementing polynomial ODEs (which have been previously shown to be Turing universal) in mass-action chemical kinetics [9]. Even though Turing complete, this translation to chemistry can result in infeasibly complex chemical reaction networks, which motivates other, more direct methods.

Modular Reactions. Adding even a single reaction to a CRN can completely change its dynamics, which makes the design process challenging. The idea of 'composable' reactions seeks a set of reactions that can be composed in a well-defined manner to implement more complex behaviors. Buisman et al. [5] compute algebraic expressions by designing the core modules that implement basic arithmetic operations, which can be further composed to achieve more complex tasks. Our goal is to make modular designs, and we follow some of the proposed design principles for achieving the goal, such as input-preserving CRNs.

Synchronous Computation. Previous work utilized synchronous logic to achieve complex tasks. Soloveichik et al. implement state machines in chemistry by relying on clock species [15]. We use the same technique, where we add clock species acting catalytically to order reactions. Jiang et al. [11], also relying on clock species, design a model of memory in chemistry to support sequential computation, demonstrating their technique on examples of a binary counter and a fast Fourier transform (FFT). Previous work shows the promise of programming synchronous logic in reactions, which we advance by providing an explicit programming language and framework for designing and testing wide-range of programs. Maybe we should criticize previous work. Extend the paragraph by adding more comparison.

Asynchronous Computation. Recall, an absence indicator is a species that is present in high concentration when a target species is present in low concentration. Absence indicators can be used to drive a reaction when a particular reaction has finished, providing a method for executing modules in desired order. Huang et al. [10] use absence indicators to implement algorithms such as integer division and GCD. Their method requires two reaction rates, 'fast' and 'slow', where the fast rate needs to be orders (2–3) of magnitude larger to ensure the proper function of the system. Since, in practice, biochemical systems allow for a restricted range of reaction rates, requiring a large spectrum of rates slows down the computation when the computation speed is dictated by the slow rates. In contrast, we allow all reactions to take the same (or comparable) rate constants. While the goal of our work is not to compare asynchronous and synchronous computation, we mention insights and intuition of their differences, which we gained through empirical studies. First, absence indicators are not robust, and typically require fine tuning to get the system right. Second, error detection is easier with synchronous logic. Since all operations follow the clock signal, there is a direct mapping from a time moment to a command that is executing, which provides a way to check correctness of a system at any point of time. Finally, we provide a framework for implementing molecular programs which is easily extensible, and can be used to compare synchronous and asynchronous logic.

We include support for absence indicators through the *ifAbsent* construct, thus allowing easy comparison of the two paradigms.

5   Discussion and Conclusions

There are multiple ways in which we can further improve *CRN++*. Note that currently every high-level module is mapped to exactly one CRN implementing the operation. Letting the tool decide which implementation to use in different contexts could boost the performance. For example, the described modules have a useful property of preserving inputs, but that property might not be needed in every case. If the input preserving property is redundant, *CRN++* could choose to use the more optimized version (for example the more compact subtraction CRN discussed above). Also, we could provide a more flexible programming experience by (a) letting the compiler automatically schedule instructions to different steps (instead of the explicit `step` construct); (b) allowing the same species as both input and output of a module and automatically generate the additional instructions.

We plan to further explore the support for nested loops in *CRN++*. Currently nested loops can be mimicked through conditional execution: the loop condition is computed through comparison and the main loop conditionally executes the instructions of the desired loop. Besides explicit support for nested loops, future work will support nested conditionals by adding multiple flag species for multiple comparisons.

An important direction for future research concerns reducing the error in our construction, and understanding how it builds up over time. We noticed that different algorithms, even computing the same function, accumulate varying levels of error. For example, as shown in the full version of this paper, the error of the Sub module increases with the magnitude of the operands, and also increases the closer they are. However, we also found an alternative way to subtract, that keeps the error constant and independent of the operands (see the full version of this paper) at the cost of a slower run-time.

Our error analysis shows that for most examples we tried, but not all, error builds up over the course of the computation. For *CRN++* programs where the error builds up in this way, there is some maximum input complexity beyond which the error overwhelms the output. Can all *CRN++* programs be refactored (preferably automatically) to bound the cumulative error of every module such that it does not build up over time? Note that if this were possible, we would obtain another, more efficient, way to achieve Turing universality.

To the best of our knowledge we are the first to provide an imperative programming language which compiles to chemical reaction networks. Moreover, we build tools that can help users get a better understanding of CRNs and improve their design. Although absolutely correct computation is not achieved, we provide tools that help understand why error occurs, and thus help improve the design of CRNs. We release our toolkit as open-source, to encourage new research and improvement of the *CRN++*, with the hope of advancing the engineering of information processing molecular systems.

Acknowledgment. We thank the fellow students of EE 381V (Programming With Molecules) at The University of Texas at Austin for constructive discussions on the material presented in this paper. We also thank Keenan Breik, Cameron Chalk, Milos Gligoric, Aleksandar Milicevic, Boya Wang and Kaiyuan Wang for their feedback on this work. This research was partially supported by the US National Science Foundation under Grants Nos. CCF-1618895, CCF-1718903, CCF-1652824, and CCF-1704790.

A Modules

Table 1. *CRN++* Modules. The first column denotes the type of the module. The restrictions column imposes compile-time restrictions for using modules, here $\not\equiv$ is used to mean different species (not values). The output column shows the value of outputs at the steady state. Finally, the CRN column shows chemical reactions implementing the module.

Type	Restrictions	Output (Steady State)	CRN
ld[A,B]	$B \not\equiv A$	$B := A$	$A \longrightarrow A + B$ $B \longrightarrow \emptyset$
add[A,B,C]	$C \not\equiv A \wedge C \not\equiv B$	$C := A + B$	$A \longrightarrow A + C$ $B \longrightarrow B + C$ $C \longrightarrow \emptyset$
sub[A,B,C]	$C \not\equiv A \wedge C \not\equiv B$	$C := \begin{cases} A - B, & A > B \\ 0, & \text{otherwise} \end{cases}$	$A \longrightarrow A + C$ $B \longrightarrow B + H$ $C \longrightarrow \emptyset$ $C + H \longrightarrow \emptyset$
mul[A,B,C]	$C \not\equiv A \wedge C \not\equiv B$	$C := A \cdot B$	$A + B \longrightarrow A + B + C$ $C \longrightarrow \emptyset$
div[A,B,C]	$C \not\equiv A \wedge C \not\equiv B$	$C := A/B$	$A \longrightarrow A + C$ $B + C \longrightarrow B$
$sqrt$[A,B]	$B \not\equiv A$	$B := \sqrt{A}$	$A \xrightarrow{1} A + B$ $B + B \xrightarrow{\frac{1}{2}} \emptyset$
am[A,B]	$A \not\equiv B$	$A := \begin{cases} A + B, & A > B \\ 0, & B > A \end{cases}$ $B := \begin{cases} 0, & A > B \\ A + B, & B > A \end{cases}$	$A + B \longrightarrow A + T$ $B + A \longrightarrow B + T$ $T + A \longrightarrow A + A$ $T + B \longrightarrow B + B$
cmp[A,B]	$A \not\equiv B$	Sets flag species	* Two CRNs (mapping and AM) triggering in two consecutive phases (as discussed in the Technique)

References

1. *CRN* + + Github page. https://github.com/marko-vasic/crnPlusPlus
2. Angluin, D., Aspnes, J., Eisenstat, D.: A simple population protocol for fast robust approximate majority. Distrib. Comput. **21**(2), 87–102 (2008)
3. Baccouche, A., Montagne, K., Padirac, A., Fujii, T., Rondelez, Y.: Dynamic DNA-toolbox reaction circuits: a walkthrough. Methods **67**(2), 234–249 (2014)
4. Bournez, O., Graça, D.S., Pouly, A.: Polynomial time corresponds to solutions of polynomial ordinary differential equations of polynomial length. J. ACM **64**(6), 38 (2017)
5. Buisman, H.J., ten Eikelder, H.M.M., Hilbers, P.A.J., Liekens, A.M.L.: Computing algebraic functions with biochemical reaction networks. Artif. Life 5–19 (2009)
6. Cardelli, L., Csikász-Nagy, A.: The cell cycle switch computes approximate majority. Sci. Rep. **2**, 656 (2012)
7. Chen, Y.J., et al.: Programmable chemical controllers made from DNA. Nat. Nanotechnol. **8**(10), 755 (2013)
8. CRNSimulator Mathematica package. http://users.ece.utexas.edu/~soloveichik/crnsimulator.html
9. Fages, F., Le Guludec, G., Bournez, O., Pouly, A.: Strong turing completeness of continuous chemical reaction networks and compilation of mixed analog-digital programs. In: Feret, J., Koeppl, H. (eds.) CMSB 2017. LNCS, vol. 10545, pp. 108–127. Springer, Cham (2017). https://doi.org/10.1007/978-3-319-67471-1_7
10. Huang, D.A., Jiang, J.H.R., Huang, R.Y., Cheng, C.Y.: Compiling program control flows into biochemical reactions. In: Proceedings of the International Conference on Computer-Aided Design, pp. 361–368 (2012)
11. Jiang, H., Riedel, M., Parhi, K.: Synchronous sequential computation with molecular reactions. In: 2011 48th ACM/EDAC/IEEE Design Automation Conference (DAC), pp. 836–841 (2011)
12. Lachmann, M., Sella, G.: The computationally complete ant colony: global coordination in a system with no hierarchy. In: Morán, F., Moreno, A., Merelo, J.J., Chacón, P. (eds.) ECAL 1995. LNCS, vol. 929, pp. 784–800. Springer, Heidelberg (1995). https://doi.org/10.1007/3-540-59496-5_343
13. Magnasco, M.O.: Chemical kinetics is Turing universal. Phys. Rev. Lett. **78**(6), 1190 (1997)
14. Salehi, S.A., Parhi, K.K., Riedel, M.D.: Chemical reaction networks for computing polynomials. ACS Synth. Biol. **6**(1), 76–83 (2017)
15. Soloveichik, D., Seelig, G., Winfree, E.: DNA as a universal substrate for chemical kinetics. Proc. Natl. Acad. Sci. **107**(12), 5393–5398 (2010)

Know When to Fold 'Em: Self-assembly of Shapes by Folding in Oritatami

Erik D. Demaine[1], Jacob Hendricks[2], Meagan Olsen[3], Matthew J. Patitz[3],
Trent A. Rogers[3], Nicolas Schabanel[4(✉)], Shinnosuke Seki[5],
and Hadley Thomas[6]

[1] CSAIL, Massachusetts Institute of Technology, Cambridge, USA
edemaine@mit.edu
[2] Department of Computer Science and Information Systems,
University of Wisconsin - River Falls, River Falls, WI, USA
jacob.hendricks@uwrf.edu
[3] Department of Computer Science and Computer Engineering,
University of Arkansas, Fayetteville, AR, USA
{mo015,patitz,tar003}@uark.edu
[4] CNRS, École Normale Supérieure de Lyon (LIP, UMR 5668) & IXXI, U. Lyon,
Lyon, France
http://perso.ens-lyon.fr/nicolas.schabanel
[5] University of Electro-Communications, Tokyo, Japan
s.seki@uec.ac.jp
[6] Colorado School of Mines, Golden, CO, USA
hadleythomas88@gmail.com

Abstract. An oritatami system (OS) is a theoretical model of self-assembly via co-transcriptional folding. It consists of a growing chain of beads which can form bonds with each other as they are transcribed. During the transcription process, the δ most recently produced beads dynamically fold so as to maximize the number of bonds formed, self-assemblying into a shape incrementally. The parameter δ is called the *delay* and is related to the transcription rate in nature.

This article initiates the study of shape self-assembly using oritatami. A shape is a connected set of points in the triangular lattice. We first show that oritatami systems differ fundamentally from tile-assembly systems by exhibiting a family of infinite shapes that can be tile-assembled but cannot be folded by any OS. As it is NP-hard in general to determine whether there is an OS that folds into (self-assembles) a given finite shape, we explore the folding of upscaled versions of finite shapes. We show that any shape can be folded from a constant size seed, at any scale $n \geqslant 3$, by an OS with delay 1. We also show that any shape can be folded at the smaller scale 2 by an OS with *unbounded* delay. This

M. J. Patitz and T. A. Rogers—Supported in part by NSF Grant CCF-1422152 and CAREER-1553166.

N. Schabanel—Supported by Moprexprogmol CNRS MI grant.

S. Seki—Supported in part by JST Program to Disseminate Tenure Tracking System, MEXT, Japan, No. 6F36, JSPS Grant-in-Aid for Young Scientists (A) No. 16H05854, and JSPS Bilateral Program No. YB29004.

© Springer Nature Switzerland AG 2018
D. Doty and H. Dietz (Eds.): DNA 2018, LNCS 11145, pp. 19–36, 2018.
https://doi.org/10.1007/978-3-030-00030-1_2

leads us to investigate the influence of delay and to prove that, for all $\delta > 2$, there are shapes that can be folded (at scale 1) with delay δ but not with delay $\delta' < \delta$.

These results serve as a foundation for the study of shape-building in this new model of self-assembly, and have the potential to provide better understanding of cotranscriptional folding in biology, as well as improved abilities of experimentalists to design artificial systems that self-assemble via this complex dynamical process.

1   Introduction

Transcription is the process in which an RNA polymerase enzyme (colored in orange in Fig. 1) synthesizes the temporal copy (blue) of a gene (gray spiral) out of ribonucleotides of four types A, C, G, and U. The copied sequence is called the *transcript*.

Fig. 1. (Left) RNA Origami [12]. (Right) An abstraction of the resulting RNA tile in the oritatami system, where a dot • represents a sequence of 3–4 nucleotides, and the solid arrow and dashed lines represent its transcript and interactions based on hydrogen bonds between nucleotides, respectively. (Color figure online)

The transcript starts folding upon itself into intricate tertiary structures immediately after it emerges from the RNA polymerase. Figure 1 (Left) illustrates *cotranscriptional folding* of a transcript into a rectangular RNA tile structure while being synthesized out of an artificial gene engineered by Geary, Rothemund, and Andersen [12]. The RNA tile is provided with a kissing loop (KL) structure, which yields a 120° bend, at its four corners, and sets of six copies of it self-assemble into hexagons and further into a hexagonal lattice. *Structure* is almost synonymous to *function* for RNA complexes since they are highly correlated, as exemplified by various natural and artificial RNAs [7]. Cotranscriptional folding plays significant roles in determining the structure (and hence function) of RNAs. To give a few examples, introns along a transcript cotranscriptionally fold into a loop recognizable by spliceosome and get excised [18], and riboswitches make a decision on gene expression by folding cotranscriptionally into one of two mutually exclusive structures: an intrinsic terminator hairpin and a pseudoknot, as a function of specific ligand concentration [24].

What is folded is affected by various environmental factors including transcription rate. Polymerases have their own transcription rate: e.g., bacteriophage 3 ms/nucleotide (nt) and eukaryote 200 ms/nt [15] (less energy would be dissipated at slower transcription [9]). Changing the natural transcription rate, by adjusting, e.g., NTP concentration [20], can impair cotranscriptional processes [2,16] (note that polymerase pausing can also facilitate efficient folding [25] but it is rather a matter of gene design). Given a target structure, it is hence necessary to know not only what to fold but at what rate to fold, that is, to know when to fold 'em.

The primary goal of both natural and artificial self-assembling systems is to form predictable structures, i.e. shapes grown from precisely placed components, because the form of the products is what yields their functions. Mathematical models have proven useful in developing an understanding of how shapes may self-assemble, and self-assembling finite shapes is one of the fundamental goals of theoretical modeling of systems capable of self-assembly. e.g. in tile-based self-assembly [3,4,23] as well as other models of programmable matter [6,26].

An oritatami system (abbreviated as OS) is a novel mathematical model of cotranscriptional folding, introduced by [11]. It abstracts an RNA tertiary structure as a triple of (1) a sequence of abstract molecules (of finite types) called *bead types*, (2) a directed path over a triangular lattice of *beads* (i.e. a location/bead type pair), and (3) a set of pairs of adjacent beads that are considered to interact with each other via hydrogen bonds. Such a triple is called a *configuration*. An abstraction of the RNA tile from [12] as a configuration is shown in Fig. 1 (Right). In the figure, each bead (represented as a dot) abstractly represents a sequence of 3–4 nucleotides, whose type is not stated explicitly but retrievable from the transcript's sequence of the tile (available in [12]); moreover, the interactions (or bonds) between pairs of beads are represented by dashed lines. An OS is provided with a finite alphabet B of bead types, a sequence w of beads over B called its *transcript*, and a rule V, which specifies between which types of beads interactions are allowed. The OS cotranscriptionally folds its transcript w, beginning from its initial configuration (*seed*), over the triangular lattice by stabilizing beads of w from the beginning one by one. Two parameters of OS govern the bead stabilization: *arity* and *delay*; arity models valence (maximum number of bonds per bead). Delay models the transcription rate in the sense that the system stabilizes the next bead in such a way that the sequence of the next bead and the $\delta - 1$ succeeding beads is folded so as to form as many bonds as possible.

Using this model, researchers have mainly explored the computational power of cotranscriptional folding (see [11] and the recent surveys [21,22]). In contrast, little has been done on self-assembly of shapes. Elonen in [8] informally sketched how an OS can fold a transcript whose beads are all of distinct types (hardcodable transcript) into a finite shape using a provided Hamiltonian path. Masuda et al. implemented an OS that folds its periodic transcript into a finite portion of the Heighway dragon fractal [17].

Our Results. We initiate a systematic study of shape self-assembly by oritatami systems. We start with the formal definitions of OS and shapes in Sect. 2. As it is NP-hard to decide if a given connected shape of the triangular lattice contains a Hamiltonian path [1], it is also NP-hard to decide if there is an OS that folds into (self-assembles) a given finite shape. We thus explore the folding of upscaled versions of finite shapes. We introduce three upscaling schemes $\mathscr{A}_n$, $\mathscr{B}_n$ and $\mathscr{C}_n$, where n is the scale factor (see Fig. 2). We first show that oritatami systems differ fundamentally from tile-assembly systems by exhibiting a family of infinite shapes that can be tile-assembled but cannot be folded by any OS (Theorem 2, Sect. 3). We then show that any shape can be folded at scale factor 2 by an OS with *unbounded* delay (Theorem 3, Sect. 4). In Sect. 5, we present various incremental algorithms that produce a delay-1 arity-4 OS that folds any shape from a seed of size 3, at any scale $n \geqslant 3$ (Theorems 6 and 8, Sect. 5). For this purpose, we introduce a universal set of 114 bead types suitable for folding any delay-1 tight OS (Theorem 4) that can be used in other oritatami designs. We then show that the delay impacts our ability to build shapes: we prove that there are shapes that can be folded (at scale 1) with delay δ but not with delay $\delta' < \delta$ (Theorem 9, Sect. 6). Omitted proofs may be found in [5].

These results serve as a foundation for the study of shape-building in this new model of self-assembly, and have the potential to provide better understanding of cotranscriptional folding in biology, as well as improved abilities of experimentalists to design artificial systems that self-assemble via this complex dynamical process.

Note that in [14] in the present proceedings, the authors study a slightly different problem: they show that one can design an oritatami transcript that folds an upscaled version of a *non-self-intersecting path* (instead of a shape). The initial path may come from the triangular grid or from the square grid. The scale of the resulting path is somewhere in between our scales 3 and 4 according to our definition. Note that the cells are only partially covered by their scheme. Combining their result with our Theorem 3, their algorithm provides an oritatami transcript partially covering the upscaled version of any shape at scale 6.

2   Definitions

2.1   Oritatami System

Let B be a finite set of *bead types*. A *routing* r of a bead type sequence $w \in B^* \cup B^{\mathbb{N}}$ is a directed self-avoiding path in the triangular lattice $\mathbb{T}$,[1] where for all integer i, vertex r_i of r is labelled by w_i. r_i is the *position* in $\mathbb{T}$ of the $(i+1)$th bead, of type w_i, in routing r. A *partial routing* of a sequence w is a routing of a prefix of r.

An Oritatami system $\mathcal{O} = (B, w, \mathbb{V}, \delta, \alpha)$ is composed of (1) a set of bead types B, (2) a (possibly infinite) bead type sequence w, called the *transcript*, (3) an *attraction rule*, which is a symmetric relation $\mathbb{V} \subseteq B^2$, (4) a parameter δ called the *delay*, and (5) a parameter α called the *arity*.

---

[1] The triangular lattice is defined as $\mathbb{T} = (\mathbb{Z}^2, \sim)$, where $(x, y) \sim (u, v)$ if and only if $(u, v) \in \cup_{\epsilon = \pm 1}\{(x + \epsilon, y), (x, y + \epsilon), (x + \epsilon, y + \epsilon)\}$. Every position (x, y) in $\mathbb{T}$ is mapped in the euclidean plane to $x \cdot X + y \cdot Y$ using the vector basis $X = (1, 0)$ and $Y = \text{RotateClockwise}(X, 120°) = (-\frac{1}{2}, -\frac{\sqrt{3}}{2})$.

We say that two bead types a and b *attract* each other when $a \lor b$. Given a (partial) routing r of a bead type sequence w, we say that there is a *potential (symmetric) bond* $r_i r_j$ between two adjacent positions r_i and r_j of r in $\mathbb{T}$ if $w_i \lor w_j$ and $|i - j| > 1$. A *set of bonds* H for a (partial) routing r is a subset of its potential bonds. A couple $c = (r, H)$ is called a (partial) *configuration* of w. The *arity* $\alpha_i(c)$ of position r_i in the partial configuration $c = (r, H)$ is the number of bonds in H involving r_i, i.e. $\alpha_i(c) = \#\{j : r_i r_j \in H\}|$. A (partial) configuration c is *valid* if each position r_i is involved in at most α bonds in H, i.e. if $(\forall i)\alpha_i(c) \leqslant \alpha$. We denote by $h(c) = |H|$ the number of bonds in configuration c.

For any partial valid configuration $c = (r, H)$ of some sequence w, an *elongation* of c by k beads (or k-*elongation*) is a partial valid configuration $c' = (r', H')$ of w of length $|c| + k$ where r' extends the self-avoiding path r by k positions and such that $H \subseteq H'$. We denote by $\mathcal{C}_w$ the set of all partial configurations of w (the index w will be omitted when the context is clear). We denote by $c^{\triangleright k}$ the set of all k-elongations of a partial configuration c of sequence w.

Oritatami Dynamics. The folding of an oritatami system is controlled by the delay δ and the arity α. Informally, the configuration grows from a *seed configuration*, one bead at a time. This new bead adopts the position(s) that maximise the number of valid bonds the configuration can make when elongated by δ beads in total. This dynamics is *oblivious* as it keeps no memory of the previously preferred positions; it differs thus slightly from the hasty dynamics studied in [11] but is more prevailing in the OS research [10, 13, 17, 19, 21] because it seems closer to experimental conditions such as in [12].

Formally, given an oritatami system $\mathcal{O} = (B, w, \lor, \delta, \alpha)$ and a *seed configuration* σ of the $|\sigma|$-prefix of w, we denote by $\mathcal{C}_{\sigma,w}$ the set of all partial configurations of the sequence w elongating the seed configuration σ. The considered *dynamics* $\mathscr{D} : 2^{\mathcal{C}_{\sigma,w}} \to 2^{\mathcal{C}_{\sigma,w}}$ maps every subset S of partial configurations of length ℓ, elongating σ, of the sequence w to the subset $\mathscr{D}(S)$ of partial configurations of length $\ell + 1$ of w as follows:

$$\mathscr{D}(S) = \bigcup_{c \in S} \arg\max_{\gamma \in c^{\triangleright 1}} \left(\max_{\eta \in \gamma^{\triangleright \min(\delta - 1, |w| - |\gamma|)}} h(\eta) \right)$$

We say that a (partial) configuration c *produces* a configuration c' over w, denoted $c \vdash c'$, if $c' \in \mathscr{D}(\{c\})$. We write $c \vdash^* c'$ if there is a sequence of configurations $c = c^0, \ldots, c^t = c'$, for some $t \geqslant 0$, such that $c^0 \vdash \cdots \vdash c^t$. A sequence of configurations $c = c^0 \vdash \cdots \vdash c^t = c'$ is called a *foldable sequence* over w from configuration c to configuration c'. The *foldable configurations* in t steps of $\mathcal{O}$ are the elongations of the seed configuration σ by t beads in the set $\mathscr{D}^t(\{\sigma\})$. We denote by $\mathcal{A}[\mathcal{O}] = \cup_{t \geqslant 0} \mathscr{D}^t(\{\sigma\})$ the set of all foldable configurations. A configuration $c \in \mathcal{A}[\mathcal{O}]$ is *terminal* if $\mathscr{D}(\{c\}) = \varnothing$. We denote by $\mathcal{A}_\square[\mathcal{O}]$ the set of all terminal foldable configurations of $\mathcal{O}$. A finite foldable sequence $\sigma = c^0 \vdash \cdots \vdash c^t$ *halts* at c^t after t steps if c^t is terminal; then, c^t is called the *result* of the foldable sequence. A foldable sequence may halt after $|w| - |\sigma|$ steps or earlier if the growth is geometrically obstructed (i.e., if no more elongation is possible because the configuration is trapped in a closed area). An infinite foldable sequence $\sigma = c^0 \vdash \cdots \vdash c^t \vdash \cdots$ admits a *unique limiting configuration* $c^\infty = \sqcup_t c^t$ (the superposition of all the configurations (c^t)), which is called the *result* of the foldable sequence.

We say that the oritatami system is *deterministic* if at all time t, $\mathscr{D}^t(\{\sigma\})$ is either a singleton or the empty set. In this case, we denote by c^t the configuration at time t, such that: $c^0 = \sigma$ and $\mathscr{D}^t(\{\sigma\}) = \{c^t\}$ for all $t > 0$; we say that the partial configuration c^t *folds (co-transcriptionally) into* the partial configuration c^{t+1} deterministically. In this case, at time t, the $(t+1)$-th bead of w is placed in c^{t+1} at the position that maximises the number of valid bonds that can be made in a $\min(\delta, |w| - t - |\sigma|)$-elongation of c^t. Note that when $\alpha \geqslant 4$ the arity constraint vanishes (as a vertex may bond to at most 4 neighbors, 5 if the growth is at a dead end) and then, there is only one maximum-size bond set for every routing, consisting of all its potential bonds.

2.2   Shape Folding and Scaling

The goal of this article is to study how to fold shapes. A *shape* is a connected set of points in $\mathbb{T}$. The *shape* associated to a configuration $c = (r, H)$ of an OS $\mathcal{O}$ is the set of the points $S(c) = \cup_i\{r_i\}$ covered by the routing of c. A shape S is *foldable* from a seed of size s if there is a deterministic OS $\mathcal{O}$ and a seed configuration σ with $|\sigma| = s$, whose terminal configuration has shape S.

Note that every shape admitting a Hamiltonian path is trivially foldable from a seed of size $|S|$, whose routing is a Hamiltonian path of the shape itself. The challenge is to design an OS folding into a given shape whose seed size is an *absolute* constant. One classic approach in self-assembly is then to try to fold an *upscaled* version of the shape. The goal is then to minimize the scale at which an upscaled version of every shape can be folded.

From now on, we denote by $(i, j) \in \mathbb{N}^2$ the point $i \cdot X + j \cdot Y$ of $\mathbb{T}$ in $\mathbb{R}^2$ where $X = (1, 0)$ (east) and $Y = (-\frac{1}{2}, -\frac{\sqrt{3}}{2})$ (south west) in the canonical basis.

As it turns out, there are different possible upscaling schemes for shapes in $\mathbb{T}$. A *scaling scheme* $\Lambda = (\lambda, \mu)$ of $\mathbb{T}$ is defined by a homothetic linear map λ from $\mathbb{T}$ to $\mathbb{T}$, and a shape μ containing the point $(0, 0)$, called the *cell mold*. For all $p \in \mathbb{T}$, the *cell* associated to p by Λ is the set $\Lambda(p) = \lambda(p) + \mu = \{\lambda(p) + q : q \in \mu\}$, i.e. the translation of the cell mold by $\lambda(p)$. $\lambda(p)$ is called the *center* of the cell $\Lambda(p)$. The Λ-scaling of a shape S is then the set of points $\Lambda(S) = \cup_{p \in S}\Lambda(p)$. We say that two cells $\Lambda(p)$ and $\Lambda(q)$ are neighbors, denoted by $\Lambda(p) \sim \Lambda(q)$, if they intersect or have neighboring points, i.e. if $\Lambda(p) \cap \Lambda(q) \neq \varnothing$ or there are two points $p' \in \Lambda(p)$ and $q' \in \Lambda(q)$ such that $p' \sim q'$. We require upscaling schemes to preserve the topology of S, in particular that $\Lambda(p) \sim \Lambda(q)$ iff $p \sim q$. We consider the following upscaling schemes (see Fig. 2):

Scaling $\mathscr{A}_n$: $\lambda_{\mathscr{A}_n}(i, j) = i \cdot (n - 1, 1 - n) + j \cdot (n - 1, 2n - 2)$ and $\mu_{\mathscr{A}_n} = H_n$
Scaling $\mathscr{B}_n$: $\lambda_{\mathscr{B}_n}(i, j) = i \cdot (n - 1, -n) + j \cdot (n, 2n - 1)$ and $\mu_{\mathscr{B}_n} = H_n$
Scaling $\mathscr{C}_n$: $\lambda_{\mathscr{C}_n}(i, j) = i \cdot (n, -n) + j \cdot (n, 2n)$ and $\mu_{\mathscr{C}_n} = H'_n$

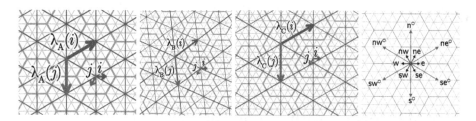

Fig. 2. The three upscaling schemes $\mathscr{A}_3$, $\mathscr{B}_3$ and $\mathscr{C}_3$ (cell boundaries are represented in orange and the upscaled triangular grid in brown); to the right: the lattice directions $\mathcal{D} = \{\mathsf{nw, ne, e, se, sw, w}\}$ in $\mathbb{T}$, and the cell directions $\mathcal{D}^\circ = \{\mathsf{nw}^\circ, \mathsf{n}^\circ, \mathsf{ne}^\circ, \mathsf{se}^\circ, \mathsf{s}^\circ, \mathsf{sw}^\circ\}$. (Color figure online)

where $H_n = \{(i, j) \in \mathbb{T} : |i| < n, |j| < n, |i - j| < n\}$ is the (filled) hexagon of radius $n - 1$ with n vertices on each side, and $H'_n = \{(i, j) \in \mathbb{T} : -n < i \leqslant n, -n < j \leqslant n, -n \leqslant i - j < n\}$ is the irregular hexagon whose sides are of alternating sizes n and $n + 1$. Note that $H_n \subset H'_n \subset H_{n+1}$. Each of these upscaling schemes have their ups and downs:

- Every cell in $\mathscr{A}_n$ is a regular hexagon. It is the most compact but, as the sides of the cells overlap, the area of $\Lambda_{\mathscr{A}_n}(S)$ scales linearly only asymptotically with the size of the original shape S. In particular empty cells are smaller than occupied cell.
- Every cell in $\mathscr{B}_n$ is a regular hexagon. It is less compact than $\mathscr{A}_n$ and twisted, but the edges of neighboring cells never overlap so the area of $\Lambda_{\mathscr{A}_n}(S)$ scales linearly with the size of the original shape S.
- $\mathscr{C}_n$ can be considered as a non-overlapping version of $\mathscr{A}_{n+1}$ where the nw°-, n°- and ne°-sides of each cell have been trimmed by 1. It is isotropic as its cells are irregular hexagons, but it is untwisted and $\Lambda_{\mathscr{C}_n}(S)$ scales linearly with the size of the original shape S. One can also see the irregular hexagons as concentric spheres growing from the center of the triangles in lattice $\mathbb{T}$.

In terms of the resulting size of $\Lambda(S)$, $\mathscr{A}_n$ is strictly more compact than $\mathscr{B}_n$ which is strictly more compact than $\mathscr{C}_n$ which is as compact as $\mathscr{A}_{n+1}$ for all $n \geqslant 2$. n is referred as the *scale* for each scheme. Our goal is to find an OS with constant seed size for each of these schemes that can fold any shape at the smallest scale n.

Before we give our algorithms, we note the importance of scaling the shape in order to self-assemble it. Figure 3(a) shows an example of a shape which cannot be self-assembled by any OS (at scale 1), as it does not contain any Hamiltonian path. In fact, [1] proves that it is NP-hard to decide if a shape in $\mathbb{T}$ has a Hamiltonian path. Note that, if we are given a Hamiltonian path, there is a (hard-coding) OS that "folds" it, by simply using this path as the seed with no transcript. The existence of an OS (with unbounded seed) self-assembling a shape is thus equivalent to the existence of an Hamiltonian path. It follows that:

Observation 1. *Given an arbitrary shape S, it is NP-hard to decide if there is an oritatami system (with unbounded seed) which self-assembles it.*

In Sect. 5, we will present three algorithms building delay-1 OS that fold into arbitrary shapes at any of the scales $\mathscr{A}_n$, $\mathscr{B}_n$, and $\mathscr{C}_n$ with $n \geqslant 3$.

3   Infinite Shapes with Finite Cut

The self-assembly of shapes in oritatami systems is fundamentally different from the self-assembly of shapes in the Tile Assembly Model due to the fact that every configuration in an OS has a routing that is a linear path of beads. To illustrate this difference, let us say an infinite shape has a *finite cut* if there is a finite subset of points K in S such that $S \smallsetminus K$ contains at least two *infinite* connected components, S_1 and S_2. As every path going between S_1 and S_2 has to pass through the cut K of finite size, after a finite number of back and forth passes it will no longer be possible and the routing will not be able to fill at least one of S_1 or S_2. Furthermore, since any scaling of S has also a finite cut, scaling cannot help here and we conclude that:

Theorem 2. *Let S be an infinite shape having a finite cut. Then for any scaling scheme Λ and any OS $\mathcal{O}$, $\Lambda(S)$ is not foldable in $\mathcal{O}$.*

4   Self-assembling Finite Shapes at Scale 2 with Linear Delay

In this section, we show how to create an oritatami system for building an arbitrary finite shape S at scales $\mathscr{A}_2$, $\mathscr{B}_2$, and $\mathscr{C}_2$, with a delay equal to $|S|$.

The theorem below proves that: every $\mathscr{A}_2$-, $\mathscr{B}_2$- and $\mathscr{C}_2$-upscaled version of a given shape S has a Hamiltonian cycle (HC); and furthermore, presents an algorithm that outputs an OS with delay $|\Lambda(S)| = O(|S|)$ that folds into this cycle from a seed of size 3. The OS relies on set of beads following the HC and custom designed to bind to all of their neighboring beads. Using a delay factor equivalent to the size of the shape, all beads after the first three of the seed are transcribed before they then all lock into their optimal placements along the HC which allows them to form the maximum number of bonds. A schematic overview of the scaling, HC, and bead path is shown in Fig. 3.

Theorem 3. *Let S be a finite shape. For each scale $s \in \{\mathscr{A}_2, \mathscr{B}_2, \mathscr{C}_2\}$, there is an OS $\mathcal{O}_S$ with delay $|\Lambda_s(S)| = O(|S|)$ and seed size 3 that self-assembles S at scale s.*

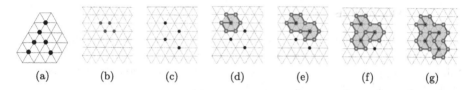

Fig. 3. (a) An example shape which cannot be self-assembled by an oritatami system without being scaled (b) Small example shape, (c) scaled to $\mathscr{A}_2$ and rotated version, (d) after addition of first gadget, (e) after second gadget, (f) after third gadget, (g) after fourth gadget and completion of HC.

5   Self-assembling Finite Shapes at Scale $\geqslant 3$ with Delay 1

All our algorithms are *incremental* and proceed by extending the foldable routing at each step, to cover a new cell, neighboring the already covered cells. They proceed by maintaining a set of *"clean edges"* in the routing, one on every *"available side"* of each cell, from which we can extend the routing. Predictably, this is getting harder and harder as the scale gets smaller and as the edges of the cells overlap. We will present our different scaling algorithms by increasing difficulty: $\mathscr{B}_n$ for $n \geqslant 3$, then $\mathscr{C}_n$ for $n \geqslant 3$, then $\mathscr{A}_n$ for $n \geqslant 5$, then $\mathscr{A}_4$ and finally our most compact scaling $\mathscr{A}_3$.

All the scaling algorithms presented in this section have been implemented in Swift on iOS.[2] All the figures in this section have been generated by this program and reflect its actual implementation.

5.1   Universal Tight Oritatami System with Delay 1

Definition 1. *We say that an OS is* tight *if (1) its delay is 1, (2) every bead makes only one bond when it is placed by the folding and there is only one location where it can make a bond at the time it is placed during the folding.*

All the OS presented in this section are tight. Tight OS can be conveniently implemented using the following result:

Theorem 4. *Every tight OS can be implemented using a universal set of* $114 = 19 \times 6$ *bead types together with a universal rule, from a seed of size 3.*

In the next subsections, all oritatami systems are tight. We will thus focus on designing routing with a single tight bond per bead, and rely on Theorem 4 for generating the transcript from the designed routing in linear time.

---

[2] Our app Scary Pacman can be freely downloaded from the app store at https://apple.co/2qP9aCX and its source code can be downloaded and compiled from the public Darcs repository at https://bit.ly/2qQjzy6.

5.2   Key Definitions

Consider a shape S and $p_1, \ldots, p_{|S|}$ a *search* of S, i.e. a sequence of distinct points covering S such that for all $i \geqslant 2$, there is a $j < i$ such that $p_i \sim p_j$. W.l.o.g., we require that the nw-neighbor of p_1 does not belong to S so that the n-neighboring cell of $\Lambda(p)$ is empty in $\Lambda(S)$.

Starting from a tight routing covering the cell $\Lambda(p_1)$, our algorithms cover each other cell $\Lambda(p_i)$ in order $i = 2 \ldots |S|$, one by one, by extending the tight routing from a previously covered cell.

Lattice and Cell Directions. We denote by $\mathcal{D} = \{\text{nw}, \text{ne}, \text{e}, \text{se}, \text{sw}, \text{w}\}$ the set of all *lattice directions* in $\mathbb{T}$, and by $\mathcal{D}^\circ = \{\text{nw}^\circ, \text{n}^\circ, \text{ne}^\circ, \text{se}^\circ, \text{s}^\circ, \text{sw}^\circ\}$ the set of all *cell directions*, joining the centers of two neighboring cells (see Fig. 2). We denote by $\bar{d}$ the direction opposite to d. We denote by $\text{cw}(d)$ and $\text{ccw}(d)$ the next direction in $\mathcal{D}$ if $d \in \mathcal{D}$ (or in $\mathcal{D}^\circ$ if $d \in \mathcal{D}^\circ$), in clockwise and counterclockwise order respectively. For $d \in \mathcal{D}$ (resp. $d \in \mathcal{D}^\circ$), we denote by $(d)^\circ$ (resp. $(d)^\triangle$) the cell direction (resp. lattice direction) next to d in counterclockwise order, e.g. $(\text{w})^\circ = \text{sw}^\circ$ and $(\text{ne}^\circ)^\triangle = \text{ne}$.

A cell $\Lambda(p)$ is *occupied* if the current routing covers it, otherwise it is *empty*. Each cell has six *sides*, its nw°-, n°-, ne°-, se°-, s°-, and sw°-sides, connecting each of its six w-, nw-, ne-, e-, se-, and sw-*corners*. Given a cell, its neighboring cell in direction $d \in \mathcal{D}^\circ$ is called its *d-neighboring cell*. At scale $\mathscr{A}_n$, the d-side of a cell is the $\bar{d}$-side of its d-neighboring cell. At scales $\mathscr{B}_n$ and $\mathscr{C}_n$, we say that the d-side of a cell and the $\bar{d}$-side of its d-neighboring cell are *neighboring sides*.

The *clockwise-most* and *second clockwise-most* edges of the d-side of a cell are the two last edges in $\mathbb{T}$ of this side in the direction $d' = \text{ccw}((d)^\triangle)$, e.g., if $d = \text{nw}^\circ$, the two sw-most edges of the nw°-side of the cell.

Routing Time. At each step of our algorithms, the routing defines a *total order over the vertices* of the currently occupied cells. For every vertex p covered by the routing, we denote by $\text{rtime}(p)$ its rank (from 0 to $|r| - 1$) in the current routing r. We say of two occupied vertices p and q, that p is *earlier* (resp. *later*) than q if $\text{rtime}(p) < \text{rtime}(q)$ (resp. $\text{rtime}(p) > \text{rtime}(q)$).

Clean Edge. The d-side of an occupied cell $\Lambda(p_i)$ is *available* if its d-neighboring cell is empty. Consider an edge uv of $\mathbb{T}$ which belongs to an available d-side of an occupied cell $\Lambda(a)$. Let $\Lambda(b)$ be the empty d-neighboring cell of $\Lambda(a)$. We say that edge uv is *clean* if: (1) it belongs to the current routing; (2) uv's orientation d' in the routing is clockwise with respect to the center $\lambda(b)$ of $\Lambda(b)$, i.e. $d' = \text{ccw}((d)^\triangle)$ (e.g., $d' = \text{e}$ if $d = \text{s}^\circ$); and (3) the $\bar{d}'$- and $\text{cw}(\bar{d}')$-neighbors p and q of its origin u are both occupied and earlier than u (e.g., the w- and nw-neighbors of u if $d = \text{s}^\circ$). p and q are resp. called the *support* and the *bouncer* of the clean edge uv. Figure 4 gives examples of clean edges for the different scaling schemes. Clean edges are a key component for our algorithms because they are the edges from which the routing is extended to cover a new empty cell. Indeed it is easy to grow a tight path from a clean edge as shown in Fig. 4.

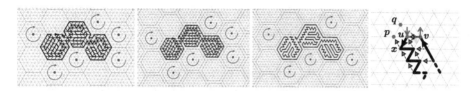

Fig. 4. Left: Examples of clean edges at scales $\mathscr{A}_5$, $\mathscr{B}_5$ and $\mathscr{C}_5$ – the current routing is displayed in black; some clean edges are highlighted in red together with the two vertices required to be occupied, and earlier than the origin of the edge; the centers of some empty cells are highlighted in blue together with their clockwise orientation. Right: Extending the routing from a clean edge – the extension, drawn in black together with its tight bonds, replaces the clean edge $u \rightarrow v$ of the current routing r (in red); because p and q are occupied and earlier than u in r, the first bead of the extension is deterministically placed at x by the folding and the zigzag pattern grows southeastwards, self-supportedly; the way back to v folds by bonding to the initial zigzag; note that all bonds are tight. (Color figure online)

Self-supported Extension. We say that a path ρ extending a routing from a clean edge uv with support p is *self-supported* if all its bond are tight and made only with the beads at u, p or within ρ. Self-supported extensions are convenient because they fold correctly independently on their surrounding.

5.3   Design of Self-supported Tight Paths Covering Pseudo-hexagons

A (a, b, c, d, e, f)-*pseudohexagon* is an hexagonal shape whose sides have length a, b, c, d, e and f respectively from the ne$^\circ$- to the n$^\circ$-side in clockwise order, i.e. is the convex shape in $\mathbb{T}$ encompassed in a path consisting in a steps to se, b to sw, c to w, d to nw, e to ne and f to e.

Theorem 5. *Let H be a (a, b, c, d, e, f)-pseudohexagon with $a, b, c, d, e, f \geqslant 5$. There is an algorithm* COVERPSEUDOHEXAGON *that outputs in linear time a self-supported tight routing covering H from a clean edge placed on either of the two eastmost edges above its n$^\circ$-side, and such that it ends with a counterclockwise tour covering the nw$^\circ$-, sw$^\circ$-, s$^\circ$-, se$^\circ$- and finally ne$^\circ$-sides.*

By Theorem 4, we conclude that all large enough pseudo-hexagons can be self-supportedly folded by a tight OS.

5.4   Scale $\mathscr{B}_n$ and $\mathscr{C}_n$ with $n \geqslant 3$

Cells in scaling $\mathscr{B}_n$ and $\mathscr{C}_n$ do not overlap. It is then enough to find one routing extension for the cell (with a clean edge on all of its all available side) from every possible neighboring clean edge.

Scale $\mathscr{B}_n$ is isotropic. Thus, there are only two cases to consider up to rotations: either the cell is the first, or it will plug onto a neighboring clean edge. For $\mathscr{B}_n$,

the clean edges that we plug onto, are the *counterclockwise-most* of each side of
an neighboring occupied cell. For $n \geqslant 7$, we rely on Theorem 5 to construct such
a routing. The two routings for $n = 3$ are given in Fig. 5. We have then:

Lemma 1. *At every step, the computed routing is self-supported and tight, covers all the cells inserted, and contains a clean edge on every available side with
the exception of the n°-side of the initial cell $\Lambda(p_1)$.*

Proof. This is immediate by induction on the size of the cell insertion sequence
by noticing that all the routing extensions are self-supported and tight and that
every available side (but the n°-side of the root cell) bears a clean edge.   □

Note that no insertion will occur on the n°-neighboring cell of $\Lambda(p_1)$ because
it is assumed w.l.o.g. to be empty. Theorem 4 thus applies and outputs, in linear
time, a corresponding OS with 114 bead types and a seed of size 3. The same
technique applies at scale $\mathscr{C}_n$ with $n \geqslant 3$ (omitted, see [5]). It follows that:

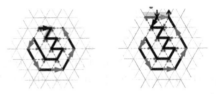

Fig. 5. *The self-supported tight routing extensions for scale $\mathscr{B}_3$:* in light purple, the
clean edge used to extend the routing in this cell; in red, the ready-to-use new clean
edges in every direction; highlighted in orange, the seed. (Color figure online)

Theorem 6. *Any shape S can be folded by a tight OS at all scales $\mathscr{B}_n$ and $\mathscr{C}_n$
with $n \geqslant 3$.*

5.5   Scale $\mathscr{A}_n$ with $n \geqslant 4$

Scale $\mathscr{A}_n$ is the most compact considered in this article. It is isotropic but its
cells do overlap. For this reason, we need to provide more extension in order to
manage all the cases. The cases $n \geqslant 5$ are the easiest because we can provide
a routing for each situation with a clean edge on every available side. Scale $\mathscr{A}_4$
is trickier because only one available side (the latest) may contain a clean edge.
Scale $\mathscr{A}_3$ requires a careful management of time and geometry in the routing
to ensure that a clean edge can be exposed when needed. Scale $\mathscr{A}_3$ is presented
separately in the next subsection. Scale $\mathscr{A}_4$ is omitted, see [5].

At scale $\mathscr{A}_n$ with $n \geqslant 5$, the clean edges are located at the *second
counterclockwise-most* edge on all of the available sides of every occupied cell
(e.g., see leftmost figure on Fig. 4). Our design guarantees this property for every
possible empty cell shape. As every occupied cell covers the d-side of all its $\bar{d}$-
neighboring empty cells, there are a priori $33 = 1 + 2^5$ different shapes to consider:

the completely empty cell, for the first cell inserted; plus the 2^5 possible shapes corresponding to the five possible states occupied/empty for the neighboring cells on which we do not plug. For $\mathscr{A}_n$ with $n \geqslant 5$, our design can extend the routing from any clean edge, regardless of its time or location. This reduces the number of shapes to consider to 14 cases, by rotating the configuration. The following definition allows to identify conveniently the various cases.

Segment and Signature. The *signature rooted on* $d \in \mathcal{D}^\circ$ of an empty cell $\Lambda(p)$ is the integer (written in binary) $\mathsf{sig}_d(p) = \sum_{i=0}^{5} s_i 2^i$ where $s_i = 1$ if the $\mathsf{cw}^i(d)$-neighboring cell of $\Lambda(p)$ is occupied, and $= 0$ otherwise. $\mathsf{sig}_d(p) = 0$ if and only if all the neighboring cells of $\Lambda(p)$ are empty; $\mathsf{sig}_d(p)$ is odd if and only if the d-neighboring cell of $\Lambda(p)$ is occupied. A *segment* of an empty cell $\Lambda(p)$ is a maximal sequence of consecutive sides already covered by its neighboring cells. *We will always root the signature of an empty cell on the clockwise-most side of a segment.* With this convention, the two least significant bits of the signature of an empty cell with at least one and at most 5 neighboring occupied cells is always 01. By rotating the patterns, we are then left with designing self-supported tight routings for 14 shapes with clean edges at the second clockwise position of every available side. For $n \geqslant 8$, the 14 pseudo-hexagons are large enough for Theorem 5 to provide the desired routings. The routing extensions for $n = 5, \ldots, 8$ may be found in [5]. Scale $\mathscr{A}_4$ is handled similarly (omitted, see [5]). We can thus conclude by an immediate induction on the size of the cell insertion sequence, as for scale $\mathscr{B}_n$, that:

Theorem 7. *Any shape S can be folded by a tight OS at scale $\mathscr{A}_n$, for $n \geqslant 4$.*

5.6   Scale $\mathscr{A}_3$

At scale $\mathscr{A}_3$, the sides of each cell have length 2, and no edge can fit in if both neighboring cells are already occupied. We must then pay extra attention to the order of self-assembly, i.e. to time. We define the *time of an occupied side* as the routing time of its middle vertex (its rank in the current routing). In $\mathscr{A}_3$, the clean edges are located at the *counterclockwise-most* position of the available sides of the occupied cells. Our routing algorithm maintains, before each insertion, an invariant for the routing that *combines time and geometry* as follows:

Invariant 1 (insertion). Around an empty cell, the clockwise-most side of any segment is always the latest of that segment, and its clockwise-most edge is clean.

As it turns out, we cannot maintain this invariant for every empty cell at every step. The middle vertex of a side violating this invariant is called a *time-anomaly.*

The anomalies around an empty cell are fixed *only* at the step the empty cell is covered by the algorithm. Because fixing anomalies consists in freeing the corresponding side (as if the neighboring cell was empty), without actually freeing the cell, we define the signature rooted on side d of an empty $\Lambda(p)$ slightly

---

Algorithm 1. Incremental routing algorithm for scale $\mathscr{A}_3$

1: **procedure** FILLEMPTYCELL(centered at: $\lambda(p)$)
2:     **if** $\Lambda(p)$ has no occupied neighboring cell **then**
3:         Fill $\Lambda(p)$ with routing 0 from Fig. 6(a), mark the n°-cell as *forbidden* and **return**.
4:     **while** the latest side of $\Lambda(p)$ is an anomaly **do**
5:         Fix this anomaly in the corresponding neighboring cell according to the diagram in Fig. 6.
6:     Compute the $\Lambda(p)$'s signature rooted on the latest side and extend the path according to the corresponding basic pattern in Fig. 6(a).

---

differently here, as: $\mathsf{sig}_d(p) = \sum_{i=0}^{5} s_i 2^i$ where $s_i = 1$ if the *vertex at the middle* of the $\mathsf{cw}^i(d)$-side is occupied, and $= 0$ otherwise.

The routing algorithm is described in Algorithm 1 and uses two series of routing extensions: the *basic* patterns in Fig. 6(a), and the *anomaly-fixing* patterns in Fig. 6(b–d). There are two types of anomalies: *path-anomalies* (marked as yellow dots) only require a local rerouting inside the cell to become clean; *time-anomalies* (marked as red dots) cannot be turned into clean edge and must be freed according to the diagram in Fig. 6(b–d). Figure 7 gives a step-by-step construction of a shape which involves fixing several anomalies.

The following key topological lemma and corollary ensure that time- and path-anomalies are very limited and can be handled locally (omitted, see [5]). And the theorem follows by immediate induction:

Lemma 2 (Key topological lemma). *At every step of the algorithm, the boundary of each empty area contains exactly one time-anomaly vertex.*

Corollary 1. *The* **while** *loop is executed at most twice, and it fixes: at most one time-anomaly, and at most one path-anomaly. After these fixes, the latest edge around the empty cell is always the clockwise-most of a segment and clean.*

Theorem 8. *Any shape S can be folded by a tight OS at scale $\mathscr{A}_3$.*

6   A Shape Which Can Be Assembled at Delay δ but Not $<\delta$

This section contains the statement of Theorem 9 and a high-level description of its proof. For full details, see [5].

Theorem 9. *Let $\delta > 2$. There exists a shape S_δ such that S_δ can be self-assembled by some OS $\mathcal{O}_\delta$ at delay δ, but no OS with delay δ' self-assembles S_δ where $\delta' < \delta$.*

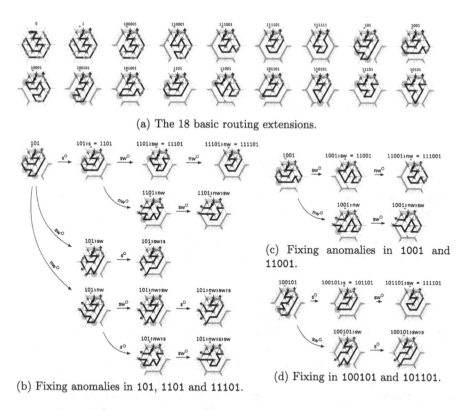

(a) The 18 basic routing extensions.

(b) Fixing anomalies in 101, 1101 and 11101.

(c) Fixing anomalies in 1001 and 11001.

(d) Fixing in 100101 and 101101.

Fig. 6. *Routing extensions at $\mathscr{A}_3$*: in purple, the latest (clockwise-most) clean edge used to extend the routing; in green, the sides already covered, earlier in the routing; in yellow, the side shared with the newly covered neighboring cell after fixing a path-anomaly; the red arrows are the new potential clean edges available to extend the routing; time- and path-anomalies, that need to be fixed to allow extension on that side, are indicated resp. by red and yellow dots; the seed is highlighted in orange in signature 0. (Color figure online)

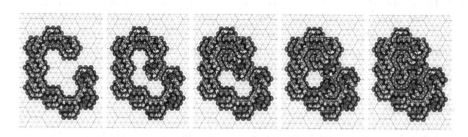

Fig. 7. The step-by-step construction of a routing folding into a shape at scale $\mathscr{A}_3$ according to Algorithm 1, involving fixing anomalies 101 → 101》nw → 101》nw》s → 101》nw》s》sw in the four last steps.

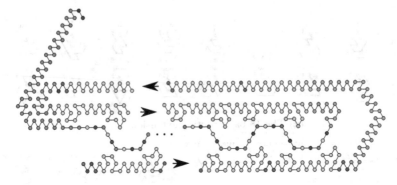

Fig. 8. A depiction of shape S_δ and a routing R'_δ for $\delta = 4$. This can be thought of as a "slice" of the shape (along with a forced routing) which cannot be self-assembled by an oritatami system with delay <4, but can be assembled by an OS with delay 4. The arrows represent the direction of the directed path in the routing and the different colored beads represent the different gadgets in the routing. (Color figure online)

We prove Theorem 9 by constructing a deterministic OS $\mathcal{O}_\delta$ for every $\delta > 2$, and we define $S_\delta = \mathrm{dom}(C_\delta)$ where $C_\delta \in \mathcal{A}_\square[\mathcal{O}_\delta]$. It then immediately follows that there exists a system at delay δ which assembles S_δ, and we complete the proof by showing that there exists no OS with delay less than δ which can assemble S_δ. A schematic depiction of the shape S_δ (for $\delta = 4$) can be seen in Fig. 8. $\mathcal{O}_\delta$ forms the shape as follows. First a "cave" is formed where the distance between the top and the bottom is δ at specified points. At regular intervals along the top and bottom, blue beads are placed. Once the cave is complete, a single-bead-wide path grows through it from right to left, and every δ beads is a red bead which interacts with the blue. To optimize bonds, each red binds to a blue, which is possible since the spacing between locations adjacent to blue beads is exactly δ, allowing the full transcription length to "just barely" discover the binding configuration. The geometry of S_δ ensures that any oritatami system forming it must have single-stranded portions that reach all the way across the cave. So, in any system with $\delta' < \delta$, since the minimal distance at which beads can form a bond across the cave is δ, when the transcription is occurring from a location adjacent to one of the sides, no configuration can be possible which forms a bond with a bead across the cave. Thus, the beads must stabilize without a bond across the cave forcing their orientation and so can stabilize in incorrect locations, meaning S_δ isn't deterministically formed.

References

1. Arkin, E.M., et al.: Not being (super)thin or solid is hard: a study of grid hamiltonicity. Comput. Geom.-Theor. Appl. **42**(6–7), 582–605 (2009)
2. Chao, M.Y., Kan, M.-C., Lin-Chao, S.: RNAII transcribed by IPTG-induced T7 RNA polymerase is non-functional as a replication primer for ColE1-type plasmids in *escherichia coli*. Nucleic Acids Res. **23**, 1691–1695 (1995)

3. Demaine, E.D., et al.: Staged self-assembly: nanomanufacture of arbitrary shapes with $O(1)$ glues. Nat. Comput. **7**(3), 347–370 (2008)
4. Demaine, E.D., Patitz, M.J., Schweller, R.T., Summers, S.M.: Self-assembly of arbitrary shapes using RNAse enzymes: meeting the Kolmogorov bound with small scale factor (extended abstract). In: STACS 2011. LIPIcs, vol. 9, pp. 201–212. Schloss Dagstuhl-Leibniz-Zentrum fuer Informatik (2011)
5. Demaine, E.D., et al.: Know when to fold 'em: Self-assembly of shapes by folding in oritatami (Full text). arXiv:1807.04682 (2018)
6. Derakhshandeh, Z., Gmyr, R., Richa, A.W., Scheideler, G., Strothmann, T.: Universal shape formation for programmable matter. In: SPAA 2016, pp. 289–299. ACM (2016)
7. Elliott, D., Ladomery, M.: Molecular Biology of RNA, 2nd edn. Oxford University Press, Oxford (2016)
8. Elonen, A.: Molecular folding and computation, Bachelor thesis, Aalto University (2016)
9. Feynman, R.P.: Feynman Lectures on Computation. Westview Press, Boulder (1996)
10. Geary, C., Meunier, P.-E., Schabanel, N., Seki, S.: Folding Turing is hard but feasible. arXiv:1508.00510v2
11. Geary, C., Meunier, P.-E., Schabanel, N., Seki, S.: Programming biomolecules that fold greedily during transcription. In: MFCS 2016. LIPIcs, vol. 58, pp. 43:1–43:14 (2016)
12. Geary, C., Rothemund, P.W.K., Andersen, E.S.: A single-stranded architecture for cotranscriptional folding of RNA nanostructures. Science **345**(6198), 799–804 (2014)
13. Han, Y.-S., Kim, H.: Ruleset optimization on isomorphic oritatami systems. In: Brijder, R., Qian, L. (eds.) DNA 2017. LNCS, vol. 10467, pp. 33–45. Springer, Cham (2017). https://doi.org/10.1007/978-3-319-66799-7_3
14. Han, Y.-S., Kim, H.: Construction of geometric structure by oritatami system. In: DNA24 (2018)
15. Isambert, H.: The jerky and knotty dynamics of RNA. Methods **49**, 189–196 (2009)
16. Lewicki, B.T.U., Margus, T., Remme, J., Nierhaus, K.H.: Coupling of rRNA transcription and ribosomal assembly in vivo: formation of active ribosomal subunits in *escherichia coli* requires transcription of rRNA genes by host RNA polymerase which cannot be replaced by bacteriophage T7 RNA polymerase. J. Mol. Biol. **231**(3), 581–593 (1993)
17. Masuda, Y., Seki, S., Ubukata, Y.: Towards the algorithmic molecular self-assembly of fractals by cotranscriptional folding. In: Câmpeanu, C. (ed.) CIAA 2018. LNCS, vol. 10977, pp. 261–273. Springer, Heidelberg (2018). https://doi.org/10.1007/978-3-319-94812-6_22
18. Merkhofer, E.C., Hu, P., Johnson, T.L.: Introduction to cotranscriptional RNA splicing. In: Hertel, K.J. (ed.) Spliceosomal Pre-mRNA Splicing. MMB, vol. 1126, pp. 83–96. Humana Press, Totowa, NJ (2014). https://doi.org/10.1007/978-1-62703-980-2_6
19. Ota, M., Seki, S.: Rule set design problems for oritatami systems. Theor. Comput. Sci. **671**, 26–35 (2017)
20. Repsilber, D., Wiese, S., Rachen, M., Schröder, A.W., Riesner, D., Steger, G.: Formation of metastable RNA structures by sequential folding during transcription: time-resolved structural analysis of potato spindle tuber viroid (-)-stranded RNA by temperature-gradient gel electrophoresis. RNA **5**, 574–584 (1999)

21. Rogers, T.A., Seki, S.: Oritatami system: a survey and impossibility of simple simulation at small delays. Fund. Inform. **154**, 359–372 (2017)
22. Seki, S.: Cotranscriptional folding: a frontier in molecular engineering - a challenge for computer scientists. SIAM News **50**(4) (2017)
23. Soloveichik, D., Winfree, E.: Complexity of self-assembled shapes. SIAM J. Comput. **36**(6), 1544–1569 (2007)
24. Watters, K.E., Strobel, E.J., Yu, A.M., Lis, J.T., Lucks, J.B.: Cotranscriptional folding of a riboswitch at nucleotide resolution. Nat. Struct. Mol. Biol. **23**(12), 1124–1133 (2016)
25. Wong, T.N., Sosnick, T.R., Pan, T.: Folding of noncoding RNAs during transcription facilitated by pausing-induced nonnative structures. PNAS **104**(46), 17995–18000 (2007)
26. Woods, D., Chen, H.-L., Goodfriend, S., Dabby, N., Winfree, E., Yin, P.: Active self-assembly of algorithmic shapes and patterns in polylogarithmic time. In: ITCS 2013, pp. 353–354. ACM (2013)

Optimizing Tile Set Size While Preserving Proofreading with a DNA Self-assembly Compiler

Constantine G. Evans[1,2(✉)] and Erik Winfree[2]

[1] Evans Foundation, Pasadena, CA, USA
cgevans@evansfmm.org
[2] California Institute of Technology, Pasadena, CA, USA

Abstract. Algorithmic DNA tile systems have the potential to allow the construction by self-assembly of large structures with complex nanometer-scale details out of relatively few monomer types, but are constrained by errors in growth and the limited sequence space of orthogonal DNA sticky ends that program tile interactions. We present a tile set optimization technique that, through analysis of algorithmic growth equivalence, potentially sensitive error pathways, and potential lattice defects, can significantly reduce the size of tile systems while preserving proofreading behavior that is essential for obtaining low error rates. Applied to systems implementing multiple algorithms that are far beyond the size of currently feasible implementations, the optimization technique results in systems that are comparable in size to already-implemented experimental systems.

1 Introduction

Self-assembling DNA tile systems provide a mechanism for implementing complex self-assembly behaviors at a molecular scale [22,30]. Both simple periodic structures with a range of attachment and lattice configurations, and "uniquely-addressed" structures of single copies of thousands of different monomers, have been demonstrated experimentally [21,26,32,33]. In between, algorithmic tile systems can employ a small number of monomer types that perform potentially arbitrary computation during growth to construct large structures with complex, small-scale details [7,34]. Additionally, using the choice of initial seed or presence of a particular monomer type as an input to a computation, the same algorithmic tile system can grow substantially different assemblies.

The number of monomer types in a tile system affects its cost and is a frequently-used measure of complexity [23,31]. The number of glues, however, is a potentially more limiting constraint. Implemented as short, single-stranded "sticky ends" of DNA, glues are limited by sequence space and spurious binding between subsequences of non-complementary sticky ends [10], particularly for the 5 to 6 nucleotide sticky ends in the widely-used double-crossover (DX) tile motifs [12]. Uniquely-addressed systems can assemble largely-correct structures

© Springer Nature Switzerland AG 2018
D. Doty and H. Dietz (Eds.): DNA 2018, LNCS 11145, pp. 37–54, 2018.
https://doi.org/10.1007/978-3-030-00030-1_3

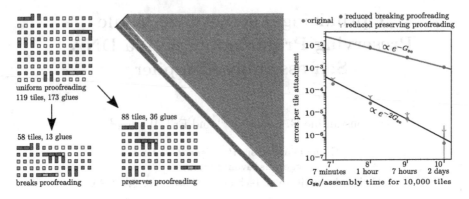

Fig. 1. An example of an algorithmic tile system designed for DNA tiles, simultaneously implementing 3 separate algorithms, reduced in size with and without preservation of proofreading behavior, and corresponding simulation results.

even if some tiles attach incorrectly: they may thus be less affected by non-complementary interactions, and sticky ends of inhomogeneous strengths may actually assist growth [15]. For algorithmic systems, however, a single incorrect tile attachment could completely change further growth, and thus spurious interactions can strongly limit the number of glues, limiting the complexity of implementable algorithms. A method to reduce the number of glues in a tile system could thus significantly increase the complexity of experimentally-implementable algorithms.

Ma and Lombardi defined the Pattern Assembling Tile-Set Synthesis (PATS) problem to consider the minimal algorithmic tile system required to assemble a unique terminal assembly of a given pattern, with research resulting in algorithms for finding such systems [6,23,24], but also establishing the problem as NP-hard [16,17,19,20,23]. These methods consider abstract tile systems in a model not allowing errors that assemble to unique final assemblies from single seeds, with all single-strength glues, in a single growth direction. While Göös et al. developed a measure of reliability for such systems in a more physically-relevant model that allows errors [14], as discussed in Sect. 4, model limitations prevented the measure from being preserved during optimization and from handling proofreading error reduction behavior [4,5,27,31,35]. Without proofreading behavior through either accident or design, systems will have error rates that decrease only with the square root of assembly speed. Thus, systems without proofreading have far higher error rates, whereas with basic proofreading, error rates decrease linearly with assembly speed. For simulations of our XOR example in Sect. 6, a reduced-size version preserving proofreading could grow a 1,000 tile assembly in 200 min with 99.7% probability, while one not preserving proofreading succeeded in the same conditions in only 26% of the trials. For slower assembly speeds, the difference becomes even more pronounced: thus, proofreading has become a practical necessity for complex tile systems used in experiments, along with other design principles such as nucleation control [9,28,29,35].

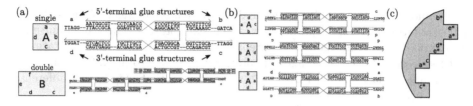

Fig. 2. Abstract tiles implemented by two distinct structures of DX tiles (a) and some of their rotations (b); (c) shows a hypothetical seed.

In this paper, we present a series of criteria and methods for reducing the size of experimentally-implementable tile systems while preserving desirable physical behavior. In contrast to the PATS, we do not seek minimal tile systems for a single terminal assembly, but instead seek to find smaller equivalents of given tile systems that behave equivalently for all producible assemblies from a set of different seeds. To do so, we provide equivalence criteria for such behavior in the abstract Tile Assembly Model (aTAM) that addresses seeded growth, tile growth in arbitrary directions, and permanently-bonded "double tiles" filling two lattice sites that are commonly used in experimental systems. We then present a tile-based analysis method of "sensitivity profiles" to characterize proofreading error rate behavior in the kinetic Tile Assembly Model (kTAM), allowing the preservation of error rate scaling in reduced systems. To address two potential physical concerns beyond the kTAM that could affect experimental systems, we also develop simple methods to algorithmically avoid lattice defect formation and spurious attachments of two assemblies in solution. We use these criteria and methods with a simple algorithm for attempting merges of different tiles and glues on three implementable example systems, showing that the systems can be reduced significantly in complexity while preserving behavior in kTAM simulations. These size reductions are significant enough that, by combining three example systems, the combined and reduced-size system can implement all three algorithms simultaneously while using a comparable or smaller number of glues than the original designs of the individual algorithms.

2 Background: Tile Systems and Merge Transformations

We consider a *glue g* as an object having some *glue structure*, and *bond strength* $b(g)$. A glue can form a *bond* of strength $b(g)$ with a glue of the same structure that is its *complement*, which we denote as $g*$, with $(g*)* = g$ and $b(g*) = b(g)$. For DX tiles [12], a glue is implemented by a glue structure of a short single-stranded region, with a set length and one of two orientations, as shown in Fig. 2. Complementary glues have Watson-Crick complement sequences; for practicality, we will require that glues not be self-complementary.

We consider a *tile T* (sometimes referred to as a "tile type" in other papers) to be $(\sigma, c, (g_i))$, where σ is the *tile structure*, c is the tile's *color*, and g_i is the glue on the ith *edge* of the tile. Each tile, as determined by its structure, will fill one or more sites in a regular lattice and will have a set number of edges facing adjacent lattice sites. In physical systems, tiles can rotate and attach in multiple orientations, but in our model, tile orientation is fixed. We include the rotations of tiles as separate tiles with fixed orientations: we define rotation functions R_i^σ, which map a tile T of structure σ to a rotation of T that may have a different structure σ'.

A seed is some structure that presents a certain number of glues on certain edges of sites on a lattice: every producible assembly will grow from a seed. For the purposes of this paper, a tile system S is a set of tiles and potential seeds, $\{T_i\} \cup \{\Sigma_j\}$; a *rotatable* tile system is the closure of a tile system under all rotations.

As in the PATS problem, we will attempt to reduce the size of a tile system by making different glues, or tiles, equivalent.

Definition 1. *The* **glue merge transformation**, *for non-complementary glues a and b of the same glue structure and bond strength, is defined as* $\mathrm{Mg}_{b,a}(X) = X'$, *where every instance of a or b in X is considered to be an identical glue in X', and every instance of a∗ or b∗ is considered to be an identical glue. X may be any object containing glues, such as a glue, a tile, a seed, or a tile system (Fig. 3).*

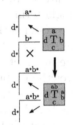

Some tiles or seeds in a tile system S may be mapped to identical tiles or seeds in $\mathrm{Mg}_{b,a}(S)$, if they are already identical except for glues a and b or $a∗$ and $b∗$. Thus tile merges can be defined as compositions of glue merges (here $\prod_i M_i = M_1 \circ M_2 \circ \dots$ denotes composition):

Fig. 3. Glue merge $\mathrm{Mg}_{b,a}$ with allowed and disallowed attachment sites shown.

Definition 2. *The* **tile merge transformation**, *for tiles T and U of the same tile structure and color, is defined as* $\mathrm{Mt}_{U,T} = \prod_i \mathrm{Mg}_{g_i(U),g_i(T)}$, *where $g_i(T)$ is the glue on the ith edge of T (Fig. 4).*

As not all pairs of glues can be merged, not all pairs of tiles have a defined tile merge transformation.

For abstract, idealized growth, we will first consider whether a series of merges will continue to result in equivalent growth in the abstract Tile Assembly Model (aTAM). In this model, starting from an initial seed, tiles attach to empty lattice sites adjacent to an assembly if they can bind by matching (complementary) glues with bond strengths that sum to at least some threshold τ, sometimes called the temperature in other papers. Once attached, tiles never detach [34]. After establishing equivalence criteria at this abstract level, more physically-accurate models can be considered.

Fig. 4. Tile merge $\mathrm{Mt}_{U,T}$.

3   aTAM Equivalence

Since different tile systems will not have the same tiles, we first define equivalence between assemblies in different tile systems. We define two assemblies A and A' as *color equivalent* if every lattice site is either empty in both or filled with a tile of the same structure and color in both (irrespective of glues and bonds). We similarly define two tile systems S and S' as color equivalent if, for every assembly A that is producible by one system, there exists a corresponding assembly A' producible by the other that is color equivalent with A. We will define the set of all assemblies that S can produce through correct growth as PA(S). Then, after some composition of merges M, we can state

Lemma 1. *If $M(\text{PA}(S)) = \text{PA}(M(S))$, i.e., if M applied to the set of producible assemblies of S is equal to the set of every producible assembly of $M(S)$, then tile systems S and $M(S)$ are* **color equivalent.**

Proof. M preserves tile color and structure, so every assembly A is color equivalent to $M(A)$. For every assembly A in PA(S), $M(\text{PA}(S)) = \text{PA}(M(S))$ means that $M(A)$ will be in PA($M(S)$), and for every assembly A' in PA($M(S)$), it means that there will be an assembly A in PA(S) such that $M(A) = A'$.   □

Intuitively, all bonds between tiles possible in S will remain possible in $M(S)$, and thus all of the same assemblies will remain producible. However, with merged glues, there may be growth possible in S' that would not be possible in S. There may also be different growth pathways that construct color equivalent assemblies. To limit equivalence to tile systems with equivalent growth pathways, we define a more restrictive goal, which is a form of bisimulation [18,25]:

Definition 3. *Tile systems S and $M(S)$ are* **growth equivalent** *if for every assembly $A \in \text{PA}(S)$, every attachment site that has $Q \subseteq S$ as the set of possible correct tile attachments has $M(Q)$ as the set of possible attachments in $M(A)$.*

Lemma 2. *If tile systems S and $M(S)$ are growth equivalent, then they are color equivalent.*

Proof. For growth equivalent S and $M(S)$, at every attachment site p in every assembly A in PA(S), if tile T in S can attach to form an assembly $A +_p T$, then $M(T)$ can attach to the corresponding site in $M(A)$, resulting in an assembly $M(A) +_p M(T)$. Similarly, for every tile T' that can attach to an attachment site p in $M(A)$, resulting in $M(A) +_p T'$, growth equivalence requires that there must be a tile T in S that can attach to the corresponding site in A where $M(T) = T'$. Thus if A is in PA(S), every attachment step $A +_p T$ will be in PA(S), and if $M(A)$ is in PA($M(S)$), every possible attachment step will result in as assembly of the form $M(A) +_p M(T) = M(A +_p T)$. Every seed Σ in S is in PA(S) and corresponds to a seed $M(\Sigma)$ in PA($M(S)$), there are no other seeds in PA($M(S)$), and all assemblies start from seeds; therefore by induction, growth equivalence requires that $M(\text{PA}(S)) = \text{PA}(M(S))$.   □

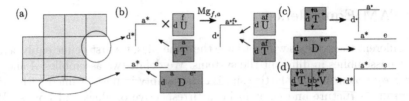

Fig. 5. (a) shows an assembly and potential attachment sites, which can be viewed as local neighborhoods (b) allowing certain tiles to attach. For a subset of tile systems, use annotations allow (c) the generation of input neighborhoods for each used tile, though for systems with double tiles, assemblies of two tiles (d) must also be considered.

Growth equivalence implies something stronger than just color equivalence: the set of assemblies producible from a specific assembly A will always be equivalent to those producible from $M(A)$. As a special case, A is a terminal assembly (i.e., no further tiles can attach) if and only if $M(A)$ is, which is not necessarily the case for color equivalence.

Since the aTAM assumes that tiles attach on a regular lattice and glues are additive and have non-negative strengths, whether a tile can attach to an attachment site can be determined by just the *local neighborhood* of edges adjacent to the attachment site (Fig. 5(b)). For systems of single and double tiles, a local neighborhood will be a subset of the edges adjacent to either one empty lattice site (potentially allowing attachment of a single tile) or two empty lattice sites (potentially allowing attachment of a double tile of one orientation), each labeled with a glue as if from a pre-existing tile in an assembly. An attachment site adjacent to an assembly may have multiple local neighborhoods, each with different subsets of edges. We define $\mathrm{PN}(S)$ to be the set of local neighborhoods present in every producible assembly of S, and $\mathrm{PT}_S(L)$ for a local neighborhood L to be the set (possibly empty) of tiles that can correctly attach. Then,

Lemma 3. *For tile system S and merge M, if for all $L \in \mathrm{PN}(S)$, $M(\mathrm{PT}_S(L)) = \mathrm{PT}_{M(S)}(M(L))$, then S and $M(S)$ are growth equivalent.*

Proof. Every attachment site in an assembly A in $\mathrm{PA}(S)$ will have some local neighborhood L, which will be in $\mathrm{PN}(S)$, and so at that attachment site, $Q = \mathrm{PT}_S(L)$ will be the set of tiles that can attach. The corresponding site in $M(A)$ will have local neighborhood $M(L)$, where $\mathrm{PT}_{M(S)}(M(L))$ can attach. Thus, if $\mathrm{PT}_{M(S)}(M(L)) = M(Q) = M(\mathrm{PT}_S(L))$, growth equivalence will be satisfied. □

Whether a local neighborhood is present in any producible assembly of a tile system is undecidable: considering a tile system that implements an arbitrary program and produces a particular local neighborhood only if the program halts, the question can be reduced to the halting problem. Thus, we only consider tile systems satisfying additional constraints. First, we require that the system include (correct) *use annotations* for each tile actually used in producible assemblies, designating edges on tiles as being used as *inputs* (edges with which the tile attaches to assemblies) or *outputs* (edges where other tiles attach): while tiles in a system may have multiple use annotations, we do not consider systems where tiles attach with intentionally mismatched glues, leaving certain edges with glues *unused*. Second, we require that for every local neighborhood $L \in \mathrm{PN}(S)$ with glues of total bond strength of at least τ, there exists a tile $T \in S$ that can attach to L with no mismatched glues, and with attachments of only input edges on the tile to output edges on the local neighborhood.

With these assumptions, for systems containing only single tiles, every $L \in \mathrm{PN}(S)$ will consist of output edges that bind to complementary glues on corresponding input edges of some tile T, so we can enumerate all possible local neighborhoods of S, at the cost of possibly including some that are not actually producible, by examining each tile in S with input-annotated edges. To do so, we will define $\mathrm{IN}(T)$ to be the local neighborhood (or neighborhoods, if the tile bound with strength greater than τ) corresponding to the input edges of T (Fig. 5(c)). Since $\mathrm{IN}(S) \supseteq \mathrm{PN}(S)$, it is clear from Lemma 3 that

Theorem 1. *For tile system S (that uses only single tiles) and merge M, if for all $L \in \mathrm{IN}(S)$, $M(\mathrm{PT}_S(L)) = \mathrm{PT}_{M(S)}(M(L))$, then S and $M(S)$ are growth equivalent.*

All parts of the requirement in this theorem—local neighborhoods from input annotations on tiles, and whether other tiles can correctly attach to them—are computable, so it can be used to verify that M and $M(S)$ are growth equivalent.

In the case of a system including double tiles, since double tiles may attach to local neighborhoods with edges adjacent to two lattice sites (Fig. 5(b)), $\mathrm{IN}(S)$ must be extended to include input neighborhoods constructed from two single tiles with matching glues and use annotations (Fig. 5(d)).

Theorem 1 provides a way of determining whether a tile system S, after a series of merges M, will continue to have only equivalent correct attachments, and thus equivalent growth in the aTAM. In more physically-relevant models, however, tiles can attach incorrectly, resulting in errors. To ensure that error behavior remains similar after a series of merges, further criteria, in a more physically-relevant model, will be needed.

4   Sensitivity Profiles and kTAM Equivalence

In the kinetic Tile Assembly Model (kTAM), any tile can attach to any potential site, and will do so at a rate $r_f = \hat{k}_f e^{-G_{\mathrm{mc}}}$ for a constant $\hat{k}_f$, where G_{mc} is an analogue of the tile concentration $[c] \propto e^{-G_{\mathrm{mc}}}$. Instead of determining whether an attachment is possible, the total bond strength of matching glues b will instead determine the rate at which a tile detaches, $r_{r,b} = \hat{k}_f e^{-bG_{\mathrm{se}}}$, where G_{se} is the (sign-reversed and unitless) free energy of a single bond. Thus, tiles will attach at the same rate, but will fall off faster if b is smaller. To approximate $\tau = 2$ aTAM, G_{mc} is typically set to $2G_{\mathrm{se}} - \epsilon$ for some small ϵ, such that tiles bound by $b < 2$ will fall off faster than they attach, and tiles bound by $b = 2$ will attach slightly faster than they detach. In this regime, the growth rate of an assembly will be dependent upon the bond free energy G_{se}, scaling approximately as $e^{-2G_{\mathrm{se}}}$.

The design of tile systems that robustly exhibit the same growth in the kTAM as in the aTAM is itself an area of continuing research. In the limit of infinitely slow growth, growth in the kTAM and aTAM is equivalent, as tiles attaching by bond strength 0 or 1 will fall off far faster than they attach [34]. Moving away from this limit, however, incorrect attachments may provide pathways for the growth of assemblies that could not be produced by the system in the aTAM, where the attachments remain as errors, and further undesired growth can continue via correct attachments [11].

One approach to approximating aTAM growth in the kTAM is to minimize the rate at which errors occur in some error rate model so that assemblies of a desired size assemble perfectly with high probability. The *kinetic trapping model* (KTM) provides a model for one type of error, a *growth error*, where a tile attaches incorrectly to a site where another tile could attach correctly, and allows further growth that effectively locks the error in place [11,34]. Another type of error, a *facet nucleation error*, can occur when a tile incorrectly attaches to a location where not all adjacent output edges are present yet [4], but these errors are beyond the scope of our analysis.

For a tile system at $\tau = 2$ containing only single tiles and where all glues have bond strengths of one, the KTM considers kTAM transition rates between empty and filled states for a single local neighborhood (Fig. 6(a)). Starting from an empty state (E), the correct tile can attach, resulting in the "correct" state C, or a tile attaching by one correct bond and one mismatch can attach, resulting in the "almost-correct" state A. C or A can revert to E by the tile falling off at the kTAM detachment rate, or, at some rate r^* related to the growth rate, can be trapped in place by further tiles correctly attaching to the tile and surrounding assembly, resulting in the trapped correct (TC) and trapped almost-correct (TA) states. When there are m possible almost-correct attachments at a site and only one possible correct attachment, the KTM predicts a growth error rate (the probability of reaching TA from E) of $P_{error} = me^{-G_{se}+\epsilon}$, with $G_{mc} = 2G_{se} - \epsilon$; as the growth rate of a system usually scales as $e^{-2G_{se}}$, this means the error rate scales as the square root of the growth rate.

The validity of the KTM error rate estimate depends on two critical assumptions, which may not always be true and may depend on the tile system or the attachment site: first, that every attachment site during the growth of an assembly has exactly m almost-correct tiles that can attach instead of the correct tile attachment, and second, that both a correct and an almost-correct tile will become kinetically trapped at the same rate by subsequent attachments. We will consider the effect of these two assumptions in turn.

As almost-correct tile attachments need one matching glue, the number of almost-correct attachments will be determined by the tile system at an abstract level, and may also depend on the local neighborhood. To analyze these attachments, we will define *first-order sensitivity*, the first of a series of *sensitivity profiles*, that will enumerate pairs of tiles (T, U) where U allows the E to A pathway in the KTM to take place in the attachment site where T would attach correctly (i.e., in the input neighborhood of T). These sensitivity profiles were

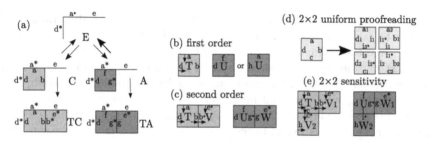

Fig. 6. (a) shows pathways in the KTM, while (b) shows potential first-order sensitive pairs for a tile, (c) shows configurations resulting in second-order pairs (black boxes represent unused edge annotations), (d) shows 2 × 2 uniform proofreading, and (e) shows configurations resulting in 2 × 2 sensitive pairs.

originally derived from glue sensitivity classes developed to analyze the effect of non-complementary glue interactions [10].

Definition 4. *A pair of tiles* (T, U) *in* S *are* **first-order sensitive** *if and only if some subset of the input edges of* T *contain glues that are the same as glues on corresponding edges (regardless of use annotation) of* U, *with total bond strength 1 or more.*

If an almost-correct attachment of a tile U in the KTM is possible in any possible local neighborhood where a tile T can attach correctly, then (T, U) is a first-order sensitive tile pair (Fig. 6(b)). For any producible local neighborhood where a tile T can attach by bond strength $b = \tau$, an almost-correct attachment in the KTM requires a tile that can attach to that local neighborhood by $b = 1$. By definition, any tile that can do so, in a system with complementary glues, will be first-order sensitive with T.

First-order sensitivity is similar to the tile system *reliability* of Göös et al. defined within the context of the PATS problem—defined, for a system constructing only a single terminal assembly, as the probability of perfectly growing that assembly in the kTAM [14]. This was calculated by combining the KTM probability of correct growth at each site in the correct assembly, considering only the C and A states and the number of potential almost-correct attachments at each site, which resulted in a reliability that decreases as the number of possible almost-correct attachments increases. Starting from uniquely-addressed systems where no almost-correct attachments were possible, their reduction techniques tended to first decrease, and then increase, their reliability measure. Similarly, one option for our methods would be reduction that attempts to only apply merges that do not add new first-order sensitive pairs, or that seeks to minimize the number of pairs.

There are two limitations to approaches such as these, related to the two assumptions underpinning the KTM error rate estimate. One, which Göös et al. address and account for, is that the number of potential almost-correct tile attachments, m, can vary from site to site. Thus, tile set reductions that decrease

m will result in a lower KTM error rate estimate. However, for algorithmic self-assembly to take advantage of the computational power at $\tau \geq 2$, there must be some correct attachment determined by two glues rather than one, and thus there must be some potential almost-correct attachments, and $m \geq 1$ for some such sites. Otherwise, the tile system will be equivalent to a $\tau = 1$ system, with its accompanying computational limitations [8]. Consequently, the lowest error rate estimate provided by this use of the KTM will still be proportional to $e^{-G_{se}}$, while the growth rate is proportional to $e^{-2G_{se}}$, resulting in an error rate that scales no better than $\sqrt{r}$ as the growth rate r is decreased.

The second limitation concerns the assumption that all almost-correct tile attachments have the potential to become trapped at the same rate as correct tile attachments. Göös et al. do not address this issue, which accounts for the main difference in our results. In particular, when an almost-correct attachment occurs in some tile systems, there may be no tile that can attach by at least τ bond strength in the resulting local neighborhoods to trap the error in place, even for tile systems where every local neighborhood in correct growth will allow tile attachment. In this case, another growth error would be required for growth to continue, making it more likely that the initial error will detach instead— and making the KTM error rate estimate invalid. Proofreading behavior [4,5, 27,31,35], where almost-correct attachments cause exactly such impediments to further correct growth, can in principle reduce error rates, for a desired $k > 1$, to scale as $e^{-kG_{se}}$, or $r^{k/2}$ for a growth rate r. In practice, this is necessary for experimental systems to have low error rates, and therefore proofreading needs to be preserved in tile system reduction.

To this end, as with the E to A transition in the KTM, we can define a *second-order sensitivity* to enumerate pairs where the A to TA transition is possible, by considering shared glues on additional tiles that can attach to first-order sensitive pairs (Fig. 6(c)):

Definition 5. *For a tile system containing only single tiles, a pair of tiles (T, U) are **second-order sensitive** if they are first-order sensitive and, for some output edge on T with glue b, some tile V that can attach by an input edge with a glue b^*, and some tile W that can attach to the corresponding edge on U with a glue g^*, taking every glue g_i that is on both an input edge of V and the corresponding edge of W, both g^* and at least one g_i are at least strength 1.*

Theorem 2. *For a tile system of only single tiles, only second-order sensitive pairs as defined above will have a potentially valid pathway in the KTM between almost-correct attachment and a trapped almost-correct attachment.*

Proof. Consider an almost-correct state in the KTM of a tile U attaching where T would have attached correctly. As shown previously, the almost-correct tile U must be first-order sensitive with T. In order to reach the trapped-almost-correct state, an additional tile must be able to attach to U and the surrounding assembly. If T had attached instead, as a correct attachment, it would have done so by input edges, and any available glues on edges adjacent to empty lattice sites would be output edges. For any of those output edges, by our requirement that correct growth in sites with glues on adjacent output edges always be possible, there must be a tile V that attaches to that output edge by an input edge and, unless the glue on the output edge has strength $b = \tau$, at least one other adjacent output edge in the local neighborhood by some input edge on V. Thus, if U were to attach instead of T, then for a tile W to lock U in place by filling the site where V would have attached, W must share a sufficient total strength of *matching* glues on edges of V labeled as inputs (as the local neighborhood where V could attach must have corresponding outputs available). These constraints, considered for each output edge of T, are the same as the criteria for second-order sensitivity.   □

In short, the KTM error rate estimate only applies for tiles that have second-order sensitivity; the true error rate in cases that have only first-order sensitivity will be insignificant in comparison. If a tile set reduction technique were to ensure that there are no second-order sensitive tile pairs, excellent proofreading error rates could be achieved. This is the aim of our methods, although we will somewhat soften this goal below.

The second-order definition and Theorem 2 above are valid only for single tiles; double tiles add additional complexity in that tile edges further away from the initial error may be involved in allowing the trapping second attachment to occur. Defining second-order sensitivity that accounts for double tiles is possible, but would require consideration of a large number of potential local configurations. Our current second-order sensitivity implementation treats double tiles as two single tiles with edges that can be inputs or outputs depending upon which results in second-order sensitivity; by doing so, it does not account for certain error pathways, but for many systems with few double tiles that do not have all six glues, it is sufficient to find most pathways.

In the ideal case of a system with any number of first-order pairs, but no second-order pairs, applying the KTM only where it is valid would predict *no* growth errors: no almost-correct attachment could be trapped in place. Proofreading transformations, however, usually satisfy the weaker constraint of requiring that an error prevent correct growth at some later point (rather than immediately), such that breathing of the growth front is still likely to remove the initial error. For 2×2 uniform proofreading [35], which is the simplest to implement experimentally, an initial almost-correct attachment of a tile U can, at worst, allow a further attachment on one edge of U, but will not allow any correct attachment on a second edge. To attempt to preserve such behavior, we can construct a further sensitivity profile to find pairs that could violate it:

Definition 6. *A pair of tiles (T, U) are 2×2 sensitive if they are second-order sensitive and the second-order criteria can be simultaneously satisfied on two different output edges of T, or the second-order criteria can be satisfied on one output edge of T, and U is a double tile that extends out along a second output edge of T.*

Intuitively, for tile systems with only strength-1 glues, only tile pairs that are 2×2 sensitive will allow growth to continue with no further impediment after an almost-correct attachment. While a perfect 2×2 uniform proofreading design will have second-order sensitive pairs, it will have no 2×2 sensitive pairs, and thus the sensitivity profile is also useful for checking proofreading implementation. However, the sensitivity profile has no rigorous significance with respect to the KTM.

5   Considerations Beyond the kTAM: Lattice Defects and Spurious Hierarchical Assembly

The aTAM and kTAM both assume that tiles assemble into perfect regular lattices. Physical DNA tile lattices, however, have some degree of flexibility, and tiles can form bonds with other tiles that fall outside of a perfect lattice, creating *lattice defects*, as shown in Fig. 7. In general, lattice defect formation depends on numerous physical factors, and would be difficult to model rigorously. However, it would be beneficial to have a method for avoiding their formation, and ensuring that in reducing tile system size, their likelihood is not increased.

To do so, in an approach similar to sensitivity profiles, we search for small assemblies of tiles that could create neighborhoods where a tile could attach by two correct bonds and form a lattice defect. For tile systems of DAO-E tiles, we speculate that the simplest, smallest lattice defects, in the orientations likeliest to allow bonds to form between non-adjacent tiles, will be the likeliest, as shown in Fig. 7(b) and (c). If in every possible combination of tiles in the pattern of one of these defects, no tile can attach by two correct bonds, then lattice defects of that size should not be possible without previous errors or other growth directions.

Another potential concern beyond the kTAM is that, for growth in solution, assemblies may bind to other assemblies, a process that has been utilized in other "hierarchical" models of self-assembly [3], but is generally undesirable in the systems designed to grow by single tile attachments. Such *spurious hierarchical attachments* have been seen in some experiments [13], but the importance of design criteria to avoid them is unclear. Many systems designed by hand, for simplicity, use each glue consistently on only input or output edges of tiles, thus avoiding assembly-assembly interactions because no glue on the edges of

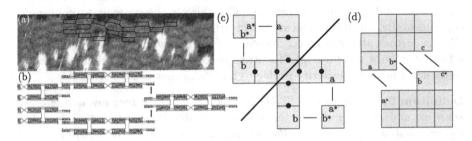

Fig. 7. (a) shows an AFM image of a DAO-E tile system lattice defect, while (b) shows a layout of a simple DAO-E lattice defect. (c) illustrates a simple algorithm for enumerating potential small lattice defects, in two orientations: circles represent arbitrary bonds of non-zero strength. (d) shows a spurious hierarchical attachment.

assemblies, which will be outputs, will be complementary to glues on edges of other assemblies. Such a distinction can be broken when merging glues, potentially allowing assemblies, while at lower concentrations than tiles, to attach by numerous bonds. The distinction can be preserved, however, by requiring that merges do not result in any glue being on both input and output edges of tiles.

6 Algorithm and Results

With the combination of criteria for aTAM equivalence, sensitivity profiles, lattice defect pathways, and spurious hierarchical attachment, a simple algorithm to attempt merges and check the resulting tile systems can be implemented. While more optimized search algorithms could improve performance [14,24], this simple algorithm suffices to demonstrate our reduction methods. In principle, as tile merges are simply the compositions of glue merges, a search through all potential glue merges could minimize a tile system, as tile merges would result automatically. In practice, for our non-exhaustive searches, we have found that first attempting possible tile merges and then glue merges is most effective at reducing the numbers of both tiles and glues.

For both searches, our algorithm is the same. For every pair of tiles, or pair of glues (filtered, if desired, by spurious hierarchical attachment criteria), we attempt to merge the pair with a transformation M. We then perform checks for aTAM equivalence per Theorem 1, and for a desired set of sensitivity profiles, check whether every pair of sensitive tiles $(M(A), M(B))$ in the merged system has a corresponding pair (A, B) of the same profile in the initial system. If either criteria fails because of a pair of tiles, the algorithm attempts, recursively, to merge those two tiles until either the criteria are satisfied or the necessary merge would be impossible. If satisfied, the resulting tile system is checked for new potential lattice defects. If all these criteria are satisfied, subsequent merge attempts are applied to the resulting system. However, in all merges, use annotations and input neighborhoods are used from the original tile system for sensitivity profile and aTAM equivalence: if they are used to generate input neighborhoods from an equivalent merged system, they will result in more local neighborhoods that will not be present in any producible assembly, thus overly constraining reduction.

This reduction algorithm is currently implemented in Alhambra, a software package for tile system design and compilation [1]. To examine the effect of the reductions on physically-implementable tile systems, we used three tile systems we had previously designed in Alhambra: XOR, Crosshatch, and Rule 110, all shown in Fig. 8. Each of the three implements 2×2 uniform proofreading, and grows from an origami seed. Additionally, we combined the three reduced systems into a "Combined" tile system implementing all three simultaneously, and reduced this system again with the same parameters.

As the algorithm can preserve different sets of sensitivity profiles, size results for several choices are shown in Table 1. Ignoring sensitivity entirely results in aTAM-equivalent systems that are similar to what might be found by PATS

Fig. 8. Structures from example tile systems. The XOR system implements a ribbon of constant, seed-defined width, with the center of the ribbon implementing the XOR function to create a Sierpinski triangle pattern, and boundaries that reflect bits. The Crosshatch (XH) system implements a ribbon with "signals" that bounce back and forth diagonally: when a signal reaches the "north" boundary, it causes the ribbon to shrink, resulting in assemblies of a finite, input-specified size. The Rule 110 system (P110) implements the cellular automata system Rule 110 using expanding boundaries, one of which uses a zig-zag growth order.

methods applied to systems that are not uniquely-addressed [14,24]: they do not preserve proofreading error rates, and, as seen in simulation results in Fig. 9 (Fig. 1 for the Combined system), have error rates that scale as $e^{-G_{se}}$. Regardless of whether spurious hierarchical attachments are avoided, preserving either 2×2 sensitivity or both second-order and 2×2 almost always results in systems that are significantly reduced in size but preserve proofreading error rate scaling of $e^{-2G_{se}}$, with error rates orders of magnitude below the sets that ignore sensitivity. The exceptions to this scaling, P110 with second-order and 2×2 preserved, both have results that fail to preserve proofreading by chance because of a pathway for errors through double tile attachments, illustrating the need for a theory and implementation of second-order sensitivity that addresses double tiles in order to most effectively reduce the size of systems such as P110 which make more extensive use of them. Fortunately, although again by chance, reductions of P110 with less stringent criteria avoided the problems with double tiles—and resulted in smaller tile systems as well.

7   Discussion

The results from our reduction methods suggest that it may be possible to implement tile systems of considerable algorithmic complexity in experimentally-viable ways using numbers of tiles and glues that are comparable with existing experimental systems. In considering experimental implementations, the unreduced Combined system, with 173 glues, uses more glues than we speculate is currently experimentally feasible for algorithmic DX tile systems. The number has been approached in uniquely-addressed DX tile systems using 152 glues [32], but uniquely-addressed systems are much less sensitive to glue quality, and so the numbers are not directly comparable. The 2×2-preserving combined system, however, preserves proofreading behavior while having fewer glues (36) than the

Table 1. Sizes of tile systems before and after reduction preserving different sets of sensitivity profiles: SHA refers to preventing spurious hierarchical attachments by restricting glue usage. Each reduction used 350 tile reduction trials, then 35 glue reduction trials on each of the 10 results with the least glues. "Combined" combines XOR, XH, and P110. Tile counts are of tiles needed for implementation, while glue are counted as sequence/complement pairs

	XOR		XH		P110		Combined	
	Tiles	Glues	Tiles	Glues	Tiles	Glues	Tiles	Glues
Before reduction	32	44	41	56	46	73	119	173
Preserve 2nd, 2 × 2, SHA	30	25	38	31	38	30	103	62
Preserve 2nd, 2 × 2	29	18	36	23	36	23	99	46
Preserve 2 × 2, SHA	27	22	33	28	31	24	91	50
Preserve 2 × 2	25	15	30	17	32	17	88	36
Ignore sensitivity	13	6	15	6	24	9	58	13

unreduced XOR system (44), which is well within the range of experimental feasibility of DX tile systems. Previously published algorithmic DX tile systems have used 35 [9], 34 [29], and 23 [2] glues, and sequence space searches have found sets around 80 glue sequences of comparable quality [10]. For systems compiled into other physical implementations, such as single-stranded tiles (SST), the larger sequence space could make even larger systems experimentally viable; uniquely-addressed SST assemblies have been demonstrated using over 10,000 glues [26]. Yet even with DX tiles, our reductions could allow experimental implementation of tile systems, using current experimental methods, far beyond the complexity of those we would otherwise be able to implement.

There are a number of other potential directions for optimizations in a tile system compiler. Preserving larger uniform proofreading transformations (e.g. $k \times k$ for $k \geq 3$) would require expanded sensitivity profiles. Other tile system properties, such as avoidance of facet nucleation errors [4] and barriers to spurious nucleation [28], would also be desirable to preserve, and it may be possible to develop similar criteria. Additionally, while our methods are intended for optimizing tile systems that are already algorithmic, it may be interesting to consider the combination of sensitivity criteria with uniquely-addressed systems and more sophisticated PATS search methods. Uniquely-addressed tile systems have no error pathways in the KTM and no sensitive pairs of any order; it is only in merging tiles that the KTM becomes applicable. Thus, preserving sensitivity profiles while reducing a uniquely-addressed assembly could result in systems that exhibit strong proofreading behavior without any need for a proofreading transformation, and avoid $e^{-G_{se}}$ error rate scaling.

Another approach might be to go beyond preserving desirable properties in tile systems that have already incorporated proofreading, and search for changes that add them to tile systems designed without proofreading. Rather than trying to reduce the size of a system, an optimizing compiler could try to split tiles and

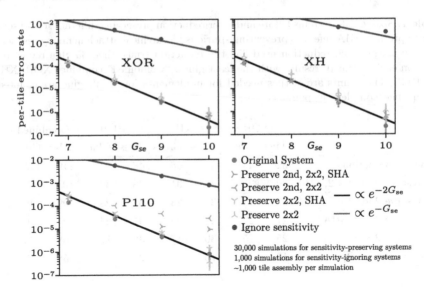

Fig. 9. Per-tile error rates in kTAM simulations, in Xgrow via Alhambra, varying G_{se}, with $G_{mc} = 2G_{se} - \log 2$. Assembly time in this regime scales approximately as $e^{2G_{se}}$: at $G_{se} = 7$, a 1,000 tile assembly will grow in about 4 min, and at $G_{se} = 9$, in about 4 h. Per-tile error rates were determined from the percentage of perfect assemblies.

glues to preserve aTAM behavior while improving or introducing proofreading, barriers to spurious nucleation, facet nucleation error rates, and lattice defect formation. Such a tile-system-specific approach could find systems with behaviors similar to those provided by general tile system transformations and design principles while being smaller, easier to design, and possibly more effective.

Acknowledgments. We thank Chigozie Nri, Philip Petersen, Lulu Qian, and Grigory Tikhomirov for discussions and collaboration on physical implementations and the Alhambra compiler, and Robert Johnson and William Poole for discussions on aTAM equivalence. This work was partially supported by the Evans Foundation and National Science Foundation award CCF-1317694.

References

1. Alhambra. https://github.com/DNA-and-Natural-Algorithms-Group/alhambra
2. Barish, R.D., Schulman, R., Rothemund, P.W.K., Winfree, E.: An information-bearing seed for nucleating algorithmic self-assembly. PNAS **106**(15), 6054–6059 (2009). https://doi.org/10.1073/pnas.0808736106
3. Cannon, S., et al.: Two hands are better than one (up to constant factors): self-assembly in the 2HAM vs. aTAM. In: Portier, N., Wilke, T. (eds.) STACS 2013. LIPIcs, vol. 20, pp. 172–184. Dagstuhl (2013). https://doi.org/10.4230/LIPIcs.STACS.2013.172

4. Chen, H.-L., Goel, A.: Error free self-assembly using error prone tiles. In: Ferretti, C., Mauri, G., Zandron, C. (eds.) DNA 2004. LNCS, vol. 3384, pp. 62–75. Springer, Heidelberg (2005). https://doi.org/10.1007/11493785_6

5. Chen, H.L., Schulman, R., Goel, A., Winfree, E.: Reducing facet nucleation during algorithmic self-assembly. Nano Lett. **7**, 2913–2919 (2007). https://doi.org/10.1021/nl070793o

6. Czeizler, E., Popa, A.: Synthesizing minimal tile sets for complex patterns in the framework of patterned DNA self-assembly. Theor. Comput. Sci. **499**, 23–37 (2018). https://doi.org/10.1016/j.tcs.2013.05.009

7. Doty, D.: Theory of algorithmic self-assembly. Commun. ACM **55**(12), 78–88 (2012). https://doi.org/10.1145/2380656.2380675

8. Doty, D., Patitz, M.J., Summers, S.M.: Limitations of self-assembly at temperature 1. Theor. Comput. Sci. **412**(1–2), 145–158 (2011). https://doi.org/10.1016/j.tcs.2010.08.023

9. Evans, C.G.: Crystals that count! Physical principles and experimental investigations of DNA tile self-assembly. Ph.D. thesis, California Institute of Technology (2014). http://resolver.caltech.edu/CaltechTHESIS:05132014-142306756

10. Evans, C.G., Winfree, E.: DNA sticky end design and assignment for robust algorithmic self-assembly. In: Soloveichik, D., Yurke, B. (eds.) DNA 2013. LNCS, vol. 8141, pp. 61–75. Springer, Cham (2013). https://doi.org/10.1007/978-3-319-01928-4_5

11. Evans, C.G., Winfree, E.: Physical principles for DNA tile self-assembly. Chem. Soc. Rev. **46**(12), 3808–3829 (2017). https://doi.org/10.1039/C6CS00745G

12. Fu, T.J., Seeman, N.C.: DNA double-crossover molecules. Biochemistry **32**, 3211–3220 (1993). https://doi.org/10.1021/bi00064a003

13. Fujibayashi, K., Hariadi, R., Park, S.H., Winfree, E., Murata, S.: Toward reliable algorithmic self-assembly of DNA tiles: a fixed-width cellular automaton pattern. Nano Lett. **8**(7), 1791–1797 (2008). https://doi.org/10.1021/nl0722830

14. Göös, M., Lempiäinen, T., Czeizler, E., Orponen, P.: Search methods for tile sets in patterned DNA self-assembly. J. Comput. Syst. Sci. **80**(1), 297–319 (2014). https://doi.org/10.1016/j.jcss.2013.08.003

15. Jacobs, W.M., Reinhardt, A., Frenkel, D.: Rational design of self-assembly pathways for complex multicomponent structures. PNAS **112**(20), 6313–6318 (2015). https://doi.org/10.1073/pnas.1502210112

16. Johnsen, A., Kao, M.Y., Seki, S.: A manually-checkable proof for the NP-hardness of 11-color pattern self-assembly tileset synthesis. J. Comb. Optim. **33**(2), 496–529 (2017). https://doi.org/10.1007/s10878-015-9975-6

17. Johnsen, A.C., Kao, M.-Y., Seki, S.: Computing minimum tile sets to self-assemble color patterns. In: Cai, L., Cheng, S.-W., Lam, T.-W. (eds.) ISAAC 2013. LNCS, vol. 8283, pp. 699–710. Springer, Heidelberg (2013). https://doi.org/10.1007/978-3-642-45030-3_65

18. Johnson, R., Dong, Q., Winfree, E.: Verifying chemical reaction network implementations: a bisimulation approach. Theor. Comput. Sci. (2018). https://doi.org/10.1016/j.tcs.2018.01.002

19. Kari, L., Kopecki, S., Meunier, P.É., Patitz, M.J., Seki, S.: Binary pattern tile set synthesis is NP-hard. Algorithmica **78**(1), 1–46 (2017). https://doi.org/10.1007/s00453-016-0154-7

20. Kari, L., Kopecki, S., Seki, S.: 3-color bounded patterned self-assembly. Nat. Comput. **14**(2), 279–292 (2015). https://doi.org/10.1007/s11047-014-9434-9

21. Ke, Y., Ong, L.L., Shih, W.M., Yin, P.: Three-dimensional structures self-assembled from DNA bricks. Science **338**(6111), 1177–1183 (2012). https://doi.org/10.1126/science.1227268

22. Lin, C., Liu, Y., Rinker, S., Yan, H.: DNA tile based self-assembly: building complex nanoarchitectures. ChemPhysChem **7**(8), 1641–1647 (2006). https://doi.org/10.1002/cphc.200600260

23. Ma, X., Lombardi, F.: Combinatorial optimization problem in designing DNA self-assembly tile sets. In: 2008 IEEE International Workshop on Design and Test of Nano Devices, Circuits and Systems, pp. 73–76 (2008). https://doi.org/10.1109/NDCS.2008.7

24. Ma, X., Lombardi, F.: Synthesis of tile sets for DNA self-assembly. IEEE Trans. Comput.-Aided Des. Integr. Circ. Syst. **27**(5), 963–967 (2008). https://doi.org/10.1109/TCAD.2008.917973

25. Milner, R.: Communication and Concurrency. Prentice Hall, Upper Saddle River (1989)

26. Ong, L.L., et al.: Programmable self-assembly of three-dimensional nanostructures from 10,000 unique components. Nature **552**(7683), 72–77 (2017). https://doi.org/10.1038/nature24648

27. Reif, J.H., Sahu, S., Yin, P.: Compact error-resilient computational DNA tiling assemblies. In: Ferretti, C., Mauri, G., Zandron, C. (eds.) DNA 2004. LNCS, vol. 3384, pp. 293–307. Springer, Heidelberg (2005). https://doi.org/10.1007/11493785_26

28. Schulman, R., Winfree, E.: Programmable control of nucleation for algorithmic self-assembly. SIAM J. Comput. **39**(4), 1581–1616 (2010). https://doi.org/10.1137/070680266

29. Schulman, R., Yurke, B., Winfree, E.: Robust self-replication of combinatorial information via crystal growth and scission. PNAS **109**(17), 6405–6410 (2012). https://doi.org/10.1073/pnas.1117813109

30. Seeman, N.C., Sleiman, H.F.: DNA nanotechnology. Nat. Rev. Mater. **3**, 17068 (2017). https://doi.org/10.1038/natrevmats.2017.68

31. Soloveichik, D., Winfree, E.: Complexity of compact proofreading for self-assembled patterns. In: Carbone, A., Pierce, N.A. (eds.) DNA 2005. LNCS, vol. 3892, pp. 305–324. Springer, Heidelberg (2006). https://doi.org/10.1007/11753681_24

32. Wang, W., Lin, T., Zhang, S., Bai, T., Mi, Y., Wei, B.: Self-assembly of fully addressable DNA nanostructures from double crossover tiles. Nucleic Acids Res. **44**(16), 7989–7996 (2016). https://doi.org/10.1093/nar/gkw670

33. Wei, B., Dai, M., Yin, P.: Complex shapes self-assembled from single-stranded DNA tiles. Nature **485**(7400), 623–626 (2012). https://doi.org/10.1038/nature11075

34. Winfree, E.: Simulations of computing by self-assembly. Technical report, CaltechCSTR:1998.22, Pasadena, CA (1998). https://doi.org/10.7907/Z9TB14X7

35. Winfree, E., Bekbolatov, R.: Proofreading tile sets: error correction for algorithmic self-assembly. In: Chen, J., Reif, J. (eds.) DNA 2003. LNCS, vol. 2943, pp. 126–144. Springer, Heidelberg (2004). https://doi.org/10.1007/978-3-540-24628-2_13

A Content-Addressable DNA Database with Learned Sequence Encodings

Kendall Stewart[1][(✉)], Yuan-Jyue Chen[2], David Ward[1], Xiaomeng Liu[1],
Georg Seelig[1], Karin Strauss[1,2], and Luis Ceze[1]

[1] Paul G. Allen School of Computer Science & Engineering,
University of Washington, Seattle, USA
kstwrt@cs.washington.edu
[2] Microsoft Research, Redmond, WA, USA

Abstract. We present strand and codeword design schemes for a DNA database capable of approximate similarity search over a multidimensional dataset of content-rich media. Our strand designs address crosstalk in associative DNA databases, and we demonstrate a novel method for learning DNA sequence encodings from data, applying it to a dataset of tens of thousands of images. We test our design in the wetlab using one hundred target images and ten query images, and show that our database is capable of performing similarity-based enrichment: on average, visually similar images account for 30% of the sequencing reads for each query, despite making up only 10% of the database.

1 Introduction

DNA-based databases were first proposed over twenty years ago by Baum [3], yet recent demonstrations of their practicality [4,6,8,9,18,28] have generated a renewed interest into researching related theory and applications.

Some of these recent demonstrations of DNA storage have used key-based random access for their retrieval schemes, falling short of the content-based associative searches envisioned by Baum. Our goal is to close this gap and design a DNA-based digital data store equipped with a mechanism for content-based similarity search.

This work contributes two advances to the field of DNA storage: first, a strand design optimized for associative search. Second, a sequence encoder capable of preserving similarity between documents, such that a query sequence generated from a given document will retrieve similar documents from the database. We validate our designs with wetlab experiments.

While our methods should generalize to databases comprising any type of media, we focus on images in this work, as there is a rich body of prior work in content-based image retrieval to draw on.

The rest of this paper is laid out as follows: Sect. 2 covers background on similarity search, DNA-based parallel search, and DNA-based data storage. Section 3 details our strand designs. Section 4 describes our methodology for mapping

D. Doty and H. Dietz (Eds.): DNA 2018, LNCS 11145, pp. 55–70, 2018.
https://doi.org/10.1007/978-3-030-00030-1_4

images to DNA sequences. Section 5 outlines our experimental protocol and the results of our experiments. Section 6 discusses the results and proposes future work. Section 7 addresses related work, and Sect. 8 concludes the paper.

2   Background

2.1   Similarity Search

The problem of *similarity search* is to retrieve documents from a database that are similar in *content* to a given query. For media such as text, images and video, this can be a difficult task. Most state-of-the-art systems convert each document into a vector-space representation using either a hand-crafted embedding, or one learned via a neural network. These *feature vectors* can then be compared with metrics like Euclidean distance, where similar documents will tend to be close together in feature-space. Therefore, a similarity search can be reduced to a k-nearest-neighbor or R-near-neighbor search.

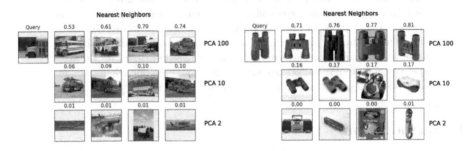

Fig. 1. A pair of sample queries from the Caltech-256 dataset, showing the four nearest neighbors in three different feature spaces. Each neighbor is annotated with its Euclidean distance to the query in that space.

Feature vectors that are effective for similarity search tend to be high dimensional. To illustrate this, Fig. 1 shows two queries using the Caltech-256 image dataset [10]. The visual features of each image in the dataset were extracted using VGG16, a publicly available convolutional neural network trained on an image classification task. We used the 4096-dimensional activations from the FC2 layer, an intermediate layer in VGG16 whose activations have shown to be effective in content-based image retrieval tasks [25]. These features were reduced down to 100, 10, and 2 dimensions using principal component analysis (PCA). The nearest neighbors in each of these subspaces (with respect to Euclidean distance) are shown to the right of each query. Qualitatively, the nearest neighbors higher-dimensional spaces appear more similar to the query than the nearest neighbors in lower-dimensional spaces.

When feature vectors have hundreds of dimensions, the well-known "curse of dimensionality" defeats efficient indexing schemes [12]. In the worst case, every item in the database must be examined to find all images within a certain distance threshold. Relaxations of the search problem that allow for errors or omissions result in much faster lookups, using algorithms such as locality-sensitive hashing (LSH) [2].

Looking toward a future where zettabytes of data are generated every year [11], even techniques such as LSH that reduce the amount of data that needs to be inspected by orders of magnitude will still burden traditional storage with a tremendous number of IO requests to a massive storage infrastructure, outstripping the time and energy cost of the feature vector distance computation itself.

Computer architects have noticed that the power required to move data from the storage device to the compute unit can be reduced by moving the compute substrate closer to the storage substrate. This class of techniques is broadly called "near-data" processing [14].

2.2   DNA-Based Parallel Search

"Adleman-style" DNA computing [1] can be thought of as an extreme version of near-data processing: each DNA strand is designed to both store and process information—the compute and storage substrates are the same.

Like Adleman's original solution to the Hamiltonian Path problem, this style of parallel processing requires exponential amounts of DNA to solve combinatorial problems. However, for less computationally intense problems like similarity search, the amount of DNA required is much less: if each of N items in the database is mapped to a single "target" molecule, then N identical copies of a "query" molecule are sufficient to react with every item in the database. If the query is equipped with a biotin tail and designed to hybridize only with relevant data, then relevant items can be "fished out" of the database using streptavidin-coated magnetic beads.

This amounts to an extremely high-bandwidth parallel search, in the vein of near-data processing techniques. Furthermore, because PCR can make exponentially many copies of the query molecule, the amount of DNA that needs to be directly synthesized is minimal. This makes DNA-based search especially appealing in the zettabyte-yottabyte future.

2.3   DNA-Based Data Storage

The current state-of-the-art DNA storage systems (Organick et al. [18] includes a good survey of recent work) focus on zero-bit-error retrieval of arbitrary digital data. Each digital file is segmented and encoded into many thousands of unique sequences, and individual files can be retrieved from a mixed database using PCR-based random access. In this work, we focus on a database for storing and retrieving *metadata*. Instead of storing sequences that contain the complete file, each file is associated with a sequence that contains the semantic features used for content-based retrieval, as well as a pointer to the file in another database (which could be either a traditional database or a DNA-based one).

3   Database Design

To take advantage of the near-data processing capabilities of DNA, we need a database design that allows each element in the database to both store and process data. We choose to separate these two concerns by associating each database element with two sequences: one that stores an ID unique to that datum, and one that is generated from the semantic features of that datum, designed as a locus for a hybridization probe. The ID is not an "active" site, but rather the information to be retrieved by the search—for instance, it could be the address of the datum in another database that stores the document's complete data.

The simplest way to retain the association between the ID sequence and the feature sequence in a DNA database is to place them on the same strand of DNA. However, this association can cause unwanted secondary structures on longer strands, and can result in cross-talk if a query reacts with a potential target's ID sequence instead of its feature sequence.

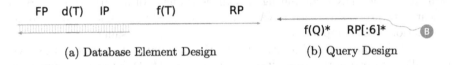

FP	d(T)	IP	f(T)	RP

(a) Database Element Design   f(Q)*   RP[:6]*   B

                                      (b) Query Design

Fig. 2. Strand designs. Blue indicates a conserved region, orange indicates a region specific to that data item. Arrow indicates the 3' end. Star (*) indicates reverse complement. RP[:6] indicates the first six bases of domain RP. (Color figure online)

Our strand designs address this issue, and are shown in Fig. 2. The database entries (Fig. 2a) are synthesized single-stranded, but are made partially double stranded using a single-step PCR reaction starting from IP (the "internal primer"), which is conserved across all elements in the database.

This process covers up the IP region, the ID sequence associated with the data $(d(T))$, and the forward primer (FP) region, which is another conserved region used to prepare samples for sequencing. This leaves the feature sequence $(f(T))$ and the conserved reverse sequencing primer (RP) available to interact with the query.

To execute a query Q, a biotinylated query strand (Fig. 2b) is mixed with the prepared targets. Because the query and target feature sequences are designed to be imperfect matches, the query strand also includes the reverse complement of first six bases of RP (denoted RP[:6]*)—this exact match is designed to prevent misalignments and ensure that hybridization only depends on the interaction between $f(T)$ and $f(Q)$. The query and targets are annealed, and then streptavidin-coated magnetic beads are added to pull down targets that have hybridized with the queries.

The resulting filtered targets are amplified using FP and RP, then sequenced to retrieve the data region associated with each target.

4   Learned Sequence Encodings

To take advantage of the strand designs described above, we need to design a mapping from images to feature domains such that a query molecule will retrieve relevant targets from the database. To simplify our task, we pre-process all images by transforming them into the 10-dimensional subspace shown in Fig. 1, and choose our feature domains to be 30 nucleotides in length.

Our general feature encoding strategy is inspired by semantic hashing [21], where a deep neural network transforms an input feature space into an output address space where similar items are "close" together. Our goal is to design a neural network sequence encoder that takes the 10-dimensional image feature vectors from the VGG16 + PCA extraction process described in Sect. 2.1, and outputs DNA sequences that are close together if and only if the feature vectors are close together. Following Tsaftaris et al. [22], we define a pair of query and target sequences as "close" if their hybridization reaction has a high thermodynamic yield: the proportion of target molecules that are converted into a query-target duplex.

To train the neural network, we want a loss function that will push the encoder's parameters to generate output sequences where a query retrieves a target if and only if the target and query represent similar images. The most appropriate choice for this is the cross-entropy loss[1], where the labels are binary similarity labels (similar vs. not similar) for each pair of query and target images, and the retrieval probabilities are the thermodynamic yields of each query-target hybridization reaction.

Using the cross-entropy loss requires us to define a binary notion of image similarity, and to define thermodynamic yield as a differentiable function of two DNA sequences. The function must be differentiable because neural networks are efficiently trained using gradient descent, which requires taking the derivative of the loss with respect to the encoder parameters.

In the sections below, we present a definition of binary image similarity, followed by an approximation for thermodynamic yield using Hamming distance, and an approximation for Hamming distance using the cosine distance between "one-hot" encodings of DNA bases. Finally, we present the results of using these approximations to train a neural network on a large image dataset.

4.1   Binary Image Similarity

As described in Sect. 2.1, a semantic notion of image "similarity" can be mapped to a real-valued number by computing the Euclidean distance between two image

---

[1] Given a set of n pairs of binary labels $y \in \{0, 1\}$ and retrieval probabilities p, the cross-entropy loss is:

$$l(y, p) = -\frac{1}{n} \sum_{i=1}^{n} y_i \cdot \log(p_i) + (1 - y_i) \cdot \log(1 - p_i).$$

feature vectors. However, to use the efficient cross-entropy loss function defined above, we must label image pairs with a binary label: "similar" or "not similar". The simplest way to do this is to apply a threshold to the Euclidean distance.

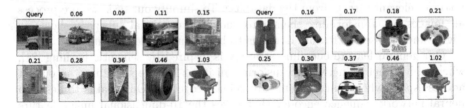

Fig. 3. Sample queries demonstrating the relationship between image similarity and distance in the 10-dimensional PCA subspace shown in Fig. 1. Distances less than 0.2 usually correspond to similar images, while those greater than 0.2 do not.

Because the definition of similarity is ultimately up to a human observer, we must determine this threshold by inspection. For the feature extraction method we used, we found a threshold of 0.2 to be fairly reliable across the Caltech-256 dataset. Figure 3 demonstrates this for a pair of sample queries.

4.2   Approximating Thermodynamic Yield

Thermodynamic yield can be calculated accurately by using the multi-stranded partition function [5], which is used by tools such as NUPACK [29]. Unfortunately, this calculation is expensive and not differentiable, and thus cannot be used directly to train a neural network.

However, Fig. 4 shows that the query-target yield and the query-target Hamming distance have a noisy sigmoid[2]. relationship. The best fit line provides us with a simple approximation of thermodynamic yield in terms of the Hamming distance. A drawback is that this approximation is less accurate for higher Hamming distances.

4.3   Approximating Hamming Distance

While we can use the Hamming distance to approximate thermodynamic yield, computing the Hamming distance requires discrete operations and is also not differentiable. Below, we define an alternative representation of DNA sequences, and a continuous approximation of Hamming distance that can be used with a neural network.

DNA sequences can be represented with a "one-hot" encoding, where each position is represented by a four-channel vector, and each channel corresponds

---

[2] Functions of the type:

$$f(x) = \frac{1}{1 + \exp(ax - b)}.$$

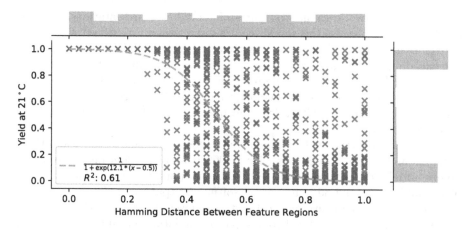

Fig. 4. Yield vs. Hamming distance for 2000 pairs of targets and queries with feature regions of length 30, as calculated by NUPACK. The dashed line shows the best sigmoid fit to the simulations.

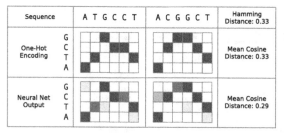

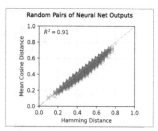

(a) Comparison of sequence representations and associated distance metrics.

(b) Effectiveness of neural network output.

Fig. 5. One-hot sequence encodings and their properties.

to a base. For instance, if that base is an A, then the channel corresponding to A will have a value of one, and the other channels will be zero.

Figure 5a shows one-hot encodings of two sequences. At each position, the one-hot encodings can be compared by computing the cosine distance[3] between them. If they represent different bases, the representations will be orthogonal, and the cosine distance will be one. If they represent the same base, the cosine distance will be zero. Therefore the mean cosine distance across positions will be equal to the mean number of mismatches, which is equivalent to the Hamming distance.

---

[3] Given two vectors $\mathbf{u}$ and $\mathbf{v}$, the cosine distance is:

$$d(\mathbf{u}, \mathbf{v}) = 1 - \frac{\mathbf{u} \cdot \mathbf{v}}{||\mathbf{u}|| \, ||\mathbf{v}||}.$$

A neural network cannot output differentiable representations that are exactly one-hot, because this would require discretization. However, if the channel values at each position are sufficiently far apart, we can approximate a one-hot encoding by normalizing them with a softmax function[4], which pushes the maximum value towards one while pushing the other values towards zero. Furthermore, we can encourage the channel values to be far apart by using a hidden-layer activation function with a large output range, such as the rectified linear unit (ReLU) function[5].

Figure 5b shows the relationship between the mean cosine distance and Hamming distance of pairs of outputs, for 10,000 pairs of random inputs to a randomly initialized neural network with 10 input units, two ReLU hidden layers of 128 units each, and 30 four-channel softmax output units. The mean cosine distance between the neural network outputs closely follows the Hamming distance between their discretized counterparts, validating our approximation. To the best of our knowledge, using this four-channel encoding technique is a novel contribution of our work.

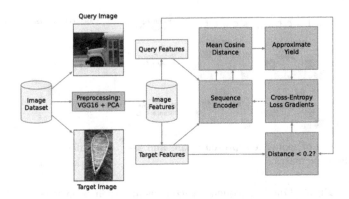

Fig. 6. The training loop, illustrating how a pair of images is used to calculate gradients for the sequence encoder. Data is in light gray, and operations are in dark gray.

---

[4] Given an N-dimensional vector $\mathbf{u}$, the softmax function is defined element-wise as follows:
$$\text{softmax}(\mathbf{u})_i = \frac{e^{u_i}}{\sum_{j=1}^{N} e^{u_j}}.$$

[5] The ReLU function is defined as:
$$\text{ReLU}(x) = \max(x, 0).$$

4.4   Neural Network Architecture

Composing the yield approximation with the Hamming distance approximation allows us to use gradient descent to train any kind of neural-network-based sequence encoder to generate good encodings for similarity search, given a suitable dataset. This process is depicted in Fig. 6. On each iteration, a pair of images is encoded, and then the mean cosine distance between the outputs is used to calculate the approximate thermodynamic yield. Combined with the actual similarity between the feature vectors, the parameters of the neural network are updated using the gradient of the cross-entropy loss with respect to the parameters.

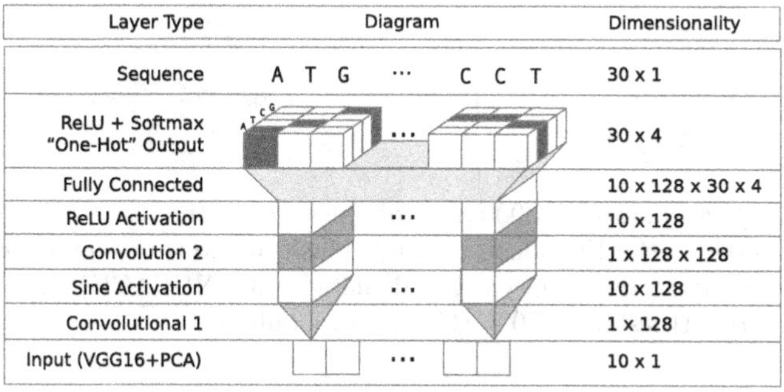

Layer Type	Diagram	Dimensionality
Sequence	A T G ⋯ C C T	30 x 1
ReLU + Softmax "One-Hot" Output		30 x 4
Fully Connected		10 x 128 x 30 x 4
ReLU Activation	⋯	10 x 128
Convolution 2		1 x 128 x 128
Sine Activation	⋯	10 x 128
Convolutional 1		1 x 128
Input (VGG16+PCA)	⋯	10 x 1

Fig. 7. The neural network architecture for the sequence encoder.

A full exploration of the design space of neural-network-based sequence encoders is outside the scope of this work. We conducted a small-scale exploration and arrived at the architecture depicted in Fig. 7, but this is not necessarily the best or only neural network for this task.

The network begins with two convolutional layers, where each input dimension is processed independently with a shared set of weights. This was done to preserve some of the "element-wise" structure of the Euclidean distance used to calculate the similarity label. The first convolutional layer has a sine-function activation, inspired by spectral hashing [26], a method for transforming an input feature space into a binary address space. The second convolutional layer uses the ReLU function to allow the outputs to be further apart.

Since the input dimensions do not have a spatial interpretation, we cap the convolutional layers with a set of fully connected weights to the four-channel sequence output, such that each input dimension's activation map is given a chance to influence each base in all positions. A ReLU activation followed by a softmax activation gives us the approximate one-hot representation discussed above.

4.5   Training Results

To train the encoder, we first split the 30,607 images of the Caltech256 dataset into 24,485 training images and 6,122 test images. We extracted the VGG16 FC2 features from all 30,607 images, and then fitted a PCA transform to the FC2 vectors from the training set. The fitted transform was applied to all images.

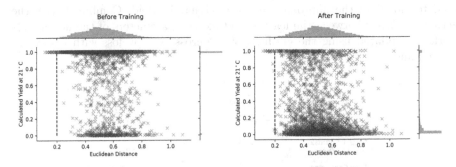

Fig. 8. Encoder performance on 3000 pairs of images from the test set, before and after training. The x-axis is the Euclidean distance between the target and the query, and the y-axis is the thermodynamic yield (calculated with NUPACK). The orange line shows the similarity threshold of 0.2. (Color figure online)

During each training iteration, a batch of random pairs of training set images was used to update the encoder weights, as depicted in Fig. 6. The encoder was trained for 65,000 iterations using 500 random pairs of images per iteration. Figure 8 shows the performance of the encoder as measured by the relationship between the thermodynamic yield (calculated with NUPACK) and the Euclidean distance between the images in the pair. NUPACK was set to simulate our experimental setup, with an equal molar ratio of target to query strands, and temperature at 21 °C.

The performance is shown before training (with random parameters), and again after training. Before training, nearly all pairs of images exhibit a high yield, indicating no selectivity by distance. After training, most pairs have a low yield, but almost no pairs of images under 0.2 in Euclidean distance (which we have defined as similar) have a low yield. However, there are still non-similar images that have high yield, indicating that any successful query will also retrieve non-similar images.

5   Experiments

5.1   Dataset Construction

To test our designs in the wetlab, we constructed a subset of the test set consisting of 10 query images and 100 target images. The queries were chosen by first clustering all images in the training set into 10 groups using k-means, and then choosing a representative query image from the test set that belonged to each cluster. The k-means step ensures that none of the query images are pairwise-similar, because they all belong to different clusters in the data.

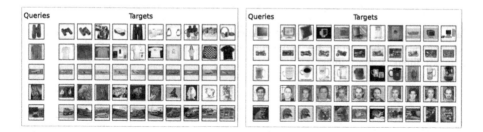

Fig. 9. The set of query and target images used in our wetlab experiments.

For each of these 10 query images, we selected its 10 nearest neighbors in the test set. This ensures that each query image has 10 similar images and 90 dissimilar images among the 100 targets. The result of this selection process is shown in Fig. 9.

For each image, we encoded its features as a 30-nucleotide DNA sequence using the trained encoder, as described in Sect. 4.5. For each target image, we assigned it a random 5-nt ID, and then constructed a 90-nt sequence as shown in Fig. 2a. For each query image, we constructed a 36-nt sequence as shown in Fig. 2b. Target and query strands were then ordered from IDT. The query strands included the addition of a biotinylated spacer at the 5' end.

5.2 Target Preparation

All target strands were mixed together in an equal molar ratio. The targets were then mixed with 20% excess of the primer IP* at 10 μM, and 20 μL of the target-primer mixture was added to 20 μL of 2x KAPA HIFI PCR enzyme mix. This 40 μL mixture was placed in a thermocycler with the following protocol: (1) 95 °C for 3 min, (2) 98 °C for 20 s, (3) 56 °C for 20 s, (4) 72 °C for 20 s, (5) go to step 2 one more time, and (6) 72 °C for 30 s. This process extends the primer to cover the 5' half of each target strand.

5.3 Query Protocol

For each of the 10 query strands, a sample of the target mixture was diluted to 200 nM and mixed with an equal molar concentration of the query, then annealed in a thermocycler from 95 °C to 21 °C at a rate of 1 °C per minute.

The annealed query-target mixture was mixed with streptavidin-coated magnetic beads, incubated at room temperature for 15 min, and placed on a magnetic

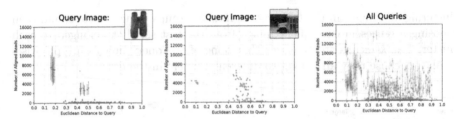

(a) Number of aligned reads per target vs. distance from target to query. Points indicate the mean across three replicates, and error bars indicate standard error. Different colors indicate different query images.

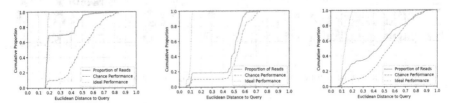

(b) Cumulative distribution of aligned reads as a function of increasing distance from target to query. For reference, the dashed lines show the cumulative distribution of targets by distance, and the dotted lines show an ideal where all reads are allocated to the nearest targets. Different colors indicate different query images (gray for all queries).

Fig. 10. Selected results for two of the ten query images, and aggregated results for all queries.

rack. The supernatant containing non-captured DNA was removed and the beads were resuspended in elution buffer, then incubated for 5 min at 95 °C and placed on a magnetic rack to separate captured DNA molecules from biotinylated query strands. The supernatant containing the captured DNA was mixed with the forward primer FP and the reverse primer RP* in a PCR reaction to amplify the captured targets. The amplified targets were ligated with Illumina sequencing adapters and then sequenced using an Illumina NextSeq.

This procedure was repeated 3 times for each of the 10 queries. Each query and replicate was given a unique sequencing index.

5.4   Results

For each query and replicate, the reads were aligned with the set of all target sequences using BWA-MEM [15]. Figure 10 shows the number of aligned reads for each target versus the distance from that target to the query, for two sample queries, and for all queries together.

Figure 10b shows the cumulative distribution of aligned reads as a function of distance from the query. The dashed line is a baseline indicating the cumulative distribution of distances across the targets. The further the solid line is from the baseline, the stronger the relationship between distance and the number of reads. The dotted line shows the ideal result, where reads are only allocated to similar targets (those less than 0.2 Euclidean distance from the query).

The first sample query (the binoculars) shows a successful result, where most of the reads are allocated to similar targets. In contrast, the second sample query (the school bus) is less successful: the reads are distributed almost evenly across similar and non-similar images.

Across all queries, our results are moderately successful—though there are many reads going to dissimilar targets, our scheme is clearly capable of performing similarity-based enrichment: roughly 30% of the sequencing resources are being used by similar targets, which by construction make up just 10% of the database.

6   Discussion

In practice, the 10-dimensional image feature subspace used for our experiments is insufficiently selective. Referring back to Fig. 1, the 100-dimensional space was more effective at relating distance to qualitative similarity. But it is difficult to train an encoder to transform this already-compressed 100-dimensional subspace into a 30-nucleotide feature sequence.

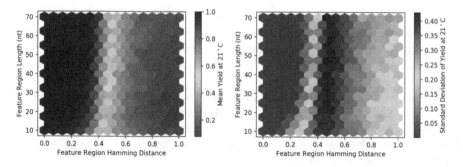

Fig. 11. Mean and standard deviation of yield as a function of feature region length and feature region Hamming distance.

We might be tempted to try longer feature regions, but this will likely experience more noise of the type seen in our results. Figure 11 illustrates this by generalizing Fig. 4 to feature regions of different sizes. These plots bin across sequence length and target-query Hamming distance, and the color indicates either the mean (on the left) or the standard deviation (on the right) of the yield values in that bin, at our protocol temperature of 21 °C. These plots tell us that selectivity decreases with increasing length, and that variance in yield for dissimilar targets increases as well.

These problems pose a difficult challenge to scaling this system. One avenue for future work is to devise a more accurate approximation for thermodynamic yield that can still be used to train a neural network. Another is to explore alternative probe designs that are meant to reduce variance, such as the toehold-exchange probes of Zhang et al. [27, 30].

7   Related Work

7.1   Content-Addressable DNA Databases

Baum was the first to propose DNA databases with associative search capabilities, noting the effectiveness of hybridization probes bound to magnetic beads [3]. Reif et al. designed and built a version of Baum's system. However, these schemes were meant to perform exact searching, while ours performs similarity search [20].

Reif and LaBean also proposed a scheme for performing similarity search in a Baum-style exact matching database [19]. This involved an *in silico* preprocessing step where the database was sorted into clusters. To retrieve similar data, a query would first be classified *in silico*, and everything in that cluster would then be retrieved *in vitro*. Because the cluster centers were static, a downside was that any data added to the database must be assigned to an existing cluster, which may not be accurate if the data belongs to a novel cluster that did not exist during training. In our system, the encoding also depends on a training set, but it is more flexible since there are no explicit cluster assignments.

7.2   Hybridization-Driven Similarity Search

Using melting temperature as a mechanism for similarity search in DNA databases was proposed by Tsaftaris et al. [22,23]. However, their work focuses on similarity search of one-dimensional data, which allows the mapping from signal values to DNA sequences to be a small lookup table. Our system maps multidimensional input to DNA sequences.

Performing similarity search on higher dimensional data has been explored by Garzon and Neel [7,16,17]. Their work leverages a technique for *in vitro* dimensionality reduction of large datasets encoded in DNA (e.g., text corpora). On the other hand, our system performs dimensionality reduction *in silico* as part of the sequence encoding.

7.3   DNA Codeword Design

Designing codewords for robust DNA computing is a large subfield within the DNA computing community [13,24]. These works focus on algorithms for computing a set of non-cross-hybridizing sequences that can be used to represent discrete signal values in an application-agnostic manner. Our system does not require non-cross-hybridizing sequences and takes an approach to codeword design, where the sequence mapping is learned from data.

8   Conclusion

We have presented a complete design, from encoding to sequencing, for a DNA database capable of performing content-based associative search by enriching database elements that are similar in content to a given query.

We have accomplished this by combining state-of-the-art research from the information retrieval and machine learning community with theoretical and experimental insights from the DNA computing and DNA storage communities to come up with novel encoding strategies and strand designs.

While it will be a challenge to scale this system to more complex features and larger datasets, this work is another step towards realizing the types of systems we will need to accommodate the storage demands of the future.

Acknowledgments. We would like to thank the anonymous reviewers for their input, which were very helpful to improve the manuscript. We also thank the Molecular Information Systems Lab and Seelig Lab members for their input, especially Max Willsey, who helped frame an early version. We thank Dr. Anne Fischer for suggesting a better way to present some of the data. This work was supported in part by Microsoft, and a grant from DARPA under the Molecular Informatics Program.

References

1. Adleman, L.M.: Molecular computation of solutions to combinatorial problems. Science **266**(5187), 1021–1024 (1994)
2. Andoni, A., Indyk, P.: Near-optimal hashing algorithms for approximate nearest neighbor in high dimensions. Commun. ACM **51**(1), 117–122 (2008)
3. Baum, E.B.: Building an associative memory vastly larger than the brain. Science **268**(5210), 583–585 (1995)
4. Church, G.M., Gao, Y., Kosuri, S.: Next-generation digital information storage in DNA. Science **337**(6102), 1628–1628 (2012)
5. Dirks, R.M., Bois, J.S., Schaeffer, J.M., Winfree, E., Pierce, N.A.: Thermodynamic analysis of interacting nucleic acid strands. SIAM Rev. **49**(1), 56–88 (2007)
6. Erlich, Y., Zielinski, D.: DNA fountain enables a robust and efficient storage architecture. Science **355**(6328), 950–954 (2017)
7. Garzon, M.H., Bobba, K., Neel, A.: Efficiency and reliability of semantic retrieval in DNA-based memories. In: Chen, J., Reif, J. (eds.) DNA 2003. LNCS, vol. 2943, pp. 157–169. Springer, Heidelberg (2004). https://doi.org/10.1007/978-3-540-24628-2_15
8. Goldman, N., et al.: Towards practical, high-capacity, low-maintenance information storage in synthesized DNA. Nature **494**(7435), 77–80 (2013)
9. Grass, R.N., Heckel, R., Puddu, M., Paunescu, D., Stark, W.J.: Robust chemical preservation of digital information on dna in silica with error-correcting codes. Angew. Chem. Int. Ed. **54**(8), 2552–2555 (2015)
10. Griffin, G., Holub, A., Perona, P.: Caltech-256 object category dataset. Technical report, California Institute of Technology (2007)
11. IDC: Where in the world is storage (2013). http://www.idc.com/downloads/where_is_storage_infographic_243338.pdf
12. Indyk, P., Motwani, R.: Approximate nearest neighbors: towards removing the curse of dimensionality. In: Proceedings of the Thirtieth Annual ACM Symposium on Theory of Computing, STOC 1998, pp. 604–613. ACM, New York (1998). https://doi.org/10.1145/276698.276876
13. Kawashimo, S., Ono, H., Sadakane, K., Yamashita, M.: Dynamic neighborhood searches for thermodynamically designing DNA sequence. In: Garzon, M.H., Yan, H. (eds.) DNA 2007. LNCS, vol. 4848, pp. 130–139. Springer, Heidelberg (2008). https://doi.org/10.1007/978-3-540-77962-9_13

14. Lee, V.T., Kotalik, J., del Mundo, C.C., Alaghi, A., Ceze, L., Oskin, M.: Similarity search on automata processors. In: 2017 IEEE International Parallel and Distributed Processing Symposium (IPDPS), pp. 523–534 (2017)

15. Li, H.: Aligning sequence reads, clone sequences and assembly contigs with BWA-MEM (2013)

16. Neel, A., Garzon, M.: Semantic retrieval in DNA-based memories with Gibbs energy models. Biotechnol. Prog. **22**(1), 86–90 (2006)

17. Neel, A., Garzon, M., Penumatsa, P.: Soundness and quality of semantic retrieval in DNA-based memories with abiotic data. In: 2004 Congress on Evolutionary Computation, pp. 1889–1895. IEEE (2004)

18. Organick, L., et al.: Random access in large-scale DNA data storage. Nat. Biotechnol. **36**(3), 242–248 (2018)

19. Reif, J.H., LaBean, T.H.: Computationally inspired biotechnologies: improved DNA synthesis and associative search using error-correcting codes and vector-quantization? In: Condon, A., Rozenberg, G. (eds.) DNA 2000. LNCS, vol. 2054, pp. 145–172. Springer, Heidelberg (2001). https://doi.org/10.1007/3-540-44992-2_11

20. Reif, J.H., et al.: Experimental construction of very large scale DNA databases with associative search capability. In: Jonoska, N., Seeman, N.C. (eds.) DNA 2001. LNCS, vol. 2340, pp. 231–247. Springer, Heidelberg (2002). https://doi.org/10.1007/3-540-48017-X_22

21. Salakhutdinov, R., Hinton, G.: Semantic hashing. Int. J. Approx. Reason. **50**(7), 969–978 (2009)

22. Tsaftaris, S.A., Hatzimanikatis, V., Katsaggelos, A.K.: DNA hybridization as a similarity criterion for querying digital signals stored in DNA databases. In: 2006 IEEE International Conference on Acoustics Speed and Signal Processing, pp. II-1084–II-1087. IEEE (2006)

23. Tsaftaris, S.A., Katsaggelos, A.K., Pappas, T.N., Papoutsakis, T.E.: DNA-based matching of digital signals. In: 2004 IEEE International Conference on Acoustics, Speech, and Signal Processing, pp. V-581–V-584. IEEE (2004)

24. Tulpan, D., et al.: Thermodynamically based DNA strand design. Nucleic Acids Res. **33**(15), 4951–4964 (2005)

25. Wan, J., et al.: Deep learning for content-based image retrieval: a comprehensive study, pp. 157–166 (2014). https://doi.org/10.1145/2647868.2654948

26. Weiss, Y., Torralba, A., Fergus, R.: Spectral hashing. In: Proceedings of the 21st International Conference on Neural Information Processing Systems, NIPS 2008, pp. 1753–1760. Curran Associates Inc. (2008)

27. Wu, L.R.: Continuously tunable nucleic acid hybridization probes. Nat. Methods **12**(12), 1191–1196 (2015)

28. Yazdi, S.M.H.T., Gabrys, R., Milenkovic, O.: Portable and error-free DNA-based data storage. Sci. Rep. **7**(1), 1433 (2017)

29. Zadeh, J.N., et al.: NUPACK: analysis and design of nucleic acid systems. J. Comput. Chem. **32**(1), 170–173 (2011)

30. Zhang, D.Y., Chen, S.X., Yin, P.: Optimizing the specificity of nucleic acid hybridization. Nat. Chem. **4**(3), 208–214 (2012)

Temporal DNA Barcodes: A Time-Based Approach for Single-Molecule Imaging

Shalin Shah[1(✉)] and John Reif[1,2]

[1] Department of Electrical and Computer Engineering, Duke University,
Durham, USA
shalin.shah@duke.edu

[2] Department of Computer Science, Duke University, Durham, NC 27701, USA
reif@cs.duke.edu

Abstract. In the past decade, single-molecule imaging has opened new opportunities to understand reaction kinetics of molecular systems. DNA-PAINT uses transient binding of DNA strands to perform super-resolution fluorescence imaging. An interesting challenge in DNA nanoscience and related fields is the unique identification of single-molecules. While wavelength multiplexing (using fluorescent dyes of different colors) can be used to increase the number of distinguishable targets, the resultant total number of targets is still limited by the number of dyes with non-overlapping spectra. In this work, we introduce the use of time-domain to develop a DNA-based reporting framework for unique identification of single-molecules. These fluorescent DNA devices undergo a series of conformational transformations that result in (unique) time-changing intensity signals. We define this stochastic temporal intensity trace as the device's *temporal barcode* since it can uniquely identify the corresponding DNA device if the collection time is long enough. Our barcodes work with as few as one dye making them easy to design, extremely low-cost, and greatly simplifying the hardware setup. In addition, by adding multiple dyes, we can create a much larger family of uniquely identifiable reporter molecules. Finally, our devices are designed to follow the principle of transient binding and can be imaged using total internal reflection fluorescence (TIRF) microscopes so they are not susceptible to photo-bleaching, allowing us to monitor their activity for extended time periods. We model our devices using continuous-time Markov chains (CTMCs) and simulate their behavior using a stochastic simulation algorithm (SSA). These temporal barcodes are later analyzed and classified in their parameter space. The results obtained from our simulation experiments can provide crucial insights for collecting experimental data.

Keywords: Molecular reporters · DNA nanodevices
Temporal reporters · TIRF · Transient binding · DNA hairpins
Single-molecule imaging

© Springer Nature Switzerland AG 2018
D. Doty and H. Dietz (Eds.): DNA 2018, LNCS 11145, pp. 71–86, 2018.
https://doi.org/10.1007/978-3-030-00030-1_5

1   Introduction

The programmable nature of deoxyribonucleic acid (DNA) has been exploited extensively in the past for a plethora of applications such as constructing complex self-assembled nanostructures [29], nanoscale logic computing [25], targeted drug-delivery [5], nanorobots [26], data storage [31], dynamic systems [12] and nanoscale imaging [20]. The programmable power of DNA is primarily due to Watson-Crick base pairing which makes it a highly desirable substrate for computing applications [8,30]. In the field of DNA computing, several logic circuits have been demonstrated. These include simple digital and analog logic gates, as well as complex feed-forward and renewable circuits [6,7,25,33]. Some recent work also focuses on DNA-based localized computing, as it has the intrinsic advantage of faster reaction kinetics [2,3].

In DNA nanotechnology and related fields, atomic force microscope (AFM) and transmission electron microscope (TEM) have been dominant characterization techniques because of their molecular-scale resolving power. However, these techniques are invasive, expensive, lack multiplexing capabilities and face difficulty in capturing dynamic behavior. Most popular non-invasive techniques used to observe single-molecule dynamic behavior use some form of light microscopy. These techniques use fluorescent particles such as fluorescent proteins, organic dyes, quantum dots (QDs), and nanoparticles (NPs) to report cellular and molecular-scale activity. Several bio-sensing techniques, *in vitro*, *in vivo*, and *in situ*, have been demonstrated [1,4,9,11,18–24,32,36]. The objective of such reporting techniques is the unique identification of target particle. These biosensors ranged from 0.5 100 µm in size, and there are three ways to broadly classify these reporters based on their information encoding process: (a) Intensity encoding (b) Geometric encoding (c) Temporal encoding. *Intensity encoding* works by identifying the difference in fluorescence intensity obtained by a linear combination of one or more dyes. They use certain thresholding mechanisms to classify intensity levels. A simple example demonstrating intensity encoding is DNA-labeled microbeads by Li et al. [19]. *Geometric encoding* stores information in the structure of a molecule such as DNA origami barcodes by Lin et al. [20]. In contrast, *temporal encoding* stores information in the fluorescence signal collected over time. A prior use of temporal encoding was in the upconversion nanocrystal by Lu and co-workers [22], who demonstrated a biosensor where photon lifetime can be controlled by manipulating the doping distance in a nanocrystal. All these luminescent single-molecules were designed to exhibit a unique identifying characteristic: geometry, wavelength, or intensity. An interesting challenge in most of these techniques are the issues of photo-bleaching and limited multiplexing capability. Both issues limit the amount of information that can be extracted from luminescent single-molecules during detection phase. In addition, most of them use multi-color dyes for multiplexing which requires a complex hardware setup for accurate detection.

A recent super-resolution microscopy technique - DNA-PAINT - by Jungmann and co-workers [14,15,20,28] used transient binding of fluorescent DNA strands to achieve sub-nm resolving power. The major benefits of the technique

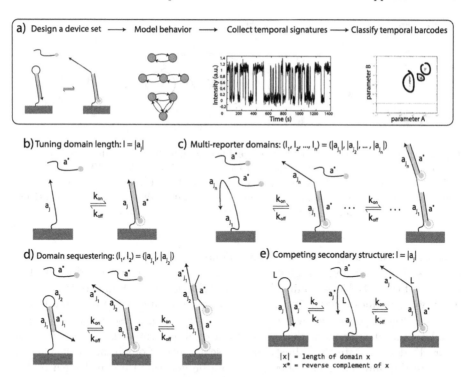

Fig. 1. A summary figure illustrating our temporal barcoding framework, with example DNA devices parametrized by domain lengths. (a) The workflow for unique identification of single-molecules using our devices. A set of devices are designed, modeled and simulated to generate temporal barcodes which are analyzed in the parameter space for clustering (or classification). (b) An example DNA device tuning domain length parameter to program the barcode behavior. (c) Designing the number and lengths of reportable domains to tune the temporal barcode. (d) Sequestering a domain to enforce event sequence. (e) Programming length of a competing secondary structure to tune dark-time of temporal barcode. Note that only one universal fluorescent is used for all the devices

include its resistance to photo-bleaching, decoupling dye photo-physics and high programmability. A drawback, though, is its multiplexing capabilities being limited by the number of dye-colors. Although Exchange-PAINT [14] addresses the issue of multiplexed imaging by using a single-dye with different DNA sequences, it still requires multiple dye-labeled DNA strands which makes it slightly expensive.

In this work, inspired from remarkable success of DNA-PAINT, we introduce a general framework to design a family of novel DNA devices that can encode information in their fluorescent pattern over time, and we use this temporal encoding to create a large number of barcodes. The stochastic conformation change that each DNA device undergoes is reported via its fluorescence signature which we refer to as the device's temporal barcode. If this emitted barcode

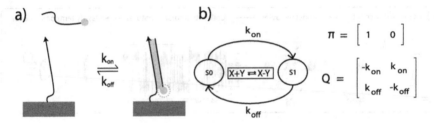

Fig. 2. A simple example illustrating the idea of modeling a single-molecule DNA device. (a) A short ssDNA device is attached on a glass surface. When fluorescent DNA strand attaches to the device, it gets reported. (b) A CTMC model showing this transient binding process along with initial probability value matrix and transition matrix. This model can be simulated to generate a state trajectory.

is captured for a long duration, it can be used to approximate the underlying device's identity with very high accuracy because of varying device kinetics. The workflow for our DNA barcoding framework is illustrated in Fig. 1. In this framework, we introduce several design strategies to program temporal barcodes, as shown in Fig. 1, generated by these DNA devices. Using these ideas, we design, simulate and classify more than 30 barcodes, all generated using a single dye-color. To demonstrate the robustness and scalability of our framework, we also estimate the number of barcodes which can be generated if wavelength multiplexing is used.

We model these devices using a continuous-time Markov chain (CTMC) and simulate the stochastic signatures of these devices using Gillespie's stochastic simulation algorithm (SSA). Prior studies have used CTMC and SSA for simulating DNA reactions [17]. These single-color dye-labeled DNA devices are immune to photo-bleaching as they follow the principle of transient binding originally proposed in DNA-PAINT literature [14,15,28]. Therefore, they inherit all the benefits of DNA-PAINT such as immunity to photo-bleaching. Additionally, they are easy to design and low cost since they use a universal dye-labeled DNA strand to report all the designed devices. In this work, we perform simulation experiments to show how design parameters can be tuned to program several distinguishable devices and identify experimental configuration which is most likely to succeed. These tiny devices can be easily combined with most of the existing biosensing techniques as they are compatible with DNA. These devices can be imaged using an inverted fluorescence microscope in total internal reflection fluorescence (TIRF) mode. Eventually, this temporal barcoding technique can be combined with wavelength multiplexing or with existing barcoding techniques to scale up the number of distinguishable reporters to several hundred.

2   Abstract Modeling of DNA Devices

One way to model the stochastic behavior of our DNA devices is by using CTMC. CTMC is a random process $X(t)_{(t>0)}$ with a finite (or countable) state space S, such that the generated state sequence follows the Markov property. This means that at any given time t, the probability to go to the next state is conditioned only on the current state and not on any past states. A CTMC is represented using a transition matrix Q, state space S, and initial probability vector π. The model assumes the holding time in each state is an exponentially distributed random variable with rate λ_{ij}. It indicates the rate of going from state i to state j. Refer Trivedi [34] for more details.

Several techniques have been suggested to simulate a CTMC, however, in this work, we will adhere to the stochastic simulation algorithm (SSA) by Gillespie since it is the computationally preferred choice for simulating a few molecules [10]. A simple single-stranded DNA (ssDNA) device and its corresponding CTMC model is shown in Fig. 2 stranded DNA (ssDNA) device and its corresponding CTMC model is shown in Fig. 2 along with the corresponding initial probability value matrix and transition matrix.

At the abstract level, we assume that a CTMC model can be converted to its corresponding DNA sequences, if desired. Therefore, we will not explicitly show toeholds and domains for in this work.

3   Results

Several parameters can be programmed to design DNA devices such as length of DNA, salt concentration, temperature, and secondary structures. In this study, we only tune DNA device parameters assuming salt concentration, imaging buffer and other experimental conditions such as temperature constant. All the simulation experiments were conducted assuming a room temperature of 22 °C and imaging buffer with sufficient quantities of Na^+ and Mg^{+2} concentration. Since these conditions were used in prior experimental studies, we can adopt rate-constants for our simulation experiments from prior literature [15].

3.1   Tuning the Length

The simplest type of device is a ssDNA, and, in such devices, the only tunable parameter is its length i.e. $|a|$ indicating the length of domain a. A recent study on super-resolution imaging showed that average hybridization time of such ssDNA devices has an exponential dependence on the length of DNA [15]. This means that these devices follow different statistics while undergoing conformation changes. To demonstrate this, we designed devices of length 7–10 nt range, given that this length allows for binding duration sufficient for current detector technology acquisition, and simultaneously allowing for transient unbinding. Shorter hybridization lengths can be used however capturing their binding events might be difficult with existing single-molecule CCD technology as the time-resolution limit lies around 1 ms. Similarly, longer hybridization length can be used however based on the calculated average binding times for such devices, they might not be immune to photo-bleaching. Hybridization and de-hybridization rate constants were adopted from Jungmann et al. [15].

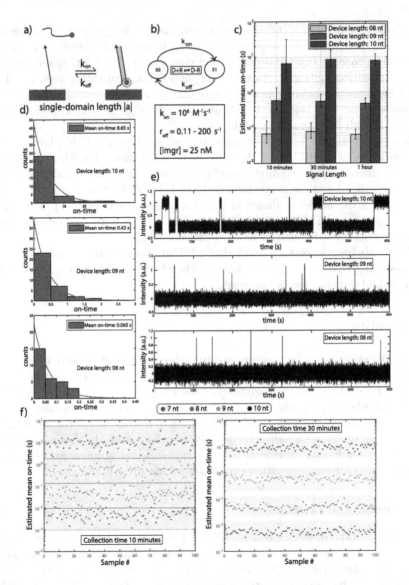

Fig. 3. A summary figure explaining the idea of tuning device length to produce distinguishable signatures. (a) A simple illustration of transiently binding fluorescent strand to ssDNA device. (b) A 2-state CTMC model representation. (c) Estimated mean value for the generated exponential distributions where error bars indicate a 95% confidence interval. (d) Histograms of on-time for ssDNA devices with length 10 nt, 9 nt and 8 nt. (e) An example of signature simulated with SSA with on-rate and off-rate adopted from Jungmann et al. [15]. Gaussian noise was added to simulated state chain before performing analysis. (f) A scatter plot for ssDNA devices of length 7, 8, 9 and 10 nt with data collected for 10 and 30 min

We modeled these devices using a 2 state CTMC as shown in Fig. 3b and simulated them using custom-written MATLAB scripts using their systems biology framework. To emulate experimental systems, we add Gaussian noise to the simulated intensity signals to account for read noise, dark current and other noise sources present in CCD detectors [28]. The devices were simulated for the time duration of 10 min, 30 min and 60 min with a concentration of the universal fluorescence strand constant at 25 nM. For device classification, we calculated the length of their on-time peaks and generated a histogram which was approximated by an exponential distribution, as shown in Fig. 3d. We define on-time as the amount of time when a fluorescent reporter strand is attached to our devices. The estimated rate value for the exponential distribution that best represents data for different collection times is shown in Fig. 3c. The error bars indicate an interval for estimating the mean value of the distribution with 95% confidence. The histogram plots in Fig. 3d show on-time distribution fits to an exponential probability density function (pdf) for a collection time of 60 min. These devices can be distinguished using a simple parameter, namely the average length of on-times (also called the average binding time). Clearly, as seen in Fig. 3c, with an increase in the data-collection time, a better parameter estimation and a tighter estimation of bounds is possible as this inherently increases the sample size of the distribution we are estimating. This can also be achieved by increasing the frequency of hybridization if shorter data-collection time is critical for reporting application. In addition, the difference in the rate values for these device is extremely large which demonstrates the potential of the time encoding technique. Several other physically tunable parameters can, therefore, be exploited to achieve a much finer distribution of the range while ensuring sufficient distinguishability. A typical simulated signature for all 3 devices are also shown in Fig. 3e for visual inspection. A quick visual inspection of devices with length 9 nt and 10 nt also indicates distinguishable behavior.

Since these devices are stochastic, we repeated the entire process for devices of length 7 to 10 nt and collect 100 samples with a data-collection time of 10 min and 30 min. As shown in Fig. 3f, there is a significant overlap among sample points of different devices if the data-collection time is only 10 min at the given concentration of fluorescent reporter strand. However, if the data-collection time is increased to 30 min, the samples are further separated allowing us to easily cluster them using a simple spatial clustering algorithm such as k-mean, nearest neighbor etc [13]. Finally, note that 10^{-4} on the vertical axis scale is numerical zero for the scatter plots shown in Fig. 3.

3.2 Tuning the Number of Domains

Since a simple ssDNA device can be easily distinguished by tuning its length, we modified the device by changing the number of domains for additional programmability as shown in Fig. 4. Such devices will have 3 observable states and 1 unobservable state, termed the dark state, as represented with a 4-state CTMC model in Fig. 4, where states $S1$ and $S3$ represents one of the device domains bound to fluorescent strand. The additional state $S2$ represents the device with multiple fluorescent strands hybridized at the same time. Such a state will have a visible jump in the fluorescence intensity since the emitted photon count is linearly proportional to the number of fluorescent dyes [27]. We represent a double domain device using the notation $(|a|, |b|)$ where $\{|a|, |b|\} \in S$ and $|x|$ indicates the length of the domain. Note that since we cannot control the order in which reporter strands attach to our devices $(|a|, |b|) = (|b|, |a|)$.

We performed a simulation experiment with 10 different devices assuming similar rates for individual domains as the previous section. Like prior simulation experiments, we restrict our domain lengths from 7 to 10 nt *i.e.* $S = \{x | x \in [7, 8, 9, 10]\}$. We analyze all the output signals to compute two parameters: a) on-time (t_{on}) and b) double-blink (t_{db}). We define double-blink time as the amount of time when both the fluorescent strands are attached to our devices. A histogram plot for both these parameters was constructed and an exponential distribution was fit to extract the rate parameters (or mean) of these distributions. The entire process was repeated for a few hundred samples and a 2D plot of the estimated parameters for all the simulated devices is shown in Fig. 4 was constructed in the parameter space. When the data-collection time was 30 min, some of the shorter devices had an overlap in the scatter plot. However, this was easily resolved with an increase in the data-collection time. A data collection time of roughly 60 min, at 25 nM fluorescent strand concentration, allows us to easily classify these 10 devices with high accuracy. For some shorter devices, there are samples without any double-blinks however these are still separable. Note that we didn't perform any simulation experiments for shorter devices since most CCDs can only capture events longer than 1 ms. However, if a CMOS camera is used, one can easily integrate shorter devices to increase the pool of distinguishable devices [28]. Finally, note that 10^{-3} on the vertical axis scale is numerical zero for the scatter plots shown in Fig. 4. They signify that the barcode signatures did not have any double-blink.

3.3 Tuning the Order by Domain Sequestering

An interesting functionality of secondary structures such as DNA hairpins is their ability to sequester information. As an improvement over ssDNA devices, this programmability can be useful to enforce the binding order or sequential binding amongst a different set of strands. This can help differentiate between devices $(|a|, |b|)$ where domain a exposed and b is sequestered, and $(|b|, |a|)$ where domain b is exposed and a is sequestered thereby increasing the number of distinguishable devices. With a hairpin-based device, it can be programmed to order the attachment of reporter strands. Therefore, by simply reversing the order of reporter domains, we can double the number of devices.

The model for hairpin-based devices with two domains is very similar to prior ssDNA devices with two domains as shown in Figs. 4b and 5b. The only difference is a fluorescent reporter's inability to bind with the hidden domain without successfully opening the hairpin. A simulation experiment with 25 nM fluorescent strand was performed with similar rate parameters as prior sections for individual domains. The noisy output signal was analyzed to compute the

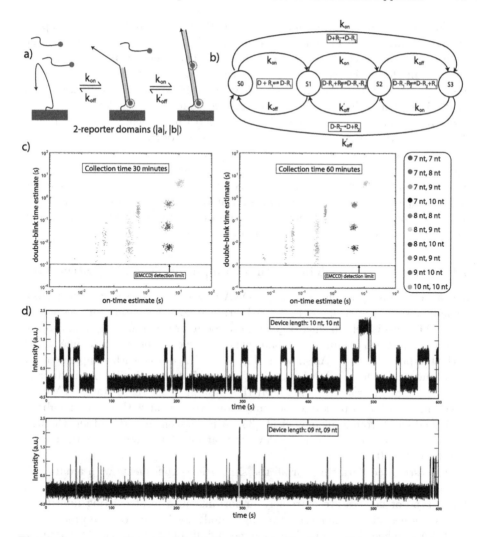

Fig. 4. A summary figure explaining the idea of tuning the number of domains to produce distinguishable single-dye signatures. (a) A simple illustration showing transient binding of fluorescent strands to our DNA device. (b) A 4-state CTMC model representation. (c) A scatter plot in the parameter space generated by learning parameters from intensity signatures of 10 different devices. (d) A typical signature of (10,10) and (9,9) device collected for 10 min

following parameters: (a) single-step time (t_{ss}), (b) double-blink time (t_{db}), and (c) double-step time (t_{ds}). A histogram was generated by analyzing all the signals to compute all 3 parameters. The exponential distributions best approximating these histograms produced estimated mean value with 95% confidence.

Note that t_{ss} and t_{ds} are computed differently as shown in Fig. 5. We compute single-step time by calculating the on-time for all the peaks that had exactly one reporter strand attached to it while double-step time here refers to the on-time time for all the peaks with double-blink time greater than zero. A 3D scatter plot in parameter space for all possible device combinations of 7 to 10 nt domain length is shown in Fig. 5. The scatter plot for data-collected for 200 min can easily be classified using popular clustering algorithms such as k-mean, mean-shift etc. [13] with high accuracy. Note that for some of the shorter devices there are samples where no double-blink was observed. Therefore, devices with at least one longer domain is the preferred choice when designing such DNA devices for reporting single-molecules. Note that this strategy assumes that we design the hairpin sequence such that after annealing it remains as a stable hairpin. This can be ensured by having longer stems. Additionally, prior studies also suggest longer hairpin stem for higher stability and therefore lower leak [35].

3.4 Tuning the Dark-Time with a Competing Secondary Structure

It is a well-known phenomenon that ssDNA can also be programmed to form a secondary structure such as the DNA-hairpin if complementary sub-sequences exists [29]. This is helpful since it gives more room for programming signatures of DNA devices. Such competing secondary structure changes the dark-time (t_{off}) of the temporal barcode. As shown in Fig. 6, a DNA device with complementary sub-sequence can form a DNA hairpin which inhibits attachment of the fluorescent reporter. Therefore, we modeled this system using the 3-state CTMC as shown in Fig. 6b and performed a simulation experiment with rates for hairpin closing adopted from Tsukanov et al. [35]. A fluorescent reporter of length 10 nt was allowed to interact with the devices that can form hairpins with a stem length of 6 to 10 nt.

The estimated dark-time for all the simulation experiments with a data collection time of 90 min yielded a distinguishable device set as shown in Fig. 6c. These type of devices are extremely important since most existing multiplexing techniques that do not use wavelength multiplexing, encode information in the DNA sequence [14]. Therefore, they need multiple dye-labeled DNA strands which increases the experimental costs significantly. With our technique, only a single dye-labeled DNA strand is required for multiple reporting devices making this reporting technique highly cost-effective.

3.5 Scaling the Number of Unique Barcodes with Multiplexing

Although our experiments were made using only one type of dye, here we estimate the number of unique barcodes we can make with the use of multiple dyes to demonstrate the robustness of our technique. Suppose we choose K different dyes such that they divide the visible spectrum equally. A simple combination of the design principles of tuning length and extending the number of domains can make a big set of ssDNA devices. If each domain length can be tuned X times we can make X^N devices. Practically, we can tune the length from 7 to 10 nt

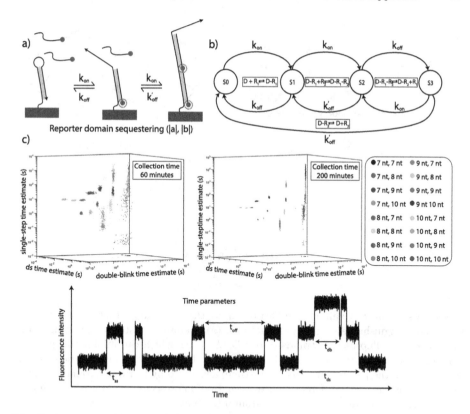

Fig. 5. A summary figure explaining the idea of tuning the sequence of domains to produce distinguishable single-dye signatures. (a) A simple illustration showing transient binding of fluorescent strands to our DNA device with hairpin secondary structure such as DNA hairpin to sequester a domain. (b) A 4-state CTMC model representation. (c) A 3D scatter plot in the parameter space generated by learning parameters from intensity signatures of 10 different devices. (d) A typical signature of a device indicating the difference between the calculated parameters single-step time and double-step time.

range, therefore, we can easily produce 4^N devices. A realistic value for N can be up to 4 with a sample dye set containing ATTO 405, ATTO 488, Cy3B, ATTO 655 giving us a total of $4^4 = 256$ devices. If we have K dyes to choose from, the number scales up to $X^N \times K^N$. For the suggested values of N, K and X, this will generate $4^4 \times 4^4 = 65536$ devices. This simple design space only tunes the length of each ssDNA device in addition to wavelength multiplexing. We can use the geometry of nanostructures [14,20] in combination with our temporal encoding to scale this number even further.

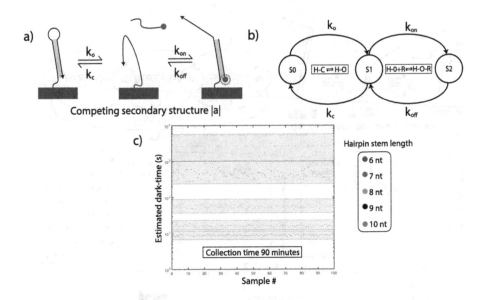

Fig. 6. A summary explaining the idea of tuning the secondary structure of device to produce distinguishable single-dye signatures. (a) A simple illustration showing transient binding of fluorescent strands to our DNA device which can inhibit this process if it forms a secondary structure. (b) A 3-state CTMC model representation. (c) A scatter plot in the parameter space (dark-time) generated by learning parameters from intensity signatures of 5 different devices. Length of fluorescent strand was constant at 10 nt while hairpin stem length ranged from 6 to 10 nt.

4   Discussion and Future Work

4.1   Experimental Demonstration of Our Devices

We are currently working on experimentally demonstrating all the devices designed and simulated in this work. We image our barcodes using fluorescence microscopes in TIRF mode. In such systems, an oil-immersion objective (100x magnification) with a high numerical aperture (N.A.) is used to achieve very high magnifications. Because the excitation light goes from a denser medium (immersion oil) to rarer medium (imaging buffer such as 1x PBS), it can undergo total internal reflection if the incident angle is higher than the critical angle. However, some light tunnels through the surface and creates an evanescent excitation wave, which can excite only the sample extremely close to the surface. To detect output fluorescence, we use highly sensitive electron-multiplying charged coupled detectors (EM-CCD) since they can collect photons with high speed and extreme sensitivity. These detectors can achieve very high frame rates in the sub-millisecond range, which is a key component to detect short-lived states.

However, there are a few challenges with the experimental data that must be addressed before we can perform successful clustering and classification. These include: (a) Thermal drift, (b) Non-specific binding of fluorescent reporters, and

(c) Poor signal to noise ratio. All these problems are well-known in the field of localization microscopy and super-resolution imaging and have already been either partially or fully addressed [28]. We adopt existing techniques to address these challenges. Finally, there is also the problem of diffraction limited imaging when working with light microscopes. To address this challenge, we work at an extremely low device concentration (a few pM). At this concentration, the probability of finding two devices in the same diffraction limited region is minimized [35]. We can also discard overlapping devices based on their temporal signature during data analysis. We are already able to distinguish more than 3 devices made by using the design principle of tuning the length of a ssDNA device. The raw data, collected for over 30 min, was processed to remove noise from the image and a simple thresholding was performed to extract spots which can be analyzed using their temporal barcode. All the experimental protocols and device data results will be published later in a full-journal article as they are beyond the scope of this paper.

4.2   Tagging DNA Nanostructures with DNA Devices

A natural application of our temporal barcoding framework is DNA nanostructure tagging. Techniques such as DNA origami [27] or DNA bricks [16] can be used to create the desired nanostructure shape. We propose, as the first step in this direction, using a 6-helix bundle dimer [20] as this structure is longer than light's diffraction limit. Such a DNA nanostructure can be reported using our DNA-based devices. As shown in Fig. 7a, the ends of a 6-helix bundle can be tagged with two devices (of similar or different types) which can independently report the tagged structure. If error correction is desirable in the detection application, each nanostructure can be tagged with the same device multiple times as identification of even a single temporal barcode should uniquely identify the structure of interest. Such redundant multi-tagging can also ensure reporting occurs even if an origami nanostructure has incomplete binding fidelity of all staples.

4.3   Tagging Cells with DNA Devices

Several demonstrations of *in situ* quantitative labeling use antigen-antibody specificity to attach a fluorescent marker to cells [14,20]. The antigen-antibody specificity is also how our body triggers necessary immune response to fight disease. Our temporal DNA devices can be directly attached to the antibodies, as shown in Fig. 7b, so that if the corresponding antigens are found in the desired cells, we can report them using our temporal barcodes. Note that we do not need multiple dyes for ob-serving several different cellular species since we use time-domain for reporting. Such single-molecule cellular activity reporting can be used for advanced applications in drug therapeutics.

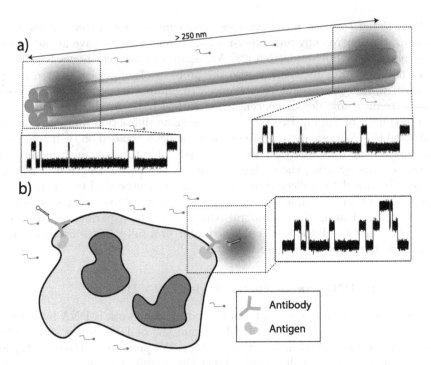

Fig. 7. An illustration demonstrating our DNA devices as taggants. (a) A simple 6-helix bundle DNA nanostructure can be tagged with our temporal reporters (without using wavelength multiplexing) in two regions to generate a unique temporal signature. These types of nanostructure tagging can also be error-resistant since only one of the two devices are required for successful identification. (b) Tagging a cell with DNA reporters using antibody-labeled devices. These antibodies can attach to antigens found on cell-surface.

5   Conclusion

In this work, we have introduced a novel framework for designing a family of DNA-based devices, each of which acts as a fluorescent reporter for the single-molecule. These devices undergo a series of dynamic transformations that result in a unique temporally-varying fluorescence signal. Since they encode information in the time domain, we can design several devices with as few as one-dye greatly simplifying the hardware setup for data-collection. These devices are easy to design and require only one universal fluorescence reporter strand making them extremely cost-effective. In addition, they follow the principle of transient binding which makes them relatively immune to photo-bleaching when imaged using TIRF microscopes.

Our framework introduces four different design methodologies to generate several distinguishable temporal barcodes, namely (a) tuning the device length (b) tuning the number of domains (c) tuning the order by domain sequestering and (d) tuning the dark-time with competing secondary structure formation.

Each of these design principles was then used to generate a family of DNA devices with different barcodes using only one fluorescent dye. We modeled the behavior of our DNA devices using CTMCs and performed several simulation experiments to demonstrate our idea and identify experimental conditions for maximum distinguishability. More than 30 DNA devices were designed, modeled, simulated and analyzed in this work. Although our barcodes can work with as few as one dye, by adding multiple dyes, we can create much larger families of uniquely identifiable reporter molecules which makes our framework highly scalable.

References

1. Braeckmans, K., De Smedt, S.C., Roelant, C., Leblans, M., Pauwels, R., Demeester, J.: Encoding microcarriers by spatial selective photobleaching. Nat. Mater. **2**(3), 169 (2003)
2. Bui, H., Shah, S., Mokhtar, R., Song, T., Garg, S., Reif, J.: Localized DNA hybridization chain reactions on DNA origami. ACS Nano **12**(2), 1146–1155 (2018)
3. Chatterjee, G., Dalchau, N., Muscat, R.A., Phillips, A., Seelig, G.: A spatially localized architecture for fast and modular DNA computing. Nat. Nanotechnol. **12**(9), 920 (2017)
4. Dejneka, M.J., et al.: Rare earth-doped glass microbarcodes. Proc. Natl. Acad. Sci. **100**(2), 389–393 (2003)
5. Douglas, S.M., Bachelet, I., Church, G.M.: A logic-gated nanorobot for targeted transport of molecular payloads. Science **335**(6070), 831–834 (2012)
6. Eshra, A., Shah, S., Reif, J.: DNA hairpin gate: a renewable dna seesaw motif using hairpins. arXiv preprint arXiv:1704.06371 (2017)
7. Fu, D., Shah, S., Song, T., Reif, J.: DNA-based analog computing. In: Braman, J.C. (ed.) Synthetic Biology. MMB, vol. 1772, pp. 411–417. Springer, New York (2018). https://doi.org/10.1007/978-1-4939-7795-6_23
8. Garg, S., Shah, S., Bui, H., Song, T., Mokhtar, R., Reif, J.: Small **14**, 1801470 (2018). https://doi.org/10.1002/smll.201801470
9. Geiss, G.K., et al.: Direct multiplexed measurement of gene expression with color-coded probe pairs. Nat. Biotechnol. **26**(3), 317 (2008)
10. Gillespie, D.T.: Stochastic simulation of chemical kinetics. Annu. Rev. Phys. Chem. **58**, 35–55 (2007)
11. Gudiksen, M.S., Lauhon, L.J., Wang, J., Smith, D.C., Lieber, C.M.: Growth of nanowire superlattice structures for nanoscale photonics and electronics. Nature **415**(6872), 617 (2002)
12. Johnson-Buck, A., Shih, W.M.: Single-molecule clocks controlled by serial chemical reactions. Nano Lett. **17**(12), 7940–7944 (2017)
13. Joshi, A., Kaur, R.: A review: comparative study of various clustering techniques in data mining. Int. J. Adv. Res. Comput. Sci. Softw. Eng. **3**(3), 55–57 (2013)
14. Jungmann, R., Avendaño, M.S., Woehrstein, J.B., Dai, M., Shih, W.M., Yin, P.: Multiplexed 3D cellular super-resolution imaging with DNA-PAINT and exchange-PAINT. Nat. Methods **11**(3), 313 (2014)
15. Jungmann, R., Steinhauer, C., Scheible, M., Kuzyk, A., Tinnefeld, P., Simmel, F.C.: Single-molecule kinetics and super-resolution microscopy by fluorescence imaging of transient binding on DNA origami. Nano Lett. **10**(11), 4756–4761 (2010)

16. Ke, Y., Ong, L.L., Shih, W.M., Yin, P.: Three-dimensional structures self-assembled from DNA bricks. Science **338**(6111), 1177–1183 (2012)

17. Lakin, M.R., Petersen, R., Gray, K.E., Phillips, A.: Abstract modelling of tethered DNA circuits. In: Murata, S., Kobayashi, S. (eds.) DNA 2014. LNCS, vol. 8727, pp. 132–147. Springer, Cham (2014). https://doi.org/10.1007/978-3-319-11295-4_9

18. Levsky, J.M., Shenoy, S.M., Pezo, R.C., Singer, R.H.: Single-cell gene expression profiling. Science **297**(5582), 836–840 (2002)

19. Li, Y., Cu, Y.T.H., Luo, D.: Multiplexed detection of pathogen DNA with DNA-based fluorescence nanobarcodes. Nat. Biotechnol. **23**(7), 885 (2005)

20. Lin, C., et al.: Submicrometre geometrically encoded fluorescent barcodes self-assembled from DNA. Nat. Chem. **4**(10), 832 (2012)

21. Lin, C., Liu, Y., Yan, H.: Self-assembled combinatorial encoding nanoarrays for multiplexed biosensing. Nano Lett. **7**(2), 507–512 (2007)

22. Lu, Y., et al.: Tunable lifetime multiplexing using luminescent nanocrystals. Nat. Photon. **8**(1), 32 (2014)

23. Nicewarner-Pena, S.R., et al.: Submicrometer metallic barcodes. Science **294**(5540), 137–141 (2001)

24. Pregibon, D.C., Toner, M., Doyle, P.S.: Multifunctional encoded particles for high-throughput biomolecule analysis. Science **315**(5817), 1393–1396 (2007)

25. Qian, L., Winfree, E.: Scaling up digital circuit computation with dna strand displacement cascades. Science **332**(6034), 1196–1201 (2011)

26. Sahu, S., LaBean, T.H., Reif, J.H.: A DNA nanotransport device powered by polymerase ϕ29. Nano Lett. **8**(11), 3870–3878 (2008)

27. Schmied, J.J., et al.: DNA origami-based standards for quantitative fluorescence microscopy. Nat. Protoc. **9**(6), 1367 (2014)

28. Schnitzbauer, J., Strauss, M.T., Schlichthaerle, T., Schueder, F., Jungmann, R.: Super-resolution microscopy with DNA-PAINT. Nat. Protoc. **12**(6), 1198 (2017)

29. Seeman, N.C.: Structural DNA nanotechnology. In: Rosenthal, S.J., Wright, D.W. (eds.) NanoBiotechnology Protocols, pp. 143–166. Springer, Heidelberg (2005). https://doi.org/10.1385/1-59259-901-X:143

30. Shah, S., Dave, P., Gupta, M.K.: Computing real numbers using DNA self-assembly. arXiv preprint arXiv:1502.05552 (2015)

31. Shah, S., Limbachiya, D., Gupta, M.K.: DNACloud: A potential tool for storing big data on DNA. arXiv preprint arXiv:1310.6992 (2013)

32. Shang, L., et al.: Photonic crystal microbubbles as suspension barcodes. J. Am. Chem. Soc. **137**(49), 15533–15539 (2015)

33. Song, T., Garg, S., Mokhtar, R., Bui, H., Reif, J.: Design and analysis of compact DNA strand displacement circuits for analog computation using autocatalytic amplifiers. ACS Synt. Biol. **7**(1), 46–53 (2017)

34. Trivedi, K.S.: Probability & Statistics with Reliability Queuing and Computer Science Applications. Wiley, Hoboken (2008)

35. Tsukanov, R., et al.: Detailed study of DNA hairpin dynamics using single-molecule fluorescence assisted by DNA origami. J. Phys. Chem. B **117**(40), 11932–11942 (2013)

36. Zhang, Y., et al.: Multicolor barcoding in a single upconversion crystal. J. Am. Chem. Soc. **136**(13), 4893–4896 (2014)

Hierarchical Growth Is Necessary and (Sometimes) Sufficient to Self-assemble Discrete Self-similar Fractals

Jacob Hendricks[1], Joseph Opseth[2], Matthew J. Patitz[3(✉)], and Scott M. Summers[4]

[1] Department of Computer Science and Information Systems, University of Wisconsin - River Falls, River Falls, WI, USA
`jacob.hendricks@uwrf.edu`
[2] Department of Mathematics, University of Wisconsin - River Falls, River Falls, USA
`joseph.opseth@my.uwrf.edu`
[3] Department of Computer Science and Computer Engineering, University of Arkansas, Fayetteville, AR, USA
`patitz@uark.edu`
[4] Computer Science Department, University of Wisconsin–Oshkosh, Oshkosh, WI 54901, USA
`summerss@uwosh.edu`

Abstract. In this paper, we prove that in the abstract Tile Assembly Model (aTAM), an accretion-based model which only allows for a single tile to attach to a growing assembly at each step, there are no tile assembly systems capable of self-assembling the discrete self-similar fractals known as the "H" and "U" fractals. We then show that in a related model which allows for hierarchical self-assembly, the 2-Handed Assembly Model (2HAM), there does exist a tile assembly systems which self-assembles the "U" fractal and conjecture that the same holds for the "H" fractal. This is the first example of discrete self similar fractals which self-assemble in the 2HAM but not in the aTAM, providing a direct comparison of the models and greater understanding of the power of hierarchical assembly.

1 Introduction

Systems composed of large, disorganized collections of simple components which autonomously self-assemble into complex structures have been observed in nature, and have also been artificially designed as well as theoretically modeled. These studies have shown the remarkable power of self-assembling systems to be

---

M. J. Patitz—This author's research was supported in part by National Science Foundation Grants CCF-1422152 and CAREER-1553166.

D. Doty and H. Dietz (Eds.): DNA 2018, LNCS 11145, pp. 87–104, 2018.
https://doi.org/10.1007/978-3-030-00030-1_6

algorithmically directed across a wide diversity of models with varying dynamics which determine the ways in which the constituent components can combine. At two ends of an important dimension in this spectrum of dynamics are models in which the atomic components can only combine to growing structures one at a time, e.g. the tile-based abstract Tile Assembly Model (aTAM) [20], and those in which arbitrarily large assemblies of previously combined components can combine with each other, e.g. the 2-Handed Assembly Model (2HAM) [2,4,5,15]. Even though models such as the aTAM which are strictly bound to one-tile-at-a-time growth have been shown to be computationally universal and very powerful in terms of the structures which can self-assemble within them, it has been shown that the hierarchical growth allowed by models such as the 2HAM can afford even greater powers [2].

In pursuit of understanding the boundaries of what is possible in these models, the self-assembly of aperiodic structures has been studied. For example, in [17], a 2HAM system with temperature parameter equal to 1 is given which self-assembles aperiodic patterns. Aperiodic structures are theoretically fundamental to the concept of Turing universal computation as well as embodied in many mathematical and natural systems as fractals. In fact, the complex aperiodic structure of fractals, as well as their pervasiveness in nature, have inspired much previous work on the self-assembly of fractal structures [6,19], especially discrete self-similar fractals (DSSF's) [1,7,12,13,16,18,19]. In a tribute to their complex structure, previous work has shown the impossibility of self-assembly of several DSSF's in the aTAM and 2HAM [1,12–14,16,18,19] yet there have also been results showing some models and systems in which their self-assembly is possible [3,7,10,11]. Quite notably, a recent result [8] is the first to achieve non-scaled self-assembly of a DSSF in the 2HAM. That work showed that DSSF's with generators (i.e. initial stages which define the shapes of the infinite series of stages) that have square, or 4-sided, boundaries can self-assemble in the 2HAM. However, they also gave an example of a DSSF with a 3-sided generator that does not. While previous work has shown sparsely-connected fractals which don't self-assemble in the aTAM or 2HAM [2,14], the recent results hinted that perhaps only extremely well-connected fractals, such as those that have 4-sided generators, may be able to self-assemble in the 2HAM, while perhaps none may be able to in the aTAM. In this paper, we continue this line of research into the self-assembly of DSSFs in the aTAM and 2HAM.

In this paper, we specifically consider aTAM and 2HAM systems which finitely self-assemble DSSFs. Finite self-assembly was defined to better understand how 2HAM systems self-assemble infinite shapes (e.g. DSSF's). Intuitively, a shape S, finitely self-assembles in a tile assembly system if any finite producible assembly of the system can continue to self-assemble into the shape S. Finite self-assembly is a less constrained version of strict self-assembly. Intuitively, a shape S strictly self-assembles in a tile assembly system if it places tiles on – and only on – points in S. Note that strict self-assembly implies finite self-assembly but the converse is not true in general. For example, a tile system could produce an infinite non-terminal producible assembly that has the property that it cannot self-assemble into the target shape S, but any finite producible assembly of the system could self-assemble into S. To further advance the possibility that no DSSF's may self-assemble in the aTAM, we provide impossibility results about fractals with more inter-stage connectivity than any previous fractal whose strict self-assembly in the aTAM was shown to be impossible. In particular, our impossibility results give two fractals which cannot be finitely self-assembled by any aTAM system, which implies that those fractals cannot be strictly self-assembled by any aTAM system either. However, our results also show that the landscape in the 2HAM is more convoluted. Namely, although [8] exhibited a fractal with a 3-sided generator that does not finitely self-assemble in the 2HAM, here we show one which does. This proves that the boundary between what can and cannot self-assemble in the 2HAM is less understood. Notably, our impossibility results and constructions are the first to give a head-to-head contrast of the powers of the aTAM and 2HAM to self-assemble DSSF's. In [2], shapes are defined which finitely self-assemble in the 2HAM but not in the aTAM, as well as shapes which strictly self-assemble in the aTAM but not in the 2HAM. In this paper, we prove that the hierarchical process of growth attainable in the 2HAM is necessary and sufficient for the self-assembly of certain DSSF's. Moreover, the construction techniques to build them in the 2HAM do not follow traditional growth patterns of "stage-by-stage" growth, but rely fundamentally on combinations of components across a spectrum of hierarchical levels. Due to space constraints, we only sketch our proofs in this version of the paper. For full details, please see the online version [9].

2 Preliminaries

Throughout this paper, we use standard definitions of, and terminology related to, the aTAM, 2HAM and discrete self-similar fractals. For more details of each, please refer to the full version of the paper [9]. In this section, we include only the few definitions unique to this paper.

2.1 Definitions for the aTAM and 2HAM

Let α be an assembly sequence of an aTAM system. In the following, $\alpha[i]$ denotes the tile that α places at assembly step i. We say that $\alpha[i]$ is the *parent* of $\alpha[j]$ if $i < j$ and $\alpha[j]$ binds to $\alpha[i]$. Furthermore, we say that tile $\alpha[i]$ is the *ancestor* of a tile $\alpha[k]$ if either $\alpha[i]$ is the parent of $\alpha[k]$, or there exists an index j, such that, $i < j < k$, $\alpha[j]$ is the parent of $\alpha[k]$ and $\alpha[i]$ is the ancestor of $\alpha[j]$. Note that $\alpha[j]$ implicitly refers to both the tile type and location, and the parent and ancestor relationships, in general, depend on the given assembly sequence α.

For an infinite shape $X \subseteq \mathbb{Z}^2$ and an aTAM or 2HAM system $\mathcal{T}$, we say that $\mathcal{T}$ *finitely self-assembles* X if every finite producible assembly of $\mathcal{T}$ has a possible way of growing into an assembly that places tiles exactly on those points in X. In this paper we consider finite self-assembly of DSSF's (in the strict sense).

2.2   The U-Fractal and H-Fractal

For the definition of discrete self-similar fractal (DSSF)[1] See [9].

Definition 1. *The* **U** *fractal is the DSSF whose generator consists of exactly the points* $\{(0,0),(0,1),(0,2),(1,0),(2,0),(2,1),(2,2)\}$.

Definition 2. *The* **H** *fractal is the DSSF whose generator consists of exactly the points* $\{(0,0),(0,1),(0,2),(1,1),(2,0),(2,1),(2,2)\}$.

3   Brief Proof of the Impossibility of Finite Self-assembly of the H fractal in the aTAM

The **H** fractal is defined as shown in Fig. 1. Let h_i be the i-th stage of **H**. We call the *center* tile of h_i, denoted as $center(h_i)$, the tile in the center of the stage that connects the *left* and *right* halves of h_i.

Let $B_0^{\mathbf{H}} = \{(0,0),(0,1),(0,2),(2,0),(2,1),(2,2)\}$. For stages $i > 1$, we call the following set of 6 points the *bottleneck* points of h_i, or $B_i^{\mathbf{H}}$:
$$B_i^{\mathbf{H}} = \left\{ \left(3^{i-1} + \tfrac{3^{i-2}-1}{2}, 3^{i-1} + \tfrac{3^{i-2}-1}{2}\right) + 3^{i-2}b \,\middle|\, b \in B_0^{\mathbf{H}} \right\}.$$ An example of the bottleneck points for a few stages of **H** can be seen in Fig. 1. In what follows, we will use the term "bottleneck tile" to refer to the tile placed (by some assembly sequence) at that bottleneck point.

The top, middle and bottom bottle-neck points of h_i are denoted as $top(i)$, $middle(i)$ and $bottom(i)$. We will refer to the points in h_i in between its center tile and left bottleneck points as its *left-center*. Assuming **H** finitely self-assembles in some TAS $\mathcal{T}$, then every tile placed in the left-center of h_i, for all $i \geq j$ for some $j \in \mathbb{N}$, has as an ancestor, relative to some $\mathcal{T}$ assembly sequence α, at least one bottleneck point. We call a tile in the left-center of h_i *top-left-placed* if $top(i)$ is its ancestor and $middle(i)$ and $bottom(i)$ are not its ancestors. We define *middle-left-placed* and *bottom-left-placed* tiles (in

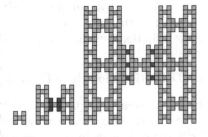

Fig. 1. First three stages of the **H** fractal, with the left-most being the generator. The bottleneck points of stages 2 and 3 (blue). (Color figure online)

---

[1] Note that we use the standard DSSF definition in which DSSF's are contained within quadrant I of $\mathbb{N}^2$. However, our impossibility result proofs could be trivially modified to hold for alternate definitions which allow for DSSFs to occupy any set of quadrants.

the left-center of h_i) similarly. Note that, if the parent of the center tile of h_i is adjacent to the left, then every tile in the left-center of h_i must have some bottleneck point (either top, middle or bottom) in the left half of h_i as an ancestor.

Theorem 1. **H** *does not finitely self-assemble in the aTAM.*

Proof. For the sake of obtaining a contradiction, assume there exists an aTAM TAS $\mathcal{T} = (T, \sigma, \tau)$ in which **H** finitely self-assembles. We will show that **H** does not finitely self-assemble in $\mathcal{T}$. Without loss of generality, we will assume that $|\sigma| = 1$, i.e. that $\mathcal{T}$ is singly-seeded but our proof technique will hold for any TAS $\mathcal{T}$ with finite seed assembly. Since the location of σ must be within **H**, let s be the stage number of the smallest stage of **H** which contains σ.

Let $c = 6|T|^6$. If **H** finitely self-assembles in $\mathcal{T}$, then every producible assembly in $\mathcal{T}$ has domain contained in **H**. Let α be the shortest assembly sequence in $\mathcal{T}$ whose result has domain h_{c+s+2}, subject to the additional constraint that, when multiple locations could receive a tile in a given step, α always places a tile in a location of the smallest possible stage.

By our choice of c, we know that there are at least 6 stages of **H** whose respective bottleneck points are identically tiled by α. Since, in any assembly sequence, the center tile of each stage of **H** either has a parent adjacent to the left or right, it follows, without loss of generality, that there are at least 3 stages, namely h_i, h_j and h_k, for $i < j < k$, whose respective bottleneck points are identically tiled by α and whose respective center tiles have parents adjacent to the left.

Relative to α, there are three cases to consider: (1) and (2) some top-left-placed (bottom-left-placed) tile of the left-center of h_j is placed at a point that is not contained in an h_{j-3}, appropriately-translated, so that $center(j-3)$, appropriately-translated, is $top(j)$ $(bottom(j))$, or (3) some middle-left-placed tile of the left-center of h_j is placed at a point that is not contained in an h_{j-2}, appropriately-translated, so that $center(j-2)$, appropriately-translated, is $top(j)$. (Intuitively, these are conditions specifying how far growth from each bottleneck tile extends toward its neighbors before utilizing cooperation with growth from them.) Note that, if none of these cases apply, then the left-center of h_j wouldn't assemble completely and **H** wouldn't finitely self-assemble in $\mathcal{T}$.

Case 1: Use α to create a new valid assembly sequence in $\mathcal{T}$ as follows. Starting from the seed, run α until the step at which it places the first bottleneck tile on the left side of h_j. Then, begin recording a sub-sequence of α and denote this sub-sequence as α'. As we run α forward from this point, until it places the last tile of h_j, whenever a top-left-placed tile in h_j is placed by α, we add that tile placement (type and location) to α'. In this way, α' becomes a sub-sequence of α that records the growth of the top-placed sub-assembly – and only the top-placed sub-assembly – of the left-center of h_j.

Now, reset α to the seed and begin its forward growth until the placement of the first bottleneck tile on the left side of h_i (recall $i < j$). At this point, merge α and α' as follows. For each tile position p in α', we translate it so that the new position, p', is the point with the same relative offset from the top-left bottleneck position of h_i as p was from the top-left bottleneck position of h_j. Continue to run α forward by performing all tile placements up to, and including, the placement of $top(i)$, with the exception of the $middle(i)$, $bottom(i)$, or any descendants thereof. As soon as α places $top(i)$, we follow the tile placements of the modified α'. The result is a valid assembly sequence up to the point of the placement of at least one tile outside of $\mathbf{H}$ (since the portion of the left-center of h_j grown by α' doesn't fit within the locations of $\mathbf{H}$ available in h_i). Thus, $\mathbf{H}$ does not finitely self-assemble in $\mathcal{T}$. A similar scenario, but for a different fractal, in which such out-of-bounds growth may occur, is depicted in Fig. 2b.

Case 2: This case is symmetric to the previous case.

Case 3: First, create an assembly sub-sequence α'' that records the tile placements of only the middle-placed tiles of h_j, similar to the construction of α' in Case 1. Then, run α forward, starting from the seed, performing all tile placements up to, and including, the placement of the $middle(k)$, with the exception of $top(k)$ or $bottom(k)$, or descendants thereof. As soon as α places $middle(k)$, we follow the tile placements of the modified α'', appropriately-translated, from h_j to h_k. Here, we are essentially replaying the assembly of a smaller stage within a larger stage. The result is a valid assembly sequence up to the point of the placement of at least one tile outside of $\mathbf{H}$ (due to the specifically different scales of portions of $\mathbf{H}$ in h_j and h_k). Thus, $\mathbf{H}$ does not finitely self-assemble in $\mathcal{T}$. □

Corollary 1. $\mathbf{H}$ *does not strictly self-assemble in the aTAM.*

Since strict self-assembly of a shape S by a system $\mathcal{T}$ implies finite self-assembly of S by $\mathcal{T}$, Corollary 1 follows from Theorem 1.

4   Impossibility of Finite Self-assembly of the U Fractal in the aTAM

The $\mathbf{U}$ fractal is defined as shown in Fig. 2a.

Theorem 2. U *does not finitely self-assemble in the aTAM.*

Due to space constraints, we only give brief description of the proof of Theorem 2. Essentially, the proof is very similar to that of Theorem 1. $\mathbf{U}$ has bottlenecks (which can be seen in Fig. 2a) similar to $\mathbf{H}$, and in a similar way, it is impossible for the portion of stages inside of the bottlenecks to self-assemble since the tiles at bottleneck locations of multiple stages must be identical, and growth which would have to be possible within one stage would be able to grow out of bounds of $\mathbf{U}$ in a different stage. An example can be seen in Fig. 2b, and more details of the proof can be found in the full version of the paper [9].

Corollary 2. U *does not strictly self-assemble in the aTAM.*

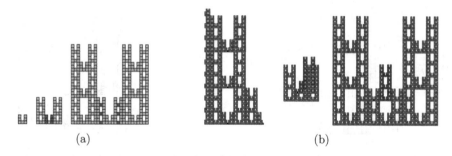

Fig. 2. (a) First three stages of the **U** fractal, with the leftmost being the generator. The bottleneck points of stages 2 and 3 are colored blue. (b) Depiction of how top-placed growth from stage 5 would go out of bounds of **U** in stage 3 and stage 4. (left) A portion of stage 5 showing the 3 bottleneck tiles in black, and possible horizontal and vertical growth from the top bottleneck tile. (middle and right) Stages 3 and 4. The black tile is the top left bottleneck tile, the green locations are those which correctly match the smaller stage, and the red are those which go out of bounds of **U**. Clearly, all tiles in green positions will be able to grow, and then erroneous growth is forced to occur immediately east of the green tiles, where no other tiles could prevent this growth. (Note that only a single tile needs to be placed in a red location to break the shape of **U**.) (Color figure online)

5 U-Fractal Finitely Self-assembles in the 2HAM

In this section we show how to finitely self-assemble the U-fractal, **U**, DSSF in the 2HAM (with scale factor of 1) at temperature 2. We will present our construction under the assumption that a particular assembly sequence is followed. We then show that the construction also holds for an arbitrary choice of assembly sequence. Due to space constraints, we present the main idea of the construction and give more detail in the full version of the paper [9]. First, we state our main positive result.

Theorem 3. *Let* **U** *be the U-fractal DSSF. There exists a 2HAM TAS* $\mathcal{T}_\mathbf{U} = (T_\mathbf{U}, 2)$ *that finitely self-assembles* **U**. *Moreover,* $\mathcal{T}_\mathbf{U}$ *has the property that for every stage* $s \geq 1$ *and every terminal assembly* $\alpha \in \mathcal{A}_\square[\mathcal{T}_\mathbf{U}]$, $U_s \subset \mathrm{dom}\,(\alpha)$ *(modulo translation).*

We now introduce notation useful for describing the sets of points (including singleton sets) in a fractal. We start with a notation for the *address* of a point in a stage U_n of **U**. Figure 3 describes this notation for U_3. Similar notation for U_n is defined recursively.

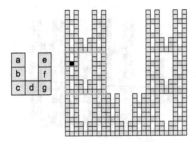

Fig. 3. (left) Address labels of each point in the generator of **U**, (right) The black location is contained within stage three, and its address is *dab* (i.e. it is location *d* in a stage one copy (outlined in red), within location *a* of a stage two copy (outlined in green), within location *b* of stage three.) (Color figure online)

Fig. 4. The set of dark gray points of U_3 are referred to as a stage-2 ladder

The address of a point in U_n is a string of n symbols of $\{a, b, c, d, e, f, g\}$. Therefore, to define a subset, S say, of points in U_n, it is convenient to use regular expressions to describe the strings corresponding to addresses of points in S. Figure 4 depicts a set of points in U_3 which we refer to as a *stage-2 ladder*. This set is defined by the regular expression $[defg][abc][ab] \mid [abcdefg]d[ab] \mid [abcd][efg][ab] \mid [defg][ab]c \mid [ef]cc \mid [abef]dc \mid [abcd][ef]c \mid [ab]gc$.

We also introduce terminology for some of the more important shapes that the 2HAM system which self-assembles **U** self-assembles. These shapes are *stage-n ladders*, *left rungs*, and *right rungs*. Figure 5 depicts a stage-2 ladder. The two rightmost supertiles in Fig. 9 depict left and right rungs where the rightmost supertile is a right rung. Let S_n by the set of points in U_{n+1} with addresses given by the expression $.\{n\}[abc]$ (i.e. strings of length $n + 1$ ending in a, b, or c). In other words, S_n is $\{(x, y + m * 3^n) \mid (x, y) \in U_n, m \in \{0, 1, 2\}\}$. Also let B be the set of westernmost, easternmost, and sothernmost points of S_n. Then, a stage-n ladder is the shape defined to be the points in $S_n \setminus B$. Figure 5 (right) depicts a supertile with the shape of a stage-3 ladder. We are now ready to present the construction which shows Theorem 3.

5.1 *U*-Fractal Construction Overview

In this section, we describe a 2HAM system that finitely self-assembles U. We do this by describing the supertiles producible in the 2HAM system and note that tiles can be defined so that these supertiles self-assemble. We first describe *base supertiles* that initially self-assemble and then describe how these base supertiles can bind to self-assemble supertiles that contain larger and larger stages of **U**. In all, the supertiles which self-assemble in $\mathcal{T}_\mathbf{U}$ are as follows.

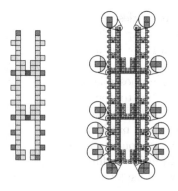

Fig. 5. A depiction of a stage-2 ladder (left) and a stage-3 ladder (right). Dark gray squares denote tile locations where tiles may contain an edge that has a special glue called an "indicating glue". The goal of the construction is to define a 2HAM system that 1) self-assembles 10 types of stage-2 ladder supertiles (the type of a stage-2 ladder supertile depends on whether or not tiles at dark gray locations contain indicating glues), and 2) for $n \geq 3$ self-assembles 10 types of stage-n ladder supertiles from stage-$(n-1)$ ladder supertiles such that the stage-n ladder supertile contains tiles that have indicating glues (at locations shown in dark gray locations in the figure on the right for stage-3 ladder supertiles)

1. 12 different types of base supertiles that are hard-coded to self-assemble, 10 of which have the shape of a stage-2 ladder, and 2 of which have the shape of either a left or right rung. We call these supertiles stage-2 ladder supertiles and left or right rung supertiles respectively. Figures 8 and 9 (left two supertiles) depict the 10 different stage-2 ladder supertiles. The two righmost supertiles shown in Fig. 9 are left and right rung supertiles.
2. For each n, 12 different types of supertiles self-assemble which have the shape of a stage-n ladder. We call these supertiles stage-n ladder supertiles. Figure 5 (right) shows a stage-3 ladder supertile.
3. Supertiles which we refer to as *grout* supertiles are hard-coded to bind to stage-n ladders for any $n \in \mathbb{N}$. For all $n \geq 2$, grout supertiles bind to stage-n ladders (and also bind to left and right rungs as a special case) to yield supertiles that expose glues which bind in some assembly sequence to yield a stage-$(n+1)$ ladder. Figure 6 depicts 6 stage-2 ladders and 6 stage-2 rungs with grout supertiles attached. We refer to a stage-n ladder supertile (resp. rung supertile) with grout supertiles attached such that no more grout supertiles can attach as a *grouted* stage-n ladder supertiles (resp. rung supertile). Finally, grout supertiles that bind to stage-n ladders are referred to as "grout for stage-$(n+1)$". As we will see there are 10 different types of grout corresponding to the 10 different types of stage-2 ladder supertiles.

Throughout this section we describe the self-assembly of the above supertiles by describing a particular assembly sequence. We note that there are many other assembly sequences for $\mathcal{T}_\mathbf{U}$ and many possible producible supertiles. This is due to the fact that proper subassemblies of the supertiles described above are themselves producible. Nevertheless, we show that this nondeterminism does not prevent $\mathbf{U}$ from being finitely self-assembled. For now, we consider assembly sequences such that for $n \geq 3$, 1) stage-$(n - 1)$ ladder supertiles completely self-assemble before grout supertiles for stage-n bind, 2) grout for stage-n binds to stage-$(n-1)$ ladder supertiles until a grouted stage-n ladder supertile self-assembles (i.e. grout supertiles bind to stage-$(n - 1)$ ladder supertiles until no other grout supertiles can bind), and 3) stage-n ladder supertiles self-assemble from grouted ladder supertiles of previous stages. Figure 7 depicts such an assembly sequence for $n = 3$. Note that grout supertiles bind to completed stage-2 ladder and rung supertiles before the stage-3 ladder self-assembles.

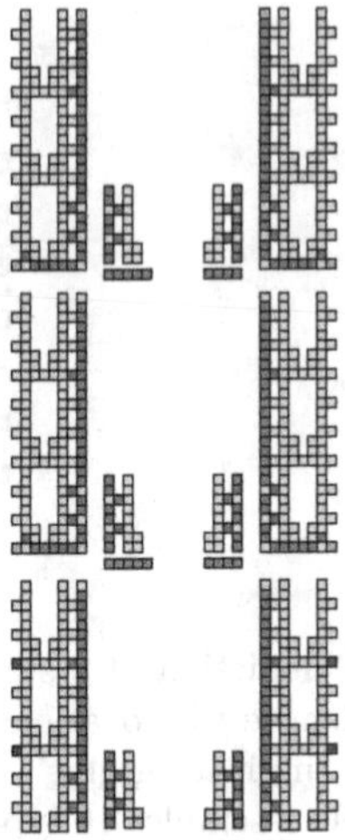

Referring to Fig. 5, the main idea behind the construction is to defined a tile set which self-assembles base supertiles and grout supertiles. Grout supertiles bind to base supertiles to yield supertiles which in turn bind to yield stage-3 ladder and rung supertiles. In particular, the stage-3 ladder and rung supertiles which self-assemble are analogous to (i.e. are higher stage versions of) stage-2 base and rung supertiles. See Fig. 5

Fig. 6. A schematic depiction of grouted stage-2 ladder supertiles and grouted rung supertiles. There are 6 types of ladder supertiles shown here. Tiles shown as yellow squares contain strength-1 glues which we call "binding glues" that allow the depicted grouted ladder supertiles to bind. Tiles shown as green or blue squares may contain edges with indicating glues and whether or not an indicating glues is on an edge of a tile at a green or blue location depends on which of the 10 typegs of grout that binds (i.e. which type of stage-3 verson of a stage-2 ladder supertile is self-assembling.) Note that tiles in locations shown as blue squares are contained in a stage-2 ladder supertile (Color figure online).

(left and right) for more detail. We now describe base and grout supertiles, the tiles that self-assemble them, as well as the assembly sequences for these supertiles and higher stages of $\mathbf{U}$ in more detail.

The 12 Base-Supertiles. The tile set which initially self-assembles stage-2 ladder supertiles and rung supertiles are defined so that these supertiles contain tiles that expose special glues in specific locations; possible locations for special glues are shown in dark gray in the Figs. 8 and 9. We call these special glues *indicating glues*. The purpose of indicating glues will be described in Sect. 5.1.

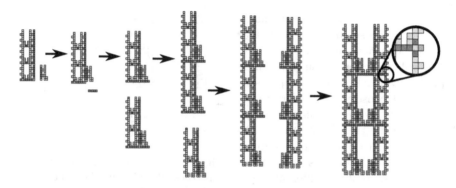

Fig. 7. An assembly sequence where grouted stage-2 ladder and rung supertiles bind to yield a stage-3 ladder supertile. Note that the result of this assembly sequence is a stage-3 ladder supertile.

In this section we describe the 12 different types of base supertiles, starting with the 10 stage-2 ladder supertiles.

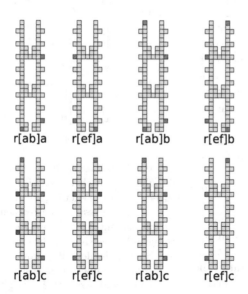

Fig. 8. (Right) A depiction of 8 types of the stage-2 ladder supertiles. Each of the 8 figures is labeled with a regular expression defining the set of points in U_4 where $r = (r1|r2)$ such that $r1 = [defg][abc]|[abcdefg]d|[abcd][efg]$ and $r2 = [defg][ab]|[ef][cd]|[ab][dg]|[abcd][ab]$. The label also describes where these stage-2 super-tiles will be located within a stage-3 ladder supertile (the tile locations of which are a subset of U_4). We will use these labels to refer to a stage-2 ladder supertile type. We also note that there are two versions of stage-2 ladder supertiles with type $r[ab]c$ and two versions with type with type $r[ef]c$.

Stage-2 ladder supertiles are hard-coded to self-assemble via particular assembly sequences described in Fig. 10. As we will see, enforcing such assembly sequences will help ensure proper self-assembly of consecutive ladder stages. For now, we assume that the stage-2 ladder supertiles completely self-assemble prior to binding to supertiles to yield larger assemblies. Tile types are defined so that 10 different types of stage-2 ladder supertiles that self-assemble. Referring to the stage-2 ladder supertiles in Figs. 8 and 9, tiles can

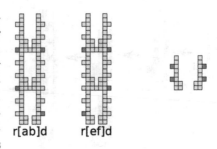

Fig. 9. A depiction of 2 stage-2 ladder supertiles labeled using the same scheme as described in Fig. 8 (right) and a depiction of stage-2 left and right rungs (right). The rightmost supertile is the right rung.

be hard-coded so that edges of tiles shown as dark gray squares expose indicating glues. The type of a stage-2 ladder supertile is uniquely determined by the locations and types of indicating glues on edges of the tiles that it contains. Moreover, for each base supertile, all of the indicating glues are distinct. We note that a stage-2 ladder supertile's type also determines its location as a subassembly of a stage-3 ladder supertile.

Except for tiles containing indicating glues, the non-abutting north (respectively south, east, and west) edges of northernmost (respectively southernmost, easternmost and westernmost) tiles of complete stage-2 ladders contain strength-1 glues, all with the same glue type which we label n (s, e, and w respectively). We call such glues *generic glues*. Generic glues are not shown in figures. The purpose of these glues is to facilitate the binding of grout supertiles as such supertiles bind to yield grouted stage-2 ladder supertiles. For each of the 10

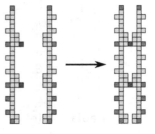

Fig. 10. To self-assemble each stage-2 ladder supertile, glues for each of the tiles in the supertile are hard-coded. In particular, the abutting edges of tiles at locations corresponding to each square of the left and middle supertiles shown here contain matching strength-2 glues and each such glue is unique for each base supertile. Tiles shown as blue squares of a stage-2 ladder supertile have strength-2 glues on their west edges and strength-1 glues on their east edge. This ensures that the "left half" (left) and "right half" (middle) (or portions of each) sufficiently self-assemble before each half binds (Color figure online).

types of stage-2 ladder supertiles, tiles at locations depicted by gray squares in Fig. 8 contain indicating glues (the purpose of which we describe in more detail next). Finally, in addition to stage-2 ladder supertiles, tiles are hard-coded so that left and right rungs self-assemble. These supertiles also contain indicating glues at tiles with locations shown as gray squares in Fig. 9 (two leftmost figures). We next describe grout supertiles.

Grout Supertiles. There are 10 different types of grout supertiles corresponding to the 10 different types of stage-2 ladder supertiles. Intuitively, grout binds to ladder supertiles to yield grouted ladder supertiles. For $n \geq 3$, appropriate grouted ladder supertiles with stage less than n bind to yield a stage-n ladder supertile. The resulting stage-n ladder supertile will contain tiles with edges that contain glues identical to the indicating glues of one of the 10 types of stage-2 ladder supertiles. Therefore, the indicating glues of edges of tiles of a stage-n ladder supertile determine the *type* for the stage-n ladder supertile. The type of stage-n ladder supertile that results is determined by the type of grout that binds to the ladder supertiles with stage less than n that bind to yield the stage-n ladder supertile. Figure 6 shows 6 different types of stage-2 ladder supertiles bound to grout supertiles (shown in red, green, and yellow). The 4 types of stage-2 ladder supertiles not shown in Fig. 6 only bind during the self-assembly of a stage-n ladder supertile for $n \geq 4$. Figure 6 also shows stage-2 left and right rungs that are bound to grout as well as grout supertiles which consist only of red tiles. Tiles belonging to supertiles depicted in Fig. 6 as yellow tiles expose binding glues which allow for the binding of these supertiles. The locations of these yellow tiles are determined by the indicating glues of the stage-2 ladder supertiles. We next describe the grout supertiles that bind and how they bind to 3 types of stage-2 ladder supertiles. The grout supertiles that bind and how they bind to the other types of stage-2 ladder supertiles is similar.

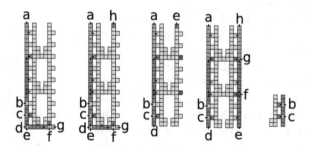

Fig. 11. A schematic depiction of 5 supertiles. From left to right, the first supertile is a grouted stage-2 ladder supertile with type $r[ef]a$, the next supertile is a grouted stage-2 ladder supertile with type $r[ef]b$, the next supertile is a grouted stage-2 ladder supertile with type $r[ef]c$, the next supertile is a grouted stage-2 with type $r[ef]d$, and the last supertile is a a grouted right rung supertile. Glue labels shown here are for reference purposes only and do not correspond to the label in the definition of the tile set for $\mathcal{T}_U$. Note that many of the glues of these supertiles are not depicted and the bound strength-1 glues shown here are intended to indicate how the grout supertiles cooperatively bind

Like stage-2 ladder and rung supertiles, grout supertiles are hard-coded to self-assemble and there are 10 different types of grout supertiles which self-assemble. We describe the grout supertiles which bind to the stage-2 ladder supertiles with types $r[ef]a$, $r[ef]b$, $r[ef]c$, and $r[ef]d$. Let L be a stage-2 ladder supertile with type $r[ef]b$. We denote as L' the supertile that is the result of grout binding to L until no more grout supertiles can bind. We refer to the labels for the glues shown in the second figure from the left in Fig. 11. First, we note that the grout supertiles shown with green tiles initially binds. The abutting edges of this supertile with no glues shown in the figure have strength-2 glues that hard-code the self-assembly of this supertile. This is also the case with the other grout supertiles shown in Fig. 11. Note that grout supertiles are defined to cooperatively bind to L to partially surround this supertile. We now describe the glues labeled a through h. The glue labeled a is a strength-1 glue that encodes the type of grout that binds to L. The glue labeled h is a non-generic "helper" glue. Together a and h cooperate to permit the binding of L' to a grouted stage-2 supertile with type $r[ef]a$, B say, iff the grout types of L' and B are the same. The glues b and c belong to a grout supertile that only ever binds stage-2 ladder supertiles; this can be enforced by the definition of the tile types which self-assemble grout supertiles. b and c do not encode the grout type as this is not necessary for the construction, but they do allow for a grouted right rung supertile (such as the one depicted in the rightmost figure of Fig. 11) to bind. As shown in Fig. 7, this is important for allowing stage-3 ladder supertile to self-assemble from L'.

Then, just as glues a and h allow for a grouted stage-2 supertile to bind to glues of north edges of tiles of L', e and f permit a grouted stage-2 supertile to bind to glues of south edges of tiles of L'. The glue labeled g will either be an indicating glue or a generic glue (an e glue in particular) depending on the type of grout that binds to L. If the grout type corresponds to type $r[ef]c$ or $r[ef]d$, then g will be an indicating glue corresponding to the indicating glue of a tile of a stage-2 ladder supertile of type $r[ef]c$ or $r[ef]d$ respectively. The d glue allows for grout supertiles to continue to bind after a grouted right rung supertiles binds. This scenario is depicted in Fig. 12. Finally, the glue labeled i in Fig. 12 encodes the grout type.

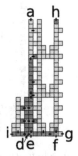

Fig. 12. A schematic depiction of a grouted stage-2 ladder supertiles bound to a grouted right rung supertiles.

Now let M be a stage-2 ladder supertile with type $r[ef]a$. We refer to the glue labels for the glues shown in the leftmost figure in Fig. 11. Most of these glues serve similar purposes to the glues of L and there are two main differences. First, a will either be a generic glue, n, or a glue which serves the same purpose as the glue h in L. In the latter case, we call a a "helper glue". If the type of grout that binds to M is type $r[ef]b$ or $r[ef]c$, then a will be a helper glue. This helper glue will facilitate the self-assembly of a stage-4 ladder supertile. If the type of grout that binds to M is any other type of grout, then, a is a generic glue. Finally, if the type of grout that binds to M is $r[ab]a$, $r[ab]b$, $r[ab]c$, or $r[ab]d$, then the glue labeled g is an indicating glue that is identical to the corresponding indicating glue of an edge of a tile in a stage-2 ladder supertile with type $r[ab]a$, $r[ab]b$, $r[ab]c$, or $r[ab]d$. Otherwise, g will be a generic e glue.

Next let N be a stage-2 ladder supertile with type $r[ef]c$. We refer to the glue labels for the glues shown in the third figure from the left in Fig. 11. Once again, most of these glues serve similar purposes to the glues of L or M. The main difference is that the d glue is a generic s glue and thus grout does not bind to the south edges of the southernmost tiles of N. This is crucial for allowing grout to bind along these south edges in the assembly of higher ladder stages. At this point, we also note that there are two versions of stage-2 ladder supertile with type $r[ef]c$. The first version has two indicating glues, one on the east edge of each of the blue tiles in Fig. 11, and the second version has generic e glues instead of these indicating glues. Moreover, there are two versions of grout supertiles with type $r[ef]c$. Grout with type $r[ab]a$, $r[ab]b$, $r[ab]c$ (both versions), or $r[ab]d$ can only bind to a stage-2 ladder with type $r[ef]c$ iff the type is of the first version. The purpose of the indicating glues on edges of these blue tiles will are utilized in the self-assembly of ladder supertiles of stage ≥ 4.

Finally let P be a stage-2 ladder supertile with type $r[ef]d$. We refer to the glue labels for the glues shown in the fourth figure from the left in Fig. 11. Once again, most of these glues serve similar purposes to the glues of N. However, in this this case, there is one major difference. Namely, grout supertiles not only bind to the west edges of tiles of P, but they also bind to east edges as well. The green supertile with tiles containing edges with glues g and h initiate such growth. The glue labeled h (resp. e) is a generic n (resp. s) glue. The glues labeled g and f are binding glues. Glues g and h do not encode a grout type and are identical to the binding glues of a right rung supertile. This allows a grouted P to serve the purpose of a grouted right rung supertile in the self-assembly of a stage-4 ladder.

Note that tile types which self-assemble grout supertiles that bind to stage-2 ladder and rung supertiles can be defined so that (1) tiles at locations corresponding to yellow squares in Fig. 6 contain edges with binding glues that permit the self-assembly a stage-3 ladder supertile, and (2) binding glues depend (though not necessarily all of the glues will) on the type of grout which binds. Binding glues enable appropriate grouted stage-2 ladder and/or rung supertiles to bind to yield a stage-3 ladder supertile. We also note that tile types which self-assemble grout supertiles can be defined so that (1) the grouted stage-2 ladder and/or rung supertiles which bind to yield a stage-3 ladder supertile all contain the same type of grout supertiles, (2) tiles at locations corresponding to green squares in Fig. 6 contain edges with indicating glues, and (3) the indicating glues of an edge of a tile in a stage-3 ladder supertile are identical to the indicating glues of exactly one type of stage-2 ladder supertile; which type

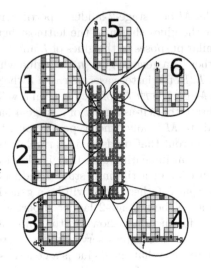

Fig. 13. A schematic depiction of a grouted stage-3 supertile. Note the similarity between the pattern of glues labeled here and the glues of the second figure from the left in Fig. 11. Many of the glues not depicted here are strength-2 glues which are hard-coded to allow either grout supertiles to self-assemble, stage-2 ladder supertiles to self-assemble, or rung supertiles to self-assemble. Glues depicted as strength-1 glues are intended to indicate how grout supertiles cooperatively bind. Glue labels shown here are for reference purposes only and are not the labels in the definition of the tile set for $\mathcal{T}_\mathbf{U}$.

depends on the type of grout supertiles contained in the stage-3 ladder supertile.

Finite Self-assembly of Stage-n Ladder Supertiles for $n \geq 2$. In Sect. 5.1 we saw that tile types can be defined to self-assemble base supertiles and grout supertiles such that there is an assembly sequence where these supertiles bind to yield stage-3 ladder supertiles. Moreover, the stage-3 ladder supertiles which self-assemble contain tiles with edges that contain indicating glues that are identical to the indicating glues to one of the stage-2 ladder supertile types, giving 10 types of stage-3 ladder supertiles.

For $n \geq 3$, we note that copies of the same grout supertiles which bind to stage-2 ladder and rung supertiles can bind to stage-$(n-1)$ ladder supertiles, yielding grouted stage-$(n-1)$ supertiles such that appropriate grouted stage-$(n-1)$ supertiles can bind to yield a stage-n ladder supertile. Moreover, the stage-n ladder supertiles which self-assemble contain tiles with edges that contain indicating glues that are identical to the indicating glues to one of the stage-$(n-1)$ ladder supertile types, and thus identical to indicating glues of one of the stage-2 ladder supertiles. See Fig. 13 for a depictions of how grout supertiles bind to a stage-3 ladder supertile with type $r[ef]b$.

5.2 Final Remarks

Theorems 1 and 2 show that the H-fractal and the U-fractal cannot be finitely self-assembled by any aTAM system. Therefore, Theorem 3 shows the power that hierarchical self-assembly has over single tile attachment by showing that there is 2HAM system which finitely self-assembles the U-fractal. We conjecture that one can also give a 2HAM system that finitely self-assembles the H-fractal.

Conjecture 1. Let **H** be the H-fractal DSSF. There exists a 2HAM TAS $\mathcal{T}_\mathbf{H} = (T_\mathbf{H}, 2)$ that finitely self-assembles **H**.

We've described the self-assembly of stage-n ladder supertiles via particular assembly sequences of $\mathcal{T}_\mathbf{U}$, ignoring many others and many producible supertiles. [9] describes how our construction ensures finite self-assembly of **U** despite these many possible assembly sequence and producible supertiles. Finally, our system self-assembles higher and higher stages of the ladder supertiles. Note that **U**, by definition, only contains points in the first quadrant of the plane. Moreover, the westernmost points (resp. southernmost points) are a vertical (resp. horizontal) line of points. We call these points the "boundary" of **U**. Only self-assembling higher and higher stages of ladder supertiles would give a system that finitely self-assembles **U** without points on the boundary. In [9] we give a simple tweak that ensures there is an assembly sequence from any producible assembly sequence to a terminal assembly with domain equal to **U** (including boundary points).

References

1. Barth, K., Furcy, D., Summers, S.M., Totzke, P.: Scaled tree fractals do not strictly self-assemble. In: Ibarra, O.H., Kari, L., Kopecki, S. (eds.) UCNC 2014. LNCS, vol. 8553, pp. 27–39. Springer, Cham (2014). https://doi.org/10.1007/978-3-319-08123-6_3
2. Cannon, S., et al.: Two hands are better than one (up to constant factors): self-assembly in the 2HAM vs. aTAM. In: Portier, N., Wilke, T. (eds.) STACS. LIPIcs, vol. 20, pp. 172–184. Schloss Dagstuhl - Leibniz-Zentrum fuer Informatik (2013)
3. Chalk, C.T., Fernandez, D.A., Huerta, A., Maldonado, M.A., Schweller, R.T., Sweet, L.: Strict self-assembly of fractals using multiple hands. Algorithmica **76**, 1–30 (2015)
4. Chen, H.-L., Doty, D.: Parallelism and time in hierarchical self-assembly. In: SODA 2012: Proceedings of the 23rd Annual ACM-SIAM Symposium on Discrete Algorithms, pp. 1163–1182. SIAM (2012)
5. Cheng, Q., Aggarwal, G., Goldwasser, M.H., Kao, M.-Y., Schweller, R.T., de Espanés, P.M.: Complexities for generalized models of self-assembly. SIAM J. Comput. **34**, 1493–1515 (2005)
6. Fujibayashi, K., Hariadi, R., Park, S.H., Winfree, E., Murata, S.: Toward reliable algorithmic self-assembly of DNA tiles: a fixed-width cellular automaton pattern. Nano Lett. **8**(7), 1791–1797 (2007)

7. Hendricks, J., Olsen, M., Patitz, M.J., Rogers, T.A., Thomas, H.: Hierarchical self-assembly of fractals with signal-passing tiles (extended abstract). In: Proceedings of the 22nd International Conference on DNA Computing and Molecular Programming (DNA 22), Munich, Germany, 4–8 September 2016, pp. 82–97. Ludwig-Maximilians-Universitt (2016)

8. Hendricks, J., Opseth, J.: Self-assembly of 4-sided fractals in the two-handed tile assembly model. In: Patitz, M.J., Stannett, M. (eds.) UCNC 2017. LNCS, vol. 10240, pp. 113–128. Springer, Cham (2017). https://doi.org/10.1007/978-3-319-58187-3_9

9. Hendricks, J., Opseth, J., Patitz, MJ., Summers, S.M.: Hierarchical growth is necessary and (sometimes) sufficient to self-assemble discrete self-similar fractals. Technical report 1807.04831, Computing Research Repository (2018)

10. Jonoska, N., Karpenko, D.: Active tile self-assembly, part 1: universality at temperature 1. Int. J. Found. Comput. Sci. **25**(02), 141–163 (2014)

11. Jonoska, N., Karpenko, D.: Active tile self-assembly, part 2: self-similar structures and structural recursion. Int. J. Found. Comput. Sci. **25**(02), 165–194 (2014)

12. Kautz, S., Shutters, B.: Self-assembling rulers for approximating generalized Sierpinski carpets. Algorithmica **67**(2), 207–233 (2013)

13. Kautz, S.M., Lathrop, J.I.: Self-assembly of the discrete Sierpinski carpet and related fractals. In: Deaton, R., Suyama, A. (eds.) DNA 2009. LNCS, vol. 5877, pp. 78–87. Springer, Heidelberg (2009). https://doi.org/10.1007/978-3-642-10604-0_8

14. Lathrop, J.I., Lutz, J.H., Summers, S.M.: Strict self-assembly of discrete Sierpinski triangles. Theor. Comput. Sci. **410**, 384–405 (2009)

15. Luhrs, C.: Polyomino-safe DNA self-assembly via block replacement. In: Goel, A., Simmel, F.C., Sosík, P. (eds.) DNA 2008. LNCS, vol. 5347, pp. 112–126. Springer, Heidelberg (2009). https://doi.org/10.1007/978-3-642-03076-5_10

16. Lutz, J.H., Shutters, B.: Approximate self-assembly of the Sierpinski triangle. Theory Comput. Syst. **51**(3), 372–400 (2012)

17. Patitz, M.J., Rogers, T.A., Schweller, R.T., Summers, S.M., Winslow, A.: Resiliency to multiple nucleation in temperature-1 self-assembly. In: Rondelez, Y., Woods, D. (eds.) DNA 2016. LNCS, vol. 9818, pp. 98–113. Springer, Cham (2016). https://doi.org/10.1007/978-3-319-43994-5_7

18. Patitz, M.J., Summers, S.M.: Self-assembly of discrete self-similar fractals. Nat. Comput. **1**, 135–172 (2010)

19. Rothemund, P.W., Papadakis, N., Winfree, E.: Algorithmic self-assembly of DNA Sierpinski triangles. PLoS Biol. **2**(12), 2041–2053 (2004)

20. Winfree, E.: Algorithmic self-assembly of DNA. PhD thesis, California Institute of Technology, June 1998

Self-assembly of 3-D Structures Using 2-D Folding Tiles

Jérôme Durand-Lose[1,2（✉）], Jacob Hendricks[3], Matthew J. Patitz[4],
Ian Perkins[4], and Michael Sharp[4]

[1] LIX, Ecole Polytechnique, UMR 7161, 91128 Palaiseau Cedex, France
[2] LIFO, Université d'Orléans, ÉA 4022, 45067 Orléans, France
jerome.durand-lose@univ-orleans.fr
[3] Department of Computer Science and Information Systems,
University of Wisconsin - River Falls, River Falls, WI, USA
jacob.hendricks@uwrf.edu
[4] Department of Computer Science and Computer Engineering,
University of Arkansas, Fayetteville, AR, USA
{patitz,irperkin,mrs018}@uark.edu

Abstract. Self-assembly is a process which is ubiquitous in natural, especially biological systems. It occurs when groups of relatively simple components spontaneously combine to form more complex structures. While such systems have inspired a large amount of research into designing theoretical models of self-assembling systems, and even laboratory-based implementations of them, these artificial models and systems often tend to be lacking in one of the powerful features of natural systems (e.g. the assembly and folding of proteins), namely the dynamic reconfigurability of structures. In this paper, we present a new mathematical model of self-assembly, based on the abstract Tile Assembly Model (aTAM), called the Flexible Tile Assembly Model (FTAM). In the FTAM, the individual components are 2-dimensional square tiles as in the aTAM, but in the FTAM, bonds between the edges of tiles can be flexible, allowing bonds to flex and entire structures to reconfigure, thus allowing 2-dimensional components to form 3-dimensional structures. We analyze the powers and limitations of FTAM systems by (1) demonstrating how flexibility can be controlled to carefully build desired structures, and (2) showing how flexibility can be beneficially harnessed to form structures which can "efficiently" reconfigure into many different configurations and/or greatly varying configurations. We also show that with such power comes a heavy burden in terms of computational complexity of simulation and prediction by proving that, for important properties of FTAM systems, determining their existence is intractable, even for properties which are easily computed for systems in less dynamic models.

M. J. Patitz and M. Sharp—This author's research was supported in part by National Science Foundation Grants CCF-1422152 and CAREER-1553166.

D. Doty and H. Dietz (Eds.): DNA 2018, LNCS 11145, pp. 105–121, 2018.
https://doi.org/10.1007/978-3-030-00030-1_7

1   Introduction

Proteins are a fantastically diverse set of biomolecules, with structures and functions that can vary wildly from each other, such as fibrous proteins (like collagen), enzymatic proteins (like catalase), and transport proteins (like hemoglobin). Truly amazing is the fact that such diversity arises solely from the linear combination of only 20 amino acid building blocks. It is the specific sequence of amino acids, interacting with each other as they are combined, which causes each chain to fold in a specific way and each protein to assume its particular three-dimensional structure, and this in turn dictates its structural and functional properties. Inspired by the prowess of nature to build molecules with such precision and heterogeneity, scientists have studied the mechanisms of protein folding - to realize that the dynamics are so complex that predicting a protein's shape given its amino acid sequence is considered to be intractable [4,8], and engineers have begun to develop artificial systems which fold self-assembling molecules into complex structures [3,5,15,18,19] - but with results that to date still lack the diversity of biology.

In order to help progress understanding of the dynamics of systems which self-assemble out of folding components, and to provide a framework for studying such systems, in this paper we introduce the *Flexible Tile Assembly Model* (FTAM). The FTAM is intended to be a simplified mathematical model of self-assembling systems utilizing components which are able to dynamically reconfigure their relative 3-dimensional locations via folding and unfolding of flexible bonds between components. It is based on the abstract Tile Assembly Model [20], and as such the fundamental components are 2-dimensional square *tiles* which bind to each other via *glues* on their edges. In contrast to the aTAM, in the FTAM each glue type can be specified to either form *rigid* bonds (which force two adjacent tiles bound by such a glue to remain fixed in co-planar positions) or *flexible* bonds (which allow two adjacent tiles bound by such a glue to possibly alternate between being in any of three relative orientations, as shown in Fig. 1). Because the FTAM is meant to be a test bed for flexible, reconfigurable self-assembling systems, we present a version of the model which makes many simplifying assumptions about allowable positions of tiles and dynamics of the self-assembly process, but which also differs greatly from previously studied self-assembling systems which allow reconfigurability [1,2,7,9–13,17], other computational studies of folding such as [1,2], and algorithmic studies focused on constructing more simple 3D structures such as [14].

Fig. 1. The three relative positions possible for two tiles bound via a flexible glue.

In Sect. 2, we formally introduce the FTAM and provide definitions and algorithms describing its dynamics. In Sect. 3, we show how to control flexibility in the model to build 3D shapes. In Sect. 4, we present a pair of constructions which demonstrate the potential utility of reconfigurability of assemblies in the FTAM. In the first construction, an FTAM system T is given which produces a single terminal assembly that may be in many different configuration. In addition, a set S of n distinct types of tiles are given such that for each subset of S, adding this subset of tiles of S to the types of tiles for T gives a system with an assembly sequence that starts from the single terminal assembly of T and yields a rigid terminal assembly (i.e., an assembly to which no tiles may bind and which, at a high-level, is in a configuration which cannot be folded via flexible glues to give another distinct configuration). Moreover, the resulting rigid assembly is distinct for each choice of subset of S. The second construction given in Sect. 3 demonstrates how a reconfigurable initial assembly can be transformed into either a volume-maximizing hollow cube or a small, tightly compressed brick by selecting between and adding one of two small subsets of tile types. These two constructions demonstrate how algorithmic self-assembling systems could be designed which efficiently (in terms of "input" specified by tile type additions) make drastic changes to their surface structures and volumes. These constructions show that FTAM systems can be designed which utilize reconfigurability. In Sect. 5, we show that this utility comes at a cost in terms of the computational complexity of determining some important properties of arbitrary FTAM systems. In particular, we show that, given an arbitrary FTAM system, the problem of determining whether it produces an assembly which cannot be reconfigured (via folding along tile edges bonded by flexible glues) is undecidable. Moreover, we show that, given an assembly, it is co-NP-complete to determine whether the assembly is rigid, i.e. has exactly one valid configuration. Our final result modifies the previous to show that the problem of deciding if a given assembly for an FTAM system is terminal is also co-NP-complete. This is especially interesting since, in the aTAM, there is a simple polynomial time algorithm to determine if a given assembly is terminal. Note that due to space constraints, many technical details are omitted from this version but can be found in the full version [6].

2 Definition of the FTAM

In this section we present definitions related to the Flexible Tile Assembly Model.

A *tile type* t in the FTAM is defined as a 2D unit square that can be translated, rotated, and reflected throughout 3-dimensional space, but can only occupy a location such that its corners are positioned on four adjacent, coplanar points in $\mathbb{Z}^3$. Each tile type t has four sides $i \in \{N, E, S, W\}$, which we refer to as t_i. Let Σ be an alphabet of labels and $\bar{\Sigma} = \{a^* | a \in \Sigma\}$ be the alphabet of *complementary labels*, then each side of each tile has a *glue* that consists of a *label* $label(t_i) \in \Sigma \cup \bar{\Sigma} \cup \epsilon$ (where ϵ is the unique *empty* label for the *null glue*), a non-negative integer *strength* $str(t_i)$, and a boolean valued *flexibility* $flx(t_i)$. (See Fig. 1 for a depiction of the positions allowable by a flexible glue.)

A *tile* is an instance of a tile type. A *placement* of a tile $p = (l, n, o)$ consists of a location $l \in \mathbb{Z}^3$, a *normal* vector n which starts at the center of the tile and points perpendicular to the plane in which the tile lies (i.e. $n \in \{+x, -x, +y, -y, +z, -z\}^1$), and an *orientation* o which is a vector lying in the same plane as the tile which starts at the center of the tile and points to the N side of the tile (i.e. $o \in \{+x, -x, +y, -y, +z, -z\}$). Note that by convention, to avoid duplicate location specifiers for a given tile, we restrict a location l to refer to only the 3 possible tile locations with corners at l and which extend in positive directions from l along one of the planes (i.e. tiles are located by their vertices with the smallest valued coordinates). For any given l, there can only be a max of one tile with $n \in \{+x, -x\}$, one tile with $n \in \{+y, -y\}$, and one tile with $n \in \{+z, -z\}$, as to avoid overlapping tiles.

Let $p = (l, n, o)$ and $p' = (l', n', o')$ be placements of tiles t and t', respectively, such that p and p' are non-overlapping[2] and for some $i, j \in \{N, E, S, W\}$, sides t_i and t'_j are adjacent (i.e. touching). We say that p and p', have *compatible* normal vectors if and only if either (1) $n = n'$, (2) n and n' intersect, or (3) $\texttt{inverse}(n)$ and $\texttt{inverse}(n')$ intersect, where the $\texttt{inverse}$ function simply negates the signs of the non-zero components of a vector. (See Figs. 2a and b.) We will refer to these three orientations as "Straight", "Up", and "Down", respectively. Furthermore, if (1) $label(t_i)$ is complementary to $label(t'_j)$, (2) $str(t_i) = str(t'_j)$, (3) $flx(t_i) = False$ and $flx(t'_j) = False$, and (4) n and n' are in a "Straight" orientation, then the glues on t_i and t'_j can *bind* with strength value $str(t_i)$ to form a *rigid bond*. Similarly, if (1) $label(t_i)$ is complementary to $label(t'_j)$, (2) $str(t_i) = str(t'_j)$, (3) $flx(t_i) = True$ and $flx(t'_j) = True$, and (4) n and n' are compatible, then the glues on t_i and t'_j can *bind* with strength value $str(t_i)$ to form a *flexible bond*. [3]

We define an *assembly* α as a graph whose nodes, denoted $V(\alpha)$, are tiles and whose edges, denoted $E(\alpha)$, represent bound complementary glues between adjacent edges of two tiles. An edge between sides i and j of tiles t and t', respectively, is represented by the tuple (t_i, t'_j), which specifies which sides of t and t' the bond is between. Whether it is flexible is denoted by $flx(t_i)$ and its strength is denoted by $str(t_i)$ (since those values must be equal for t_i and t'_j).

We define a *face* to be a set of coplanar tiles that are all bound together through rigid bonds. Additionally, we define a *face graph* to be a graph minor of the assembly graph where every maximal subgraph in which every node can be reached from every other node using a path of rigid tiles is replaced by a single node in the face graph. Two nodes in the face graph that correspond to two groups of nodes in the assembly graph have an edge if and only if there is at

---

[1] We refer to the vectors $\{(1, 0, 0), (-1, 0, 0), (0, 1, 0), (0, -1, 0), (0, 0, 1), (0, 0, -1)\})$ by the shorthand notation $\{+x, -x, +y, -y, +z, -z\}$ throughout this paper.

[2] Non-overlapping placements refer to different tile locations. Formally, two tile placements are non-overlapping if (1) $l! = l'$ or (2) $n! = n'$ and $n! = \texttt{inverse}(n')$.

[3] Note that any glue can only bind to a single other glue. Also, we do not allow two pairs of coplanar tiles to bind through the same space (i.e. the two partial surfaces created by two pairs of bounded coplanar tiles are not allowed to intersect). Therefore, 4 glues from 4 different tiles that are all adjacent to each other can all form bonds only if they form two flexible bonds in non-straight orientations.

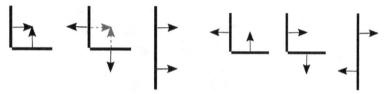

(a) Compatible normal vectors.   (b) Incompatible normal vectors.

Fig. 2. Possible normal vectors of pairs of tiles. Those in (a) are compatible and allow a bond to form between complementary glues in the orientations "Up", "Down", and "Straight", respectively. Those in (b) are not compatible.

least one flexible bond between any single node in the first group of the assembly graph and any single node in the second group of the assembly graph.

An FTAM system is a triple $\mathcal{T} = (T, \sigma, \tau)$ where T is a finite set of tile types (i.e. tile set), σ is an initial *seed* assembly, and $\tau \in \mathbb{Z}^+$ is a positive integer called *temperature* which specifies the minimum binding threshold for tiles. An assembly is τ-stable if and only if every cut of edges of α which separates α into two or more components must cut edges whose strengths sum to $\geq \tau$. We will only consider assemblies which are τ-stable (for a given τ), and we use the term assembly to refer to a τ-stable assembly.

Given an assembly α, a *configuration* c_α is a mapping from every flexible bond in α to an orientation from {"Up", "Down", "Straight"}. An *embedding* e_α is a mapping from each tile in α to a placement. Given an assembly and a configuration, we can obtain an embedding by choosing any single initial tile and assigning it a placement and computing the placement of each additional tile according to how it is bonded with tiles that are already placed. Note that, given tiles to which it is bound, their placements, and an orientation, there is only one tile location at which each additional tile can be placed. We say a configuration c_α is *valid* if and only if an embedding obtained from the configuration (1) does not place more than one tile at any tile location, (2) doesn't bond tiles through the same space, and (3) does not have contradicting bond loops. To elaborate on (2), while 4 glues can all be adjacent at one point, we allow them to bind in pairs in "Up" or "Down" orientations but do not allow both pairs to bind across the gap in "Straight" orientations. To elaborate on (3), contradicting bond loops occur when placing a series of tiles that are all bound in a loop causes the last tile to be placed at a location that is not adjacent to the first tile, therefore making the loop unable to close. Examples of configurations that follow and contradict (3) are given in Fig. 3. Note that two embeddings that use different initial tiles and initial placements but the same configuration will be equivalent up to rotation and translation.

Let α be an assembly and c_α and c'_α be valid configurations of α. If for every flexible bond $b \in \alpha$ either $c_\alpha(b) = Up$ and $c'_\alpha(b) = Down$, $c_\alpha(b) = Down$ and $c'_\alpha(b) = Up$, or $c_\alpha(b) = Straight$ and $c'_\alpha(b) = Straight$, we say that c_α is the *chiral* configuration of c'_α and vice versa. Note that the embeddings achieved from

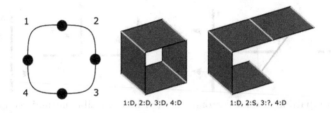

Fig. 3. Here we see an assembly, a valid configuration, and an invalid configuration. In the third image, because of the orientations of bonds 1, 2, and 4, bond 3 is between two tiles that are not connected, making the configuration invalid.

c_α and c'_α are reflections of each other. We refer to the special reconfiguration of an assembly to its chiral as *inversion*.

Given an assembly α and two different embeddings e_α and e'_α, we say that e_α and e'_α are *equivalent*, written $e_\alpha \equiv e'_\alpha$, if one can be rotated and/or translated into the other. If two embeddings are equivalent, this means they were computed from the same configuration, although possibly using a different placement for the initial tile.

We define the set of all valid configurations of α as $\mathcal{C}(\alpha)$. We say that an assembly α is *rigid* if (1) $|\mathcal{C}(\alpha)| = 1$, or (2) $|\mathcal{C}(\alpha)| = 2$ and the two valid configurations are chiral versions of each other. Conversely, if α is not rigid, we say that it is *flexible*.

The *frontier* of a configuration c_α, denoted $\partial^T c_\alpha$, is the set composed of all pairs (t, B) where $t \in T$ is a tile type from tile set T and B is a set of up to 4 tile/glue pairs such that an embedding of c_α would place each tile adjacent to one location such that a tile of type t could bind to each glue for a collective strength greater than or equal to the temperature parameter τ. Given an assembly α and a set of valid configurations $\mathcal{C}(\alpha)$, we define the multiset of frontier locations of assembly α across all valid configurations to be $\hat{\partial}^T \alpha = \bigcup_{c_\alpha \in \mathcal{C}(\alpha)} \partial^T c_\alpha$, i.e. $\hat{\partial}^T \alpha$ is the multiset resulting from the union of the sets of frontier locations of all valid configurations of α.

Given assembly α and valid configuration c_α, $\#(c_\alpha)$ is the maximum number of new bonds which can be formed across adjacent tile edges in an embedding of α which are not already bound in α (i.e. these are tile edges which have been put into placements allowing bonding in configuration c_α but whose bonds are not included in α). We then define $\mathcal{C}_{max}(\alpha) = \{c_\alpha | c_\alpha \in \mathcal{C}(\alpha) \text{ and } \forall c'_\alpha \in \mathcal{C}(\alpha), \#(c_\alpha) \geq \#(c'_\alpha)\}$. Namely, $\mathcal{C}_{max}(\alpha)$ is the set of valid configurations of α in which the maximum number of bonds can be immediately formed.

Given an assembly α in FTAM system $\mathcal{T}$, a single step of the assembly process intuitively proceeds by first randomly selecting a frontier location from among all frontier locations over all valid configurations of α. Then, a tile is attached at that location to form a new assembly α'. Next, over all valid configurations of α', a configuration is randomly selected in which the maximum number of additional new bonds can be formed (i.e. the addition of the new tile may allow for additional bonds to form in alternate configurations, and a configuration which maximizes these is chosen), and all possible new bonds are formed in that configuration, yielding assembly α''. Assuming that α was not *terminal* and thus $\alpha'' \neq \alpha$, we denote the single-tile addition as $\alpha \rightarrow_1^T \alpha''$. To denote an arbitrary number of assembly steps, we use $\alpha \rightarrow_*^T \alpha''$. For an FTAM system $\mathcal{T} = (T, \sigma, \tau)$, assembly begins from σ and proceeds by adding a single tile at a time until the assembly is terminal (possibly in the limit). (See the full version [6] for pseudocode of the assembly algorithms.) For any α' such that $\sigma \rightarrow_*^T \alpha'$, we say that α' is a *producible* assembly and we denote the set of producible assemblies as $\mathcal{A}[\mathcal{T}]$. We denote the set of terminal assemblies as $\mathcal{A}_{\square}[\mathcal{T}]$.

Note that in this section we have provided what is intended to be an intuitively simple version of the FTAM in which the full spectrum of all possible configurations of an assembly are virtually explored at each step, and only those which maximize the number of bonds formed at every step are selected. Logically, this provides a model in which assemblies reconfigure into globally optimal configurations, in terms of bond formation, between each addition of a new tile. Clearly, depending on the size of an assembly and the degrees of freedom of various components afforded by flexible bonds, such optimal reconfiguration could conceivably be precluded by faster rates of tile attachments. Various parameters which seek to balance the amount of configuration-space exploration versus tile attachment rates have been developed to study more kinetically realistic dynamics, but are beyond the scope of this paper.

3   Controlling Flexibility to Build Structures

Our goal in this section is to deterministically assemble certain shapes in the FTAM at temperature two. We define a *shape* to be a collection of connected tile locations. A shape is invariant through translation and rotation. Rather than go through an endless case-by-case analysis of all possible shapes, we focus on collections of 2D tile locations that form the outlines of three-dimensional shapes. We refer to these 3D shapes as *polycubes* and the set of 2D tile locations on their outer surface as an *outline*. We say that an FTAM system $\mathcal{T} = (T, \sigma, \tau)$ *deterministically assembles* a shape s if the embedding of all configurations $\mathcal{C}_\alpha$ of all terminal assemblies $\mathcal{A}_{\square}[\mathcal{T}]$ of the system T have shape s.

Due to the definition of the model, the most prominent additional challenge that is present in FTAM systems over traditional 2D aTAM systems is controlling the orientation of different faces in the assembly relative to one another as the assembly process is occurring. In which case, the approach that we use to demonstrate shape building in the FTAM is to make an *edge frame* for each polycube using unique tile types and filling in each face. We define an edge frame to be the collection of the outer-most tiles of each face in the outline of a polycube. For now, we will make the assumption that every edge of the shape is connected and will address this later in the section. We claim that studying edge frames is sufficient for unveiling the power of the FTAM to orient new faces in the assembly process since, intuitively, the cooperation of other tiles on the edges of adjacent faces doesn't provide additional help in correctly orienting those faces over just the tiles at the vertex. This intuition stems from the idea that the faces of a shape incident on a vertex interact on the same axes that the individual tiles incident on a vertex do.

One big deciding factor about whether the outline of a specific polycube can be made in the FTAM comes down to the types of vertices in that polycube. Because of this, we continue our analysis by breaking down the types of vertices that can exist on a polycube. Every type of vertex possible on a polycube can be enumerated by enumerating all polycubes that can fit inside a $2 \times 2 \times 2$ space that are distinct up to rotation and reflection. You can see the outcome of this enumeration in Fig. 4. In each polycube, the vertex type is illustrated at the center point of the $2 \times 2 \times 2$ space. The illustration has labels to later reference each vertex type.

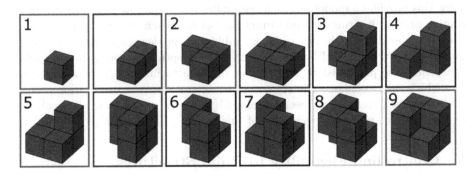

Fig. 4. All possible polycubes that can fit inside of a $2 \times 2 \times 2$ space, and furthermore, all possible vertex types that could exist on a polycube.

This yields 6 distinct vertex types. Vertices 1, 8, and 9 are all the same, which we refer to as a *convex* vertex. Vertices 3 and 5 are the same, which we refer to as a *concave* vertex. Vertex 3, 4, 6, and 7 are all distinct and we refer to them collectively as the *complex* vertices. In addition to the vertex type, the system must also be able to deterministically assemble the vertex from the correct perspective. A *perspective* is the relative direction that the new edges that form with the vertex are pointing with respect to the tiles of the original edge that first grows up to the vertex in the assembly process. Each vertex can have any number of perspectives from 1 (*symmetric* vertex) to the number of edges (*asymmetric* vertex), inclusive.

Collectively, there are 15 unique perspectives among the 6 distinct vertices. Each perspective requires its own tiling protocol to get the vertex to configure correctly. We construct these protocols using (a) the number of tiles that are incident on the vertex that are bound in a loop (which we refer to as the *loop length*) and (b) the sequence of flexibility values in the bonds of the loop (which we refer to as the *bond sequence*). If a perspective has a unique protocol, then attaching a loop of tiles using the protocol will result in the only possible configuration available for the loop of tiles being the correct perspective. Of the 15 perspectives previously mentioned, 11 perspectives among 4 of the vertices will have their own unique protocol and will therefore be deterministic. The other 4 perspectives among 2 vertices will all share one protocol and will therefore not be deterministic. These 2 vertices are types 3 and 7, which we will subsequently refer to as *reconfigurable* vertices. For a full enumeration and discussion of vertices, perspectives, and tiling protocols, see [6].

Fig. 5. (a) Original edge, (b) convex vertex, (c) concave vertex, from one unique perspective, (d) concave vertex, from another perspective

Assembly Process. Now, we consider the assembly process. Let's assume we start with a seed that is just the three tiles in a simple convex vertex. Notice that as the assembly process starts, the seed vertex and the edges that are growing out from it can invert as a whole but cannot otherwise reconfigure (since that would require removing a bond from the assembly). (For assembling an edge, we outline a trivial protocol in [6].) Each time the assembly grows up to a vertex, it will attach the loop of tiles that make this new vertex. As long as the new vertex is not a reconfigurable vertex, it will be forced to take a configuration that agrees with configuration of the seed vertex. By this, we mean that, if the seed vertex were to invert at this point, the edge connecting the two vertices would invert, and the new vertex would therefore be forced to invert. This cause-effect relationship is true for any vertices (excluding reconfigurable vertices) connected by an edge, which means that, if any bond in the partial assembly were to reorient, the whole partial assembly must invert, i.e. inversion is the only possible reconfiguration. An example of an edge frame started from a potential seed is shown in Fig. 6.

We now prove a claim that assembling in the correct configuration or the chiral configuration is identical (since both configurations have the same frontier) and will therefore yield the same shape.

Claim 1. Every frontier location f in an assembly α for a given configuration c_α has a corresponding frontier location f' in α in the chiral configuration c'_α,

Fig. 6. An assembling edge frame starting from a potential seed. Each edge grows up to a vertex and initializes other edges until the whole frame has filled out.

such that attaching f to α in c_α produces the same assembly but in the chiral configuration of attaching f' to α in c'_α.

Proof. Notice that a frontier location in the FTAM is dependent on 12 neighboring tile locations, an "Up", "Straight", and "Down" location for each of the 4 sides of the tile. Also remember chiral configurations of an assembly α produce embeddings of α that are the reflections of each other. Now, take any frontier location f in c_α. By reflecting an embedding of c_α over the plane that f exists in, the 12 tile locations that make f into a frontier location will still be neighboring f, with the "Up" and "Down" neighboring locations switching places and also reflecting, thereby keeping the same glues incident on the location of f. Since all the same glues are incident on the tile location, this location, which we will call f', is also a frontier location in c'_α with the same tile type as in c_α, even if c'_α includes some translation or rotation. Since the frontier locations are on the plane of symmetry that we used to get the chiral configurations, adding the tile to the assembly in either configuration will produce two configurations that are also chiral configurations of each other.

Once the assembly process has finished, the terminal assembly could also flip between the correct shape in its chiral. When there is at least one plane of symmetry in the shape, then reconfiguration in the assembly process actually will not prevent the system from being deterministic. This is because the chiral of a symmetric polycube is itself. Therefore, although the system will technically make two different terminal assemblies, one can be rotated into the other, meaning that the two different terminal assemblies have the same shape by definition, making the system deterministic.

Multiple Edge Frames. Up to this point, we have assumed all the edges in a polycube are connected. However, this is not always the case. For example, anytime two pieces of a shape are connected by a set of coplanar tiles (i.e. when the face graph has a cut vertex). Shapes like this are a problem because they require multiple edge frames to build, and similar to the chirality of asymmetric shapes, additional edge frames can also have chiral reconfigurations. Therefore, disagreeing chiralities of the edge frames can configure the terminal assembly of a system into a shape that is neither the intended shape nor its chiral. In

general, each additional edge frame doubles the number of configurations that
the terminal assembly can exist in, only one of which (or two, if symmetric) is
the desired shape. There are some exceptions to this (as discussed in [6]) such
as blocking and symmetry.

Summary. Combining the results of this section, we get the following theorem.

Theorem 1. *A temperature two FTAM system can deterministically assemble
the outline of any polycube that meets the following conditions:*

1. *the polycube is symmetric,*
2. *there are no reconfigurable vertices in the polycube, and*
3. *the edges of the polycube are all connected.*

4   Utilizing Flexibility

As discussed previously, reconfigurability may be able to provide assembly systems with interesting properties that enable diverse applications. For example,
changing geometry on the surface of a synthetic structure may allow it to interact with varying other structures in a system, or contracting/expanding volumes
may impact how well it can diffuse through narrow channels. With a simple
extension to the base FTAM model which allows an initial terminal assembly
to form, and then at a later stage the addition of a new set of tile types allows
the assembly to reconfigure, an assembly's final shape can be locked in based on
these additional tiles. As previously mentioned, we extend the FTAM here to
allow such staged assembly as the simplest mechanism for leveraging this type
of reconfigurability, but note that alternative mechanisms could also work, such
as glue activation and deactivation [16].

4.1   Staged Functional Surface: Maximizing the Number
of Reconfigurations

For our first demonstration of a construction utilizing flexibility as a tool, we
present a construction which maximizes the number of rigid configurations which
a flexible assembly (formed during a first stage of assembly) can be locked into,
based on the number of new tile types added during a second stage of assembly.
Figure 7 gives a high-level schematic of a simple example of such a system. (Note
that we omit full details of each tile type as these components can all be easily
constructed using standard aTAM techniques and techniques from Sect. 3.) It
shows the inner-makings of an initial structure that can later be modified by
adding new tiles types into solution. We refer to this structure as a *film*. The
film works by allowing the tiles in the very top layer to move freely. By adding
select subsets of tile types during the second stage, prescribed tiles can be pinned
up from the surface or pinned to the bottom layer of the assembly. Pinning up
works by using the second layer of the film (from the bottom) to block the
incoming tiles from folding down into the assembly, thereby forcing them to fold

up. Pinning down works by connecting the top layer to the bottom layer of the
film, forcing the tiles to fold down. The bumps formed from pinning up, also
called *pixels*, can be arranged into a specified geometry, or *image*. (More images
can be found in [6].) The eight tiles on top are used to pin up the pixels in the
image. The other tiles specified on the bottom can be used to pin down the rest
of the free pieces in the assembly if this is required instead.

For this system, if the side lengths of the film are n, note that there are
$O(n^2)$ potential pixel locations, meaning that there are a maximum of $O(2^{n^2})$
possible pixel configurations (i.e. each can be either up or down in any given
configuration). To transform the flexible film into a rigid configuration with a
particular set of pixels projecting upward, it is necessary to add tiles of $O(n^2)$
tile types corresponding to the up or down orientations, which is optimal as each
tile type is encoded by a constant number of bits and $\log(O(2^{n^2})) = O(n^2)$ bits
are necessary to uniquely identify each of the $O(2^{n^2})$ configurations. Note that
although these reconfigurations are relatively trivial, the differences in the sizes
of the reconfigurable sections can be arbitrarily large without requiring more
unique tile types to be added in the second stage. This construction displays a
maximum number of resulting rigid configurations from an optimal number of
additional tile types in the second stage.

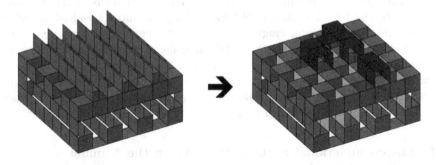

Fig. 7. An example of reconfigurable shape that can be used in a staged environment
to display a functional surface only after additional tiles are added.

4.2 Compressing/Expanding Structures

We now demonstrate a construction that is able to take advantage of the flexibility of bonds in the FTAM to allow a base assembly to lock into an expansive,
rigid but hollow configuration given the addition of one subset of tile types in
the second stage, or to instead lock into a compressed, compact and dense configuration given the addition of a different subset of tile types.

Figure 8(f) shows an assembly of six approximately $n \times n$ squares attached
together and in a flattened "sheet" configuration. Such an assembly can be efficiently self-assembled using $O(\log(n))$ tile types in the first stage. In the second

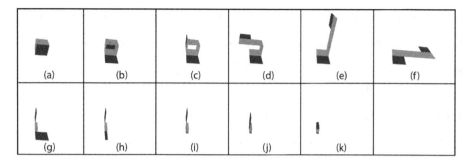

Fig. 8. Series of images giving a schematic depiction of a transformation from a hollow $n \times n \times n$ cube into a compressed, approximately $n \times \sqrt{n} \times \sqrt{n}$ configuration.

stage, one of two sets of a constant number of additional tile types could be added so that either (1) the sheet folds into a hollow, volume-maximizing cube of dimensions $n \times n \times n$ (i.e. volume n^3). A schematic representation of the transformation can be seen going backward from Fig. 8(f) to (a), or (2) the sheet folds into a compressed, compact "brick" of dimensions $O(n) \times O(\sqrt{n}) \times O(\sqrt{n})$ (i.e. volume n^2). A schematic representation of the transformation can be seen going forward from Fig. 8(f) to (k).

5   Complexity of FTAM Properties

In this section we consider the problem of deciding if a system produces rigid assemblies, the problem of deciding for a given assembly, if the assembly is rigid, and the problem of deciding for a given assembly, if the assembly is terminal. We first consider the problem of deciding if a system produces rigid assemblies.

5.1   Determining if a System Produces a Rigid Assembly is Uncomputable

We first show that, given an arbitrary FTAM system, determining if it produces a rigid terminal assembly is undecidable.

Problem 2 (Rigidity-from-system). Given an FTAM system $\mathcal{T}$, does there exist assembly $\alpha \in \mathcal{A}_\square[\mathcal{T}]$ such that α is rigid?

Theorem 3. *Rigidity-from-system is undecidable.*

For any given Turing machine M, we show that M can be simulated by an FTAM system that produces a single terminal rigid assembly iff M halts. The full proof of Theorem 3 is given in [6].

5.2   Determining the Rigidity of an Assembly is Co-NP-complete

Now, we look at the complexity of determining the rigidity of a given assembly.

Problem 4 (Rigidity-from-assembly). Given an FTAM system T and assembly $\alpha \in A[T]$, is α rigid?

Theorem 5. *Rigidity-from-assembly is co-NP-complete.*

To prove Theorem 5, we prove the following two lemmas.

Lemma 6. *The complement of rigidity-from-assembly is in NP.*

Proof. To illustrate this, we take an instance of the problem that contains the FTAM system T and assembly $\alpha \in A[T]$. Our certificate in this instance will be configurations c_α and c'_α. Since a configuration is simply a mapping from every flexible bond in α to an orientation, each configuration requires $O(|\alpha|)$ space, and thus the certificate is polynomial in the size of α. To determine if the certificate is valid, and thus if α is flexible (and therefore not rigid), we first check that c_α and c'_α are valid encodings of a configurations, meaning they each map every flexible bond in α to an orientation from { "Up", "Down", "Straight" }. Then we must ensure that c'_α is different than c_α. Both of these can be done in linear time with respect to the number of flexible bonds in the assembly. Next, we compute embeddings of α from c_α and c'_α, taking linear time in the number of tiles in the assembly. While computing the embeddings, we simply check that no tile is assigned a placement already taken by another tile, that no bonds overlap the same space, and that every tile is adjacent to the tiles it is connected to in α such that their glues line up correctly. Computing the embeddings and checking these conditions takes linear time with respect to the number of tiles in the assembly. If all of these conditions are met, then both c_α and c'_α are valid configurations of α, and therefore α is not rigid. Since the certificate has polynomial size in relation to α and can be verified in polynomial time to show that α is not rigid, the problem of determining if α is rigid is in co-NP.

Lemma 7. *The complement of rigidity-from-assembly is NP-hard.*

We prove Lemma 7 by a 3SAT reduction. In particular, we give an FTAM system, T say, and show how to encode a 3SAT formula as a producible assembly of T in a configuration, c say, such that there exists a configuration c' of α that is distinct from c iff the 3SAT formula is satisfiable. (See [6] for details.)

Finally, Theorem 5 is proven by Lemmas 6 and 7.

5.3   Determining the Terminality of an Assembly is Co-NP-complete

In addition to rigidity, terminality is another useful-to-know property of assemblies. Using much of the same logic from the previous result, we can prove a similar result regarding the terminality of arbitrary assemblies.

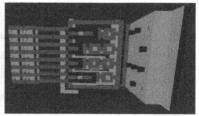

Fig. 9. Example assembly representing a 3SAT instance, visualized in FTAM simulator, used in the proof of Lemma 7.

Problem 8 (Terminality-from-assembly). Given an FTAM system T and assembly $\alpha \in \mathcal{A}[T]$, is α terminal?

Theorem 9. *Terminality-From-Assembly is co-NP-complete.*

To prove Theorem 9, we prove the following two lemmas.

Lemma 10. *The complement of terminality-from-assembly is in NP.*

Proof. For an instance of the problem, we are given an FTAM system $T = (T, \sigma, \tau)$ and assembly α. Our certificate in this case includes a configuration c_α for the assembly α and a frontier location f. Similar to in the proof of Lemma 6, (and since the encoding of f requires space $\leq |\alpha|$) we know that the certificate is polynomial in size to α. Also, we can check the validity of configuration c_α in polynomial time. Now, we simply need to verify the frontier location f (a) isn't already occupied by a tile and (b) is adjacent to tiles in α while it's in configuration c_α such that the adjacent glues allow the tile specified by f to bind to α with bonds collectively $\geq \tau$ strength, which can be done in time $O(|T|) + O(|\alpha|)$. Since the certificate has polynomial size in relation to α and can be verified in polynomial time to show that α is not terminal, the problem of determining if α is terminal is in co-NP.

Now, we will also show that the complement of terminality is NP-hard. A slight augmentation to the 3SAT machine assembly can be used to achieve this.

Lemma 11. *The complement of terminality-from-assembly is NP-hard.*

To prove Lemma 11, we use almost identical techniques as for the proof of Lemma 7, with a slight modification to the 3SAT machine so that, if and only if the 3SAT instance is satisfiable, then there will be a valid configuration of the assembly which represents the satisfying assignment, and in that configuration - and no other valid configuration - there will be a frontier location, which means that the assembly is not terminal.

Theorem 9 is proven by Lemmas 10 and 11.

References

1. Aichholzer, O., et al.: Folding polyominoes into (poly) cubes. arXiv preprint arXiv:1712.09317 (2017)
2. Aloupis, G., et al.: Common unfoldings of polyominoes and polycubes. In: Akiyama, J., Bo, J., Kano, M., Tan, X. (eds.) CGGA 2010. LNCS, vol. 7033, pp. 44–54. Springer, Heidelberg (2011). https://doi.org/10.1007/978-3-642-24983-9_5
3. Barish, R.D., Schulman, R., Rothemund, P.W.K., Winfree, E.: An information-bearing seed for nucleating algorithmic self-assembly. Proc. Natl. Acad. Sci. **106**(15), 6054–6059 (2009). https://doi.org/10.1073/pnas.0808736106
4. Crescenzi, P., Goldman, D., Papadimitriou, C., Piccolboni, A., Yannakakis, M.: On the complexity of protein folding. J. Comput. Biol. **5**(3), 423–465 (1998)
5. Dill, K.A., et al.: Principles of protein folding a perspective from simple exact models. Protein Sci. **4**(4), 561–602 (1995). https://doi.org/10.1002/pro.5560040401
6. Durand-Lose, J., Hendricks, J., Patitz, M.J., Perkins, I., Sharp, M.: Self-assembly of 3-D structures using 2-D folding tiles. Technical report 1807.04818, Computing Research Repository (2018). http://arxiv.org/abs/1807.04818
7. Fochtman, T., Hendricks, J., Padilla, J.E., Patitz, M.J., Rogers, T.A.: Signal transmission across tile assemblies: 3D static tiles simulate active self-assembly by 2D signal-passing tiles. Nat. Comput. **14**(2), 251–264 (2015)
8. Fraenkel, A.S.: Complexity of protein folding. Bull. Math. Biol. **55**(6), 1199–1210 (1993)
9. Hendricks, J., Patitz, M.J., Rogers, T.A.: Reflections on tiles (in self-assembly). Nat. Comput. **16**(2), 295–316 (2017). https://doi.org/10.1007/s11047-017-9617-2
10. Jonoska, N., Karpenko, D.: Active tile self-assembly, part 1: universality at temperature 1. Int. J. Found. Comput. Sci. **25**(02), 141–163 (2014). https://doi.org/10.1142/S0129054114500087
11. Jonoska, N., Karpenko, D.: Active tile self-assembly, part 2: self-similar structures and structural recursion. Int. J. Found. Comput. Sci. **25**(02), 165–194 (2014). https://doi.org/10.1142/S0129054114500099
12. Jonoska, N., McColm, G.L.: A computational model for self-assembling flexible tiles. In: Calude, C.S., Dinneen, M.J., Păun, G., Pérez-Jímenez, M.J., Rozenberg, G. (eds.) UC 2005. LNCS, vol. 3699, pp. 142–156. Springer, Heidelberg (2005). https://doi.org/10.1007/11560319_14
13. Jonoska, N., McColm, G.L.: Complexity classes for self-assembling flexible tiles. Theor. Comput. Sci. **410**(4–5), 332–346 (2009). https://doi.org/10.1016/j.tcs.2008.09.054
14. Ming-Yang, K., Ramachandran, V.: DNA self-assembly for constructing 3D boxes. In: Eades, P., Takaoka, T. (eds.) ISAAC 2001. LNCS, vol. 2223, pp. 429–441. Springer, Heidelberg (2001). https://doi.org/10.1007/3-540-45678-3_37
15. Liu, W., Zhong, H., Wang, R., Seeman, N.C.: Crystalline two-dimensional DNA-origami arrays. Angewandte Chemie Int. Ed. **50**(1), 264–267 (2011). https://doi.org/10.1002/anie.201005911
16. Padilla, J.E., et al.: Asynchronous signal passing for tile self-assembly: fuel efficient computation and efficient assembly of shapes. In: Mauri, G., Dennunzio, A., Manzoni, L., Porreca, A.E. (eds.) UCNC 2013. LNCS, vol. 7956, pp. 174–185. Springer, Heidelberg (2013). https://doi.org/10.1007/978-3-642-39074-6_17
17. Padilla, J.E., Patitz, M.J., Schweller, R.T., Seeman, N.C., Summers, S.M., Zhong, X.: Asynchronous signal passing for tile self-assembly: fuel efficient computation and efficient assembly of shapes. Int. J. Found. Comput. Sci. **25**(4), 459–488 (2014)

18. Rothemund, P.W.K.: Design of DNA origami. In: ICCAD 2005: Proceedings of the 2005 IEEE/ACM International Conference on Computer-aided Design, pp. 471–478. IEEE Computer Society, Washington, DC (2005)
19. Rothemund, P.W.K.: Folding DNA to create nanoscale shapes and patterns. Nature **440**(7082), 297–302 (2006). https://doi.org/10.1038/nature04586
20. Winfree, E.: Algorithmic self-assembly of DNA. Ph.D. thesis, California Institute of Technology, June 1998

Forming Tile Shapes with Simple Robots

Robert Gmyr[1], Kristian Hinnenthal[2(✉)], Irina Kostitsyna[3], Fabian Kuhn[4],
Dorian Rudolph[2], Christian Scheideler[2], and Thim Strothmann[2]

[1] University of Houston, Houston, USA
rgmyr@uh.edu
[2] Paderborn University, Paderborn, Germany
{krijan,dorian,scheidel,thim}@mail.upb.de
[3] TU Eindhoven, Eindhoven, The Netherlands
i.kostitsyna@tue.nl
[4] University of Freiburg, Freiburg im Breisgau, Germany
kuhn@cs.uni-freiburg.de

Abstract. Motivated by the problem of manipulating nanoscale materials, we investigate the problem of reconfiguring a set of tiles into certain shapes by robots with limited computational capabilities. As a first step towards developing a general framework for these problems, we consider the problem of rearranging a connected set of hexagonal tiles by a single deterministic finite automaton. After investigating some limitations of a single-robot system, we show that a feasible approach to build a particular shape is to first rearrange the tiles into an intermediate structure by performing very simple tile movements. We introduce three types of such intermediate structures, each having certain advantages and disadvantages. Each of these structures can be built in asymptotically optimal $O(n^2)$ rounds, where n is the number of tiles. As a proof of concept, we give an algorithm for reconfiguring a set of tiles into an equilateral triangle through one of the intermediate structures. Finally, we experimentally show that the algorithm for building the simplest of the three intermediate structures can be modified to be executed by multiple robots in a distributed manner, achieving an almost linear speedup in the case where the number of robots is reasonably small.

Keywords: Finite automata · Reconfiguration · Tiles
Shape formation

1 Introduction

Various models and approaches for designing and manipulating nanoscale materials have already been proposed. A prominent approach in the DNA community

This work was begun at the Dagstuhl Seminar on Algorithmic Foundations of Programmable Matter, July 3–8, 2016. A preliminary version of this paper was presented at EuroCG 2017. This work is partly supported by DFG grant SCHE 1592/3-1. Fabian Kuhn is supported by ERC Grant 336495 (ACDC).

D. Doty and H. Dietz (Eds.): DNA 2018, LNCS 11145, pp. 122–138, 2018.
https://doi.org/10.1007/978-3-030-00030-1_8

has been to use DNA tiles [14]. In the most basic *abstract tile-assembly model* (aTAM), there are square tiles with a specific glue on each side [17]. Here, standard problems are to minimize the tile complexity (i.e., the number of different tile types) in order to form certain shapes, and to intrinsically perform computations guiding the assembly process. While in aTAM only individual tiles can be attached to an existing assembly, in more complex hierarchical assembly models, partial assemblies can also bind to each other (e.g., [4,5]). However, these approaches are based on strictly passive elements, so any changes to the structure have to be enforced externally (e.g., by changing the temperature or exposing the structure to certain kinds of radiation). A limited number of approaches has been proposed that are based on active elements instead [7,9,24]. However, since these elements are presumably more difficult to build, it might be far more costly to realize these approaches than the approaches based on DNA tiles.

In this paper, we investigate a *hybrid approach* for the *shape formation problem*, in which we are given a set of *passive* tiles, which are uniform and stateless, and (a limited number of) *active* robots. The robots, which only have the computational power of a finite automaton, can transport tiles from one position to another in order to form a desired shape. Compared to the DNA tile-based approach, this approach has the advantage that all tiles are of the same type and movements are exclusively performed by the robots. Furthermore, in contrast to the approaches based entirely on active elements, we believe that many problems can be solved in our hybrid model using only a few active elements. In this paper, we support this claim by showing that already a single robot is able to solve simple shape formation problems. Our ultimate goal is to investigate how multiple robots can cooperate to speed up the process of shape formation.

Although the complexity of our model is very restricted, actually realizing such a system, for example using complex DNA nanomachines, is currently still a challenging task. However, in recent years there has been significant progress in this direction. For example, nanomachines have been demonstrated to be able to act like the head of a finite automaton on an input tape [16], to walk on a one- or two-dimensional surface [10,13,23], and to transport cargo [18,20,22]. We therefore believe that, in principle, it should be feasible to build nanomachines with the capabilities assumed in this paper.

1.1 Model and Problem Statement

We assume that a single *active* agent (a *robot*) operates on a set of n *passive* hexagonal *tiles*. Each tile occupies exactly one node of the infinite triangular lattice $G = (V, E)$ (see Fig. 1a). A *configuration* (T, p) consists of a set $T \subset V$ of all nodes occupied by tiles, and the robot's position $p \in V$. We assume that the initial position of the robot is occupied by a tile. Note that every node $u \in V$ is adjacent to six neighbors, and, as indicated in the figure, we describe the relative positions of adjacent nodes by six compass directions.

Whereas tiles cannot perform any computation nor move on their own, the robot may change its position and carry a tile, thereby modifying a configuration. We require that the robot's position p is always adjacent to a node occupied by

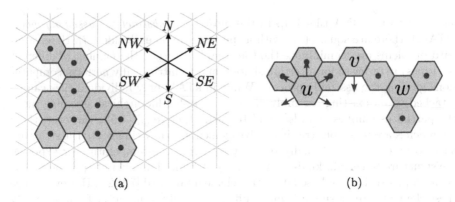

(a)   (b)

Fig. 1. (a) A set of tiles placed on nodes of the infinite triangular lattice. The top right part of the figure shows the compass directions we use to describe the movement of a robot. (b) Possible movements of tiles u, v, and w. Tile w cannot be moved anywhere without violating connectivity.

a tile. Additionally, if the robot does not carry a tile, we require the subgraph of G induced by T to be connected; otherwise, the subgraph induced by $T \cup \{p\}$ must be connected. In a scenario where a tile structure swims in a liquid, for example, this restriction prevents the robot or parts of the tile structure from floating apart. Some examples of possible tile-moving steps are shown in Fig. 1b.

The robot acts as a *deterministic finite automaton* and operates in rounds of *look-compute-move* cycles. In the *look* phase of a round the robot can observe its node p and the six neighbors of that node. For each of these nodes it can determine whether it is occupied or not. In the *compute* phase the robot potentially changes its state and determines its next move according to the observed information. In the *move* phase the robot can either (1) pick up a tile from p, if $p \in T$, (2) place a tile it is carrying at that node, if $p \notin T$, or (3) move to an adjacent node while possibly carrying a tile with it. The robot can carry at most one tile.

Note that even though we describe the algorithms as if the robot knew its global orientation, we do not actually require the robot to have a compass. For the algorithms presented in this paper, it is enough for the robot to be able to maintain its orientation with respect to its initial orientation.

We are interested in *Shape Formation* problems, in which the goal is to transform any initial configuration into a configuration in which the tiles form a certain shape on the lattice. Particularly, the goal of the *Triangle Formation Problem* is to bring the set of all tiles into a triangular form.

1.2   Related Work

There is a number of approaches to shape formation in the literature that use agents that fall somewhere in the spectrum between passive and active. For example, *tile-based self-assembly* [14] uses passive tiles that bond to each other to form shapes. A variant of *population protocols* proposed in [11] uses agents that are partly passive (i.e., they cannot control their movement) and partly active (i.e., upon meeting another, they can perform a computation and decide whether they want to form a bond). Finally, the *amoebot model* [7], the *nubot model* [24], and the modular robotic model proposed in [9] use agents that are completely active in that they can compute and control their movement. Shape formation has also been investigated in the field of *modular robotics* (see, e.g., [2,12,21]); here, the robots typically have much greater computational capabilities than in our model. All of these approaches have in common that they consider a *single type* of agent. In contrast, we investigate a model that uses a *combination* of *active* and *passive* agents.

When arguing about a robot traversing a tile structure without actually moving tiles, our model reduces to an instance of the ubiquitous *agents on graphs* model. The vast amount of research on this model covers many fascinating problems, including *Gathering* and *Rendezvous* (e.g., [15]), *Intruder Caption* and *Graph Searching* (e.g. [1,8]), and *Graph Exploration* (e.g., [3]). Other approaches allow agents to move tiles (e.g., [6,19]) but these focus on computational complexity issues or agents that are more powerful than finite automata.

1.3   Our Contribution

In this paper we mainly focus on the Triangle Formation Problem with a single robot. We begin with pointing out one of the limitations of our model: It is in general impossible for one robot to find a tile that can be removed without disconnecting the tile structure. We contrast this result by showing that having a single *pebble* already suffices to solve this problem.

We then show how to construct *intermediate structures* by using simple tile movements that allow for easy navigation and tile removal. More specifically, we present three intermediate structures. The simplest among them is a *line* structure; it can be constructed in $O(n^2)$ rounds. The second structure we introduce is a *block*. It has $O(D)$ diameter (D being the initial diameter of the tile set), and often can be constructed more efficiently than the line, namely in $O(nD)$ rounds. Finally, we describe a *tree* structure, which, in contrast to the previous structures, can be built completely inside the convex hull of the original tile set in $O(n^2)$ rounds. Using the block structure as an example, we argue that each of these intermediate structures can be transformed into a triangle by performing an additional $O(nD)$ rounds (D being the intermediate structure's diameter).

We finally discuss how the algorithm to construct a line can be transferred to the multi-robot case. We provide some first simulation results showing that a small number of robots can speed up line formation by a significant amount. As the number of robots becomes high, we observe the anticipated decline in speedup.

2   A Naive Approach

In a naive approach to shape formation, the robot could iteratively search for a tile that can be removed without disconnecting the tile structure (a *safely removable tile*) and then move that tile to some position such that the shape under construction is extended. While there always is a safely removable tile, the following theorem shows that, in general, a single robot cannot find it, which makes this naive approach infeasible.

Theorem 1. *A single robot cannot find a safely removable tile.*

Proof. Suppose that there is an algorithm that allows the robot to find such a tile. Let s be the number of states used by the algorithm. Consider the execution of the algorithm on a hollow hexagon of side length ℓ where the robot is initially placed on a vertex of the hexagon as depicted in Fig. 2a. We define the set of *border nodes* to be all vertex nodes of the hexagon, all empty nodes inside the hexagon that are adjacent to a vertex, and all empty nodes outside the hexagon whose only neighbor is a vertex (see Fig. 2a). We subdivide the execution of the algorithm into *phases* where we define a new phase to start whenever the robot visits a border node. Note that since there are at most 18 border nodes, the algorithm runs for at most $18s$ phases before the robot chooses a tile to be safely removed. Otherwise, the robot would visit a border node twice in the same state and therefore the algorithm would enter an infinite loop.

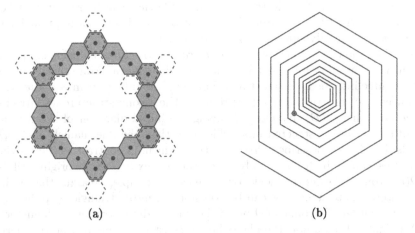

(a)   (b)

Fig. 2. (a) The hollow hexagon of side length $\ell = 4$. The border nodes of the hexagon are marked by dashed frames. (b) An example of the tile structure T. The red mark represents the initial position of the robot. (Color figure online)

The way the robot traverses the hexagon depends on the side length ℓ. We define the *traversal sequence* associated with ℓ as $((v_1, q_1), (v_2, q_2), \ldots, (v_k, q_k))$, where k is the number of phases the algorithm takes until the tile is chosen, v_i is the border node occupied by the robot at the beginning of phase i, and q_i is the state of the robot at the beginning of phase i. Note that a traversal sequence may be of length 1, i.e., if the robot never visits a border node except for its initial position. Since the algorithm takes at most $18s$ phases to choose the tile (for any choice of ℓ), there can only be at most $(18s)^{18s}$ distinct traversal sequences for different choices of ℓ. Hence, there is a finite number of traversal sequences and an infinite number of side lengths, which, according to the pigeonhole principle, implies that there must be an infinite set of side lengths L corresponding to the same traversal sequence.

Based on this observation, we now define a tile structure T for which the algorithm fails to find a tile that can be safely removed. This tile structure essentially consists of a spiral as depicted in Fig. 2b. We start at an arbitrary node of the triangular lattice and construct an outward spiral consisting of $72s$ line segments. The first line segment of the spiral goes north and each subsequent line segment takes a $60°$ clockwise turn. The lengths of the line segments are chosen from L in such a way that the segments stay well-separated. This is possible since L is an infinite set and therefore we can always choose sufficiently large segment lengths. We initially place the robot at the end of the $36s$-th line segment.

It remains to show that the algorithm fails to find a tile that can be safely removed when being executed on T. As above, we subdivide the execution of the algorithm into phases where we define a new phase to start whenever the robot visits a border node of the spiral (which we define correspondingly). It is easy to show using induction on the phases that the robot traverses T in a way that corresponds to the traversal sequence associated with the side lengths in L. Consequently, the robot chooses a tile that is neither the start tile nor the end tile of the spiral. Since these two tiles are the only tiles that can be safely removed from T, the algorithm fails. This contradicts the assumption that the algorithm works correctly and therefore shows that there is no such algorithm.

$\square$

In contrast, we obtain the following theorem for a robot and a *pebble*. Here, we additionally assume that the robot is given a single pebble which it can pick up, carry, or place on a tile. More specifically, in the *look* phase of a round, the robot can additionally observe whether the pebble is placed on any tile in its neighborhood, and, alternatively to the other options in the *move* phase, it may either pick up or place a pebble. The proof of the theorem can be found in the full version of this paper.

Theorem 2. *A robot with a pebble can always find a safely removable tile in* $O(n^2)$ *rounds.*

3   Forming an Intermediate Structure

Although the robot cannot generally determine whether tiles can be safely removed, it is easy to see that there are local tile movements that preserve

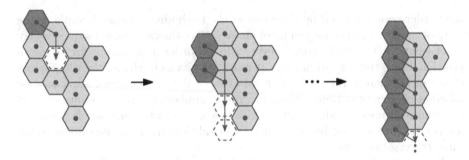

Fig. 3. First several steps of Algorithm 1. The green tiles are moved to the positions marked by dashed frames. (Color figure online)

connectivity. In this section we show how to construct *intermediate structures* by performing such movements. In the resulting structures the robot can easily navigate and remove tiles. Therefore, it can easily disassemble such a structure and rearrange its tiles into the desired shape.

We say a tile configuration is *simply connected* if it has no *holes*, i.e., finite maximal sets of connected unoccupied nodes. We aim to construct simply connected intermediate structures as removability of a tile can easily be determined locally in such a structure: a tile is safely removable if and only if the structure solely consisting of its neighbors is connected. Furthermore, since any simply connected structure clearly has a safely removable tile, it can be found by a robot moving along the structure's boundary. Note that although in the presented intermediate structures it is easy to determine a location where an arbitrarily sized shape can be built, a robot may not easily find such a location in an arbitrary simply connected structure.

We show how to construct three different intermediate structures. As a first simple example, we demonstrate how to construct a *line* in time $O(n^2)$. Clearly, the main drawback of this algorithm is that tiles might need to be moved by a distance linear in n. Our second algorithm avoids this pitfall by building a structure called a *block* in time $O(nD)$. Here, D is the *diameter* of the initial tile configuration, which is defined as the maximal length of a shortest node path between any two occupied nodes of the triangular lattice. The algorithm further ensures that no tile is moved farther than by a distance of D. The last and most complex algorithm builds a simply connected structure called a *tree* in time $O(n^2)$. The main advantage of this solution is that no tile is ever placed outside of the *convex hull* of the initial configuration. Here, we refer to the convex hull of the corresponding set of hexagonal tiles in the Euclidean plane.

3.1   Forming a Line

In this section we present an algorithm for one robot to rearrange a tile configuration into a straight line in $O(n^2)$ rounds. The pseudocode is given in Algorithm 1.

Algorithm 1. Algorithm to form a line.

1: Move S until there is no tile at S
2: **do**
3:    Set flag is_line to TRUE
4:    *Tile searching phase:* at every step, until the robot can no longer move,
5:     – if there is an adjacent tile at NW, SW, NE, or SE, set is_line to FALSE,
6:     – move NW, SW or N (in that precedence) if there is a tile in this direction
7:    *Tile moving phase:* if is_line is FALSE, pick up the tile at the current position,
    and move it to the bottom of the adjacent column, starting at position SE
8: **while** is_line is FALSE

We use the labels N, NE, SE, S, SW and NW (corresponding to cardinal directions) to refer to the six neighbors of the robot (see Fig. 1a). We define a *column*
to be a maximal sequence of connected tiles from N to S, and a *row* to be a
maximal sequence of connected tiles from NW to SE.

At the beginning of every iteration of the algorithm, the robot is located
at a tile that has no neighbor in the S direction. During one iteration of the
algorithm, the robot finds a locally most north-western tile (i.e., a tile with no
neighbors at N, NW, and SW) and moves it to the bottom of the column of
tiles to the east from it. Figure 3 illustrates the first several iterations of the
algorithm. To check whether the desired tile configuration has been achieved,
the robot inspects adjacent tiles at each step in the search phase.

The following theorem, which is proven in the full version of the paper,
establishes the correctness of the algorithm.

Theorem 3. *Following Algorithm 1, a single robot rearranges any tile configuration into a straight line in $O(n^2)$ rounds.*

Proof. (sketch) The correctness of the algorithm follows from the following observations: (1) the tile searching phase terminates in a locally most north-western
tile, (2) if there is more than one column in the tile configuration, the tile searching phase does not terminate in the northernmost tile of an easternmost column,
(3) the tile moving phase does not disconnect the tile configuration and (4) the
algorithm terminates when a line is formed.   □

Note that it is not hard to see that $\Omega(n^2)$ rounds are necessary to rearrange
an arbitrary initial tile configuration into a straight line by a single robot. If
starting from an initial configuration with diameter $O(\sqrt{n})$, a constant fraction
of the tiles has to be moved by a distance linear in n and thus, in total, $\Omega(n^2)$
move steps are necessary.

3.2   Forming a Block

Although a line can be constructed efficiently, its linear diameter might make it
an undesirable intermediate structure. In fact, if both the initial diameter and the
diameter of the desired shape are small, moving tiles by a linear distance seems

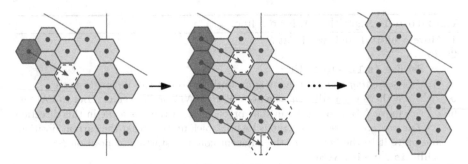

Fig. 4. Transformation of an initial structure into a block. The gray lines indicate some fixed x- and y-coordinates for reference.

to be an excessive effort. Therefore, we introduce another intermediate structure, which is called a *block*: In a block, all tiles except for the globally westernmost tiles have a neighbor at NW. That is, there is only one westernmost column, and every row begins with a tile from that column (see Fig. 4 (right)). Our algorithm builds a block in $O(nD)$ time and does not move any tile farther than by a distance D (recall that D is the diameter of the initial structure). An example of a transformation of an initial structure into a block is shown in Fig. 4.

We present the algorithm in two steps. First, we describe a non-halting algorithm by giving simple tile moving rules similar to the rules of the line construction algorithm. Eventually this algorithm will build a block structure. We then extend the algorithm with additional checks to detect whether a block structure has been built.

As in the line algorithm, the robot alternates between a searching and a moving phase: It first searches for a locally most north-western tile by repeatedly moving NW, SW, or N (in that precedence). The robot then picks up the tile, moves SE until it reaches an empty node, and places the tile there.

We first show the correctness of this simple algorithm in the following sequence of lemmas. In the following, we assign coordinates to each node, where the x-coordinate grows from west to east and the y-coordinate grows from north to south (e.g., moving N increases y by 1 while moving SW decreases x by 1 and y by $\frac{1}{2}$). Let 0 be the maximum x-coordinate of all tiles in the initial tile configuration, i.e., the x-coordinates of the easternmost tiles are 0 and all others have negative x-coordinates.

Lemma 1. *During the algorithm's execution, any two tiles with x-coordinate 0 are connected via a simple path of tiles whose x-coordinates are at most 0.*

Proof. The claim initially holds. Let P be the simple path connecting two tiles u and v with x-coordinate equal to 0. We show that after the robot has moved any other tile there remains a path between u and v. Note, that the robot does not violate the claim by picking a tile with x-coordinate greater than 0. If the robot picks up a tile t with x-coordinate equal to 0, then t cannot lie on P, as t does not have adjacent tiles at N, NW, and SW. Thus, moving t does not affect the path. Now, assume the robot picks up a tile t with x-coordinate smaller than 0. If t lies on P, then, since P is simple, t must have two adjacent tiles t' and t'' at *NE*, *SE*, or *S* that are part of P. If the *SE* position is not empty, t' and t'' remain connected after the removal of t. Otherwise, t will be placed there. In both cases a path between u and v is maintained.   □

Lemma 2. *As long as there is a tile with x-coordinate 0, the robot only picks up tiles with x-coordinate at most 0.*

Proof. The first tile the robot picks up has x-coordinate at most 0. Now assume the robot picks up a tile at some node v of the triangular lattice with x-coordinate x_v. If there is a tile at the S neighbor of v, then the next tile the robot will pick up has x-coordinate at most x_t. If there is no tile at the S neighbor of v, the next tile the robot will pick up is at the *SE* neighbor of v.

This implies that in order for the robot to first pick up a tile t_2 with x-coordinate greater than 0, it has to have previously picked up a tile t_1 at 0 with no neighbor at S. Therefore, t_1 cannot have been connected to any other tile at 0 via a path of tiles with x-coordinate at most 0. Thus, by Lemma 1, t_1 was the only tile at 0 when it was picked up. Therefore, there is no tile with x-coordinate 0 when t_2 is picked up.   □

Note that in the next lemma we do not yet assume that the algorithm will terminate when a block structure has been built, but only show that a block will eventually be built.

Lemma 3. *Let the maximum x-coordinate of the tiles in the initial tile structure be 0. Then the algorithm rearranges the tiles into a block, in which the westernmost column of tiles has x-coordinate 1, in $O(nD)$ rounds.*

Proof. We first show the correctness of the algorithm. First, note that the robot always finds a tile to move. By Lemma 2, the robot will repeatedly pick tiles with x-coordinate at most 0 until there is no such tile anymore. At this point, every tile with x-coordinate at least 2 has a neighbor at *NW*. This is due to the fact that each such tile must have had a *NW* neighbor at the time of its placement, and by Lemma 2 none of these tiles have been moved yet. Therefore, the tiles are arranged as a block in which the westernmost tile has x-coordinate at most 1.

We now turn to the runtime of the algorithm. It is easy to see that each tile is moved for at most $2D$ steps until the block is established, which implies that at most $O(nD)$ move steps are performed in total. Note that each time a tile is moved the sum of the robot's coordinates increases by $\frac{3}{2}$. On the other hand, each search step decreases this sum by at least $\frac{1}{2}$. Thus, the total number of search steps is bounded by $3m + O(n)$, where $m = O(nD)$ is the total number of move steps. Therefore, the total number of search steps is also bounded by $O(nD)$. Since each step is performed within a constant number of rounds, the number of steps the algorithm takes until it builds a block structure, with x-coordinate of a westernmost tile equal to 1, is $O(nD)$.   □

Next, we show how the robot can detect when a block has been successfully built by performing a series of tests alongside the algorithm's execution. Consider a block as a stack of *rows*, i.e., sequences of consecutive tiles from NW to SE. Note that according to the above algorithm the robot will move each tile of the westernmost column of a finished block, starting with the northernmost tile, placing each at the first empty position SE of it. Thereby, the robot can detect that a block has been built by verifying the following conditions: (1) after placing a tile, the robot performs at most one SW movement before it takes the next tile, (2) while moving a tile t, the robot does not traverse a node (except for t's previous position) that has a neighbor at NE, but not at N, or a neighbor at S, but not at SW, (3) the robot never places a tile at a node that has a neighbor at SE. A test verifying the above conditions is initiated whenever the robot picks a tile that does not have a NE neighbor. If thereafter any of the above conditions gets violated, the test is aborted. If otherwise the robot places the southernmost tile without encountering any violation, the algorithm terminates.

The following theorem follows from Lemma 3 and an analysis of the termination conditions. The formal proof can be found in the full version of the paper.

Theorem 4. *Following the above algorithm, a single robot rearranges any tile configuration into a block and terminates within $O(nD)$ rounds.*

Note that since tiles are exclusively moved SE, the resulting block has at most D rows consisting of at most D tiles each, and therefore diameter $O(D)$. Similar to the construction of a line, it can be easily seen that the runtime to construct a block is asymptotically optimal: Consider a line of tiles from SW to NW. In order to transform the initial structure into a block, a constant fraction of tiles needs to be moved by a distance linear in D.

3.3 Forming a Tree

So far we have been mainly focusing on how to *quickly* construct suitable intermediate structures. However, regarding potential practical applications, it may also be desirable to minimize the required work space. Whereas the previous structures are in many cases built almost completely outside of the initial configuration's convex hull, in this section we present an algorithm that builds a simply connected structure by exclusively moving tiles inside the structure's convex hull.

First we introduce some additional notation. An *overhang* is a set of vertically adjacent empty nodes such that (1) the northernmost node has a tile at N, (2) the southernmost node has a tile at S, and (3) all nodes have adjacent tiles at NW and SW. A *tree* is a connected tile configuration without an overhang. Examples of an overhang and a tree are shown in Fig. 5a and b, respectively. Since the westernmost nodes of a hole are part of an overhang, a tree is simply connected. The *branches* of a tree's column are defined as its western adjacent columns, where two columns are called adjacent if at least two of their tiles

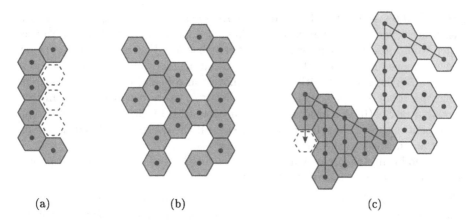

Fig. 5. (a) An overhang. (b) A tree. (c) Triangle formation (in blue) starting from a block (in gray). (Color figure online)

are adjacent. Finally, define a *local tree* as a column of tiles whose connected component, obtained by removing all of its eastern neighbors, is a tree.

We present an algorithm that transforms any initial tile configuration into a tree in $O(n^2)$ rounds and without ever placing a tile outside the initial structure's convex hull. The pseudocode of the algorithm can be found in the full version of this paper. From a high-level perspective, the algorithm works as follows. The robot first traverses the tile structure in a recursive fashion until it encounters an overhang. It then fills the overhang with tiles and afterwards restarts the algorithm. Once the whole structure can be traversed without encountering any overhang, the tiles are arranged in a tree and the robot terminates.

More precisely, the robot does the following. In the `initialize` phase, it first successively moves to eastern columns until it reaches a locally easternmost column. Then the robot starts moving west. Upon entering a column, it moves N and then enters the northernmost branch. If the column has no branches, a locally westernmost column has been reached. In this case the robot checks whether the current column has an adjacent eastern overhang by traversing the column from N to S. If so, it fills the overhang as described in the next paragraph and afterwards restarts the algorithm. Otherwise, the robot searches for an adjacent eastern column (of which there can be at most one). If there is none, then the algorithm terminates. Otherwise, the robot either continues its traversal in the first branch S to the branch from which it entered the current column, or, if no such branch exists, verifies whether the current column has an adjacent eastern overhang and proceeds as described above.

We now describe how the robot fills an overhang. First, to find a tile to place into the overhang, the robot moves in a way that assures that it will find its way back. The robot alternates between moving N as long as there is a tile at N (`get_tile_N` phase), and moving NW as long as there is a tile at NW and no tile at SW or N (`get_tile_NW` phase). The robot's path either ends in the get_tile_N phase at a tile that does not have a neighbor at NW or SW, in which case it is taken, or in the get_tile_NW phase at a locally most north-western tile, which would also be taken, or at a tile t that has a SW neighbor. In the latter case t is moved one step S. If thereafter t has a neighbor at S or SW, the robot takes t's NE neighbor t'. Otherwise, it moves onto t' and continues its search. Once the robot has picked up a tile, it returns to its originating column by moving S or SE (in this order of precedence), until it reaches the overhang. The robot continues to bring tiles as described until the overhang is filled, in which case it again turns to the initialize phase.

The following theorem, which is proven in the full version of this paper, concludes the correctness of the algorithm.

Theorem 5. *Following the above algorithm, a single robot rearranges any tile configuration into a tree in $O(n^2)$ rounds and without placing a tile outside the initial configuration's convex hull.*

4   Forming a Triangle

We will now describe how the robot can transform an intermediate structure into a *triangle*. More precisely, a triangle consists of columns whose northernmost tiles form a row, and each column consists of exactly one tile more than its eastern adjacent column (except for the westernmost column, which is only partially filled if n is not a triangular number). In the following we assume that a block has already been built. It can be easily seen that a line and a tree can be transformed in a similar way. The robot builds a triangle by repeatedly taking the easternmost tile of the northernmost row of the block, carrying it to the bottom of the westernmost column, and placing it at the next position of the westernmost column of the triangle, see Fig. 5c.

First, the robot creates the tip (i.e., the easternmost column) of the triangle by placing the first tile below the westernmost column of the block. The second tile is placed NW of the tip. Every other tile of the triangle is then placed as follows. The robot first brings a tile to the triangle's tip. It then walks NW and S (in that precedence) until there is no tile in these directions anymore. If there is a tile at SE, the robot moves one step S and drops the tile. Otherwise, the robot moves to the top of the layer, takes one step in NW direction and places the tile there. In this manner, the robot continues to extend the triangle tile by tile until the whole block has been disassembled. By Theorem 4, and since each tile can be brought and placed within $O(D)$ rounds, we conclude the following theorem.

Theorem 6. *A single robot can rearrange any tile configuration into a triangle in $O(nD)$ rounds.*

It is not hard to see, using similar arguments as in the previous sections, that the runtime is asymptotically optimal. In the case that an initial configuration's diameter is low, i.e., $D = O(n^{1/2})$, we conclude that it can be rearranged into a triangle in $O(n^{3/2})$ rounds. Note that if the number of tiles is not a triangular number, one side of the triangle is only partially occupied by tiles.

5   Towards Multiple Robots

As a first step towards extending our algorithms to the multi-robot case, we show that multiple robots can cooperatively construct a line. We believe that some of our ideas, which we only sketch due to space constraints, may also be useful to solve more difficult problems. First, we present and discuss the underlying model assumptions. Then, we briefly describe how Algorithm 1 can be adapted for multiple robots. Finally, we experimentally show that the construction of a line can be sped up significantly by using multiple robots.

Model Discussion. We consider the following extension of our model to incorporate multiple robots. Each node is occupied by at most one robot at any time. We adapt our notion of connectivity and require all robots to be adjacent to occupied nodes, and the subgraph induced by all occupied nodes and the positions of all robots carrying tiles to be connected. In the look phase, for each adjacent node a robot can additionally observe whether the node is occupied by another robot, and determine the state of that robot. It then uses this information to determine its next state and move in the compute phase, and may change the state of each adjacent robot. In the move phase, the robot is further allowed to pass a carried tile to an adjacent robot that does not yet carry a tile.

We assume the standard asynchronous model from distributed computing in which robots are *activated* in an arbitrary sequence of *activations*, where a robot performs exactly one look-compute-move cycle before the next robot is activated. Correspondingly, a round is over whenever each robot has been activated at least once. For simplicity, we not only assume that all robots have the same chirality, but share a common compass. In fact, lifting this restriction imposes difficult challenges outside the scope of this paper, since symmetry breaking is very hard in our deterministic model. We leave this issue as a future research question.

Distributed Line Algorithm. In order to extend the line algorithm to work with multiple robots, we propose three main modifications of Algorithm 1. The pseudocode and full description of the algorithm can be found the full version of this paper. First, a robot r that carries a tile and is blocked in S or SE direction by a robot that searches for a tile can pass its tile and state to the blocking robot. Additionally, if r stands on a tile, it turns to the search phase. Otherwise, r has left the tile structure (we say it is *hanging*) and subsequently traverses its boundary in clockwise order, maintaining its connectivity to the outline of the tile structure (i.e., the outermost tiles of the tile structure), until it reaches an empty tile to step on. We make sure that no hanging robot is disconnected from the tile structure by a robot picking up a tile by performing additional checks.

Secondly, we ensure that no hanging robot ever ends up in a deadlock whilst traversing the boundary by avoiding to walk into *bottlenecks*, i.e., empty nodes with tiles on two non-adjacent sides. A traversal that avoids bottlenecks is depicted in Fig. 6a. Finally, in order to eventually let each robot detect that the line has been built, we slightly modify the way tiles are moved.

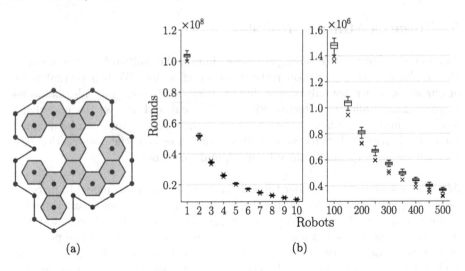

(a)   (b)

Fig. 6. (a) Boundary traversal that does not pass trough bottlenecks. (b) Simulation results for 10000 tiles.

Simulation Data. We experimentally evaluated the number of rounds until all robots halt. The results for $n = 10000$ and a varying number k of robots can be found in Fig. 6b. We conducted 50 simulations for each k, each initialized with a randomly generated tile configuration on which the robots were randomly placed. The robots were activated in a random order, each exactly once in every round. Each tile configuration was generated by the following procedure: First, randomly choose $10000 \cdot 16^2/2.02$ nodes of an equilateral parallelogram with side length $\sqrt{10000} \cdot 16$ to be occupied by a tile. Then, repeat the experiment until the largest connected component of the generated tile set contains at most 10500 tiles. The final configuration is obtained by repeatedly removing random tiles from the component whose removal does not disconnect the structure until 10000 tiles remain.

The simulations show that using a reasonably small number of robots significantly reduces the required number of rounds compared to using a single robot. The curve on the left part of Fig. 6b first decreases almost linearly (e.g., going from one to two robots essentially halves the runtime). However, for a large number of robots the benefit gained from employing more robots is almost negligible (right part of Fig. 6b). This phenomenon can likely be explained by the fact that the likeliness of robots waiting on each other increases with the number of robots. Nevertheless, these preliminary results suggest that the model indeed allows multi-robot algorithms whose runtime drastically decreases if the number of robots is reasonably small.

References

1. Bonato, A., Nowakowski, R.J.: The game of cops and robbers on graphs. AMS (2011)
2. Chirikjian, G., Pamecha, A., Ebert-Uphoff, I.: Evaluating efficiency of self-reconfiguration in a class of modular robots. J. Robot. Syst. **13**(5), 317–338 (1996)
3. Das, S.: Mobile agents in distributed computing: network exploration. Bull. Eur. Assoc. Theor. Comput. Sci. **109**, 54–69 (2013)
4. Demaine, E., Tachi, T.: Origamizer: a practical algorithm for folding any polyhedron. In: Proceedings of 33rd International Symposium on Computational Geometry (SoCG), pp. 34:1–34:16 (2017)
5. Demaine, E.D., Fekete, S.P., Scheffer, C., Schmidt, A.: New geometric algorithms for fully connected staged self-assembly. Theor. Comput. Sci. **671**, 4–18 (2017)
6. Demaine, E., Demaine, M., Hoffmann, M., O'Rourke, J.: Pushing blocks is hard. Comput. Geom. **26**(1), 21–36 (2003)
7. Derakhshandeh, Z., Gmyr, R., Richa, A.W., Scheideler, C., Strothmann, T.: Universal shape formation for programmable matter. In: Proceedings of 28th ACM Symposium on Parallelism in Algorithms and Architectures (SPAA), pp. 289–299 (2016)
8. Fomin, F.V., Thilikos, D.M.: An annotated bibliography on guaranteed graph searching. Theor. Comput. Sci. **399**(3), 236–245 (2008)
9. Hurtado, F., Molina, E., Ramaswami, S., Sacristán, V.: Distributed reconfiguraiton of 2D lattice-based modular robotic systems. Auton. Rob. **38**(4), 383–413 (2015)
10. Lund, K., et al.: Molecular robots guided by prescriptive landscapes. Nature **465**(7295), 206–210 (2010)
11. Michail, O., Spirakis, P.G.: Simple and efficient local codes for distributed stable network construction. Distrib. Comput. **29**(3), 207–237 (2016)
12. Murata, S., Kurokawa, H., Kokaji, S.: Self-assembling machine. In: Proceedings of IEEE International Conference on Robotics and Automation (ICRA), pp . 441–448 (1994)
13. Omabegho, T., Sha, R., Seeman, N.: A bipedal DNA Brownian motor with coordinated legs. Science **324**(5923), 67–71 (2009)
14. Patitz, M.J.: An introduction to tile-based self-assembly and a survey of recent results. Nat. Comput. **13**(2), 195–224 (2014)
15. Pelc, A.: Deterministic rendezvous in networks: a comprehensive survey. Networks **59**(3), 331–347 (2012)
16. Reif, J.H., Sahu, S.: Autonomous programmable DNA nanorobotic devices using DNAzymes. Theor. Comput. Sci. **410**, 1428–1439 (2009)
17. Rothemund, P., Winfree, E.: The program-size complexity of self-assembled squares. In: Proceedings of 32nd Annual ACM Symposium on Theory of Computing (STOC), pp. 459–468 (2000)
18. Shin, J., Pierce, N.: A synthetic DNA walker for molecular transport. J. Am. Chem. Soc. **126**, 4903–4911 (2004)
19. Terada, Y., Murata, S.: Automatic modular assembly system and its distributed control. Int. J. Robot. Res. **27**(3–4), 445–462 (2008)
20. Thubagere, A.: A cargo-sorting DNA robot. Science **357**(6356), eaan6558 (2017)
21. Tomita, K., Murata, S., Kurokawa, H., Yoshida, E., Kokaji, S.: Self-assembly and self-repair method for a distributed mechanical system. IEEE Trans. Robot. Autom. **15**(6), 1035–1045 (1999)

22. Wang, Z., Elbaz, J., Willner, I.: A dynamically programmed DNA transporter. Angewandte Chemie Int. Ed. **51**(48), 4322–4326 (2012)
23. Wickham, S., Bath, J., Katsuda, Y., Endo, M., Hidaka, K., Sugiyama, H., Turberfield, A.: A DNA-based molecular motor that can navigate a network of tracks. Nat. Nanotechnol. **7**(3), 169–173 (2012)
24. Woods, D., Chen, H., Goodfriend, S., Dabby, N., Winfree, E., Yin, P.: Active self-assembly of algorithmic shapes and patterns in polylogarithmic time. In: Proceedings of 4th Conference of Innovations in Theoretical Computer Science (ITCS), pp. 353–354 (2013)

Transcript Design Problem
of Oritatami Systems

Yo-Sub Han[1], Hwee Kim[2(✉)], and Shinnosuke Seki[3]

[1] Department of Computer Science, Yonsei University,
50 Yonsei-Ro, Seodaemun-Gu, Seoul 03722, Republic of Korea
emmous@yonsei.ac.kr
[2] Department of Mathematics and Statistics, University of South Florida,
12010 USF Cherry Drive, Tampa, FL 33620, USA
hweekim@mail.usf.edu
[3] Department of Computer and Network Engineering,
University of Electro-Communications, 1-5-1 Chofugaoka,
Chofu, Tokyo 1828585, Japan
s.seki@uec.ac.jp

Abstract. RNA cotranscriptional folding refers to the phenomenon in which an RNA transcript folds upon itself while being synthesized out of a gene. Oritatami model is a computation model of this phenomenon, which lets its sequence (transcript) of beads (abstract molecules) fold cotranscriptionally by the interactions between beads according to its ruleset. We study the problem of designing a transcript that folds into the given conformation using the given ruleset, which is called the transcript design problem. We prove that the problem is computationally difficult to solve (NP-hard). Then we design efficient poly-time algorithms with additional restrictions on the oritatami system.

1 Introduction

A single-stranded RNA is synthesized sequentially from its DNA template by an RNA polymerase enzyme (*transcription*). The RNA transcript folds upon itself according to the base pairing rule—(A, U) and (C, G)—with respect to hydrogen bonds and gives rise to functional 3D-structures. Note that a synthesis direction and a rate at which nucleotides are added allow an RNA to fold over a predefined pathway into a non-equilibrium structure while being transcribed [14]. This phenomenon is called *cotranscriptional folding*.

Cotranscriptional folding plays an important role in algorithmic self-assembly. For example, Geary et al. [6] studied the architecture for RNA tiles (called RNA origami) and proposed a method to design a single-stranded RNA that cotranscriptionally folds into a target structure. Oritatami model (OM) is the first mathematical model for algorithmic self-assembly by cotranscriptional folding [5]. Given a sequence of molecules, OM assumes that the sequence is transcribed linearly, and predicts a geometric structure of the folding based on the reaction rate of the folding. An oritatami system (OS) in OM defines a

D. Doty and H. Dietz (Eds.): DNA 2018, LNCS 11145, pp. 139–154, 2018.
https://doi.org/10.1007/978-3-030-00030-1_9

sequence of beads (which is the transcript) and a set of rules for possible inter-molecular reactions between beads. Here is how OS runs: Given a sequence of beads, the system takes a single bead (we call a current bead) together with a lookahead of a few succeeding beads, and determines the best location of the current bead that maximizes the number of possible interactions from a possible transcription of the lookahead. The lookahead represents the reaction rate of the cotranscriptional folding and the number of interactions represents the energy level. Researchers designed several OSs including a binary counter [4] and a Boolean formula simulator [9]. It is known that OM is Turing complete [5] and there are several methods to optimize OSs [8, 10] (Fig. 1).

RNA Origami	Oritatami System
Nucleotides	Beads
Transcript	Sequence of beads connected by a line
h-bonds between nucleotides	Interactions
Cotranscriptional folding rate	Delay
Resulting secondary structure	Conformation

(a)

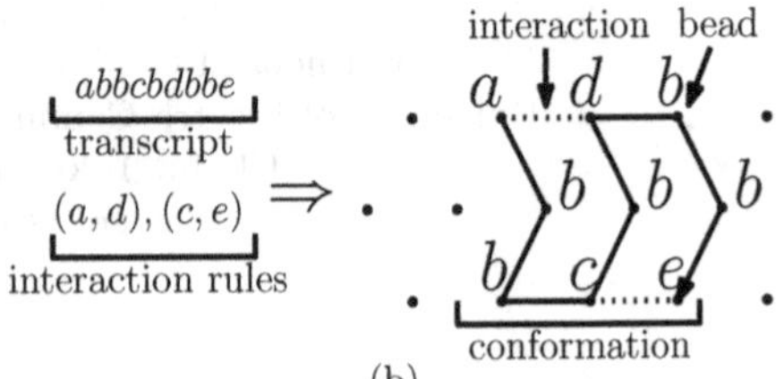

(b)

Fig. 1. (a) Analogy between RNA origami and oritatami system. (b) Visualization of oritatami system and its terms.

The inverse of RNA folding is RNA design: given a secondary structure, find a sequences of beads that uniquely folds into the input structure. If there are several possible foldings that the sequence can fold, then all the others must have less pairs than the input structure. We call this problem the RNA design problem. Hofacker et al. [12] introduced the RNA design problem and the complexity of the problem is still unknown [1]. The problem has applications in pharmaceutical research, biochemistry, synthetic biology or RNA nanostructures [2,7]. We consider the RNA design problem of an OS. In particular, we consider the case when we have the complete information about an OS including the bead type alphabet, pairing ruleset, delay, arity, and its final conformation except for beads on the conformation, and we need to find the transcript that folds the target conformation. Similar to the RNA design problem, this problem can be useful in several applications. For example, given a target structure and a generating system (OS), we can determine whether or not the generating system can produce the target structure and, if so, what is the correct transcript that indeed produces the target structure.

We first propose a general parameterized algorithm to solve the transcript design problem (TDP). We then tackle the CTDP, a restricted version of TDP where the ruleset is complementary. We prove that the CTDP is computationally difficult (NP-hard). Yet we also show that with a few restrictions on delay δ, arity α and the size $|\mathcal{H}|$ of the ruleset, we can solve the CTDP in linear time.

– CTDP is NP-hard (Theorem 2).

- CTDP is NP-complete when $\delta = 3$ and $|\mathcal{H}| = 3$ (Theorem 3).
- CTDP can be solved in linear time when $\delta = 1, |\mathcal{H}| = 1$, $\alpha = 1$ or $\alpha \geq 4$ (Lemmas 1 and 2).

2   Preliminaries

Let $w = a_1 a_2 \cdots a_n$ be a string over Σ for some integer n and bead types $a_1, \ldots, a_n \in \Sigma$. The *length* $|w|$ of w is n. For two indices i, j with $1 \leq i \leq j \leq n$, we let $w[i, j]$ be the substring $a_i a_{i+1} \cdots a_{j-1} a_j$; we use $w[i]$ to denote $w[i, i]$. We use w^n to denote the catenation of n copies of w.

Oritatami systems operate on the triangular lattice $\mathbb{T}$ with the vertex set V and the edge set E. A conformation instance, or *configuration*, is a triple (P, w, H) of a directed path P in $\mathbb{T}$, $w \in \Sigma^* \cup \Sigma^{\mathbb{N}}$, and a set $H \subseteq \{(i, j) \mid 1 \leq i, i + 2 \leq j, \{P[i], P[j]\} \in E\}$ of hydrogen-bond-based interactions (interactions for short). This is to be interpreted as the sequence w being folded while its i-th bead $w[i]$ is placed on the i-th point $P[i] \in V$ along the path and there is an interaction between the i-th and j-th beads if and only if $(i, j) \in H$. The fact that $i + 2 \leq j$ implies that $w[i]$ and $w[i+1]$ cannot form an interaction, since they are covalently bonded. Configurations (P_1, w_1, H_1) and (P_2, w_2, H_2) are *congruent* provided $w_1 = w_2$, $H_1 = H_2$, and P_1 can be transformed into P_2 by a combination of a translation, a reflection, and rotations by $60°$. The set of all configurations congruent to a configuration (P, w, H) is called the *conformation* of the configuration and denoted by $C = [(P, w, H)]$. We call w a *primary structure* of C.

A ruleset $\mathcal{H} \subseteq \Sigma \times \Sigma$ is a symmetric relation specifying between which bead types can form an interaction. A ruleset is *complementary* if for all $a \in \Sigma$, there exists a unique $b \in \Sigma$ such that $(a, b) \in \mathcal{H}$. For a complementary ruleset, we denote the pairing bead type b as $\overline{a}$. An interaction $(i, j) \in H$ is *valid with respect to* $\mathcal{H}$, or simply $\mathcal{H}$-*valid*, if $(w[i], w[j]) \in \mathcal{H}$. We say that a conformation C is $\mathcal{H}$-*valid* if all of its interactions are $\mathcal{H}$-valid. For an integer $\alpha \geq 1$, C is *of arity* α if the maximum number of interactions per bead is α, that is, if for any $k \geq 1$, $\left|\{i \mid (i, k) \in H\}\right| + \left|\{j \mid (k, j) \in H\}\right| \leq \alpha$ and this inequality holds as an equation for some k. By $\mathcal{C}_{\leq \alpha}$, we denote the set of all conformations of arity at most α.

Oritatami systems grow conformations by elongating them under their own ruleset. For a finite conformation C_1, we say that a finite conformation C_2 is an *elongation* of C_1 by a bead $b \in \Sigma$ under a ruleset $\mathcal{H}$, written as $C_1 \xrightarrow{\mathcal{H}}_b C_2$, if there exists a configuration (P, w, H) of C_1 such that C_2 includes a configuration $(P \cdot p, w \cdot b, H \cup H')$, where $p \in V$ is a point not in P and $H' \subseteq \{(i, |P|+1) \mid 1 \leq i \leq |P| - 1, \{P[i], p\} \in E, (w[i], b) \in \mathcal{H}\}$. This operation is recursively extended to the elongation by a finite sequence of beads as follows: For any conformation C, $C \xrightarrow{\mathcal{H}}_\lambda C$; and for a finite sequence of beads w and a bead b, a conformation C_1 is elongated to a conformation C_2 by $w \cdot b$, written as $C_1 \xrightarrow{\mathcal{H}}_{w \cdot b} C_2$, if there is a conformation C' that satisfies $C_1 \xrightarrow{\mathcal{H}}_w C'$ and $C' \xrightarrow{\mathcal{H}}_b C_2$.

An *oritatami system* (OS) is a 6-tuple $\varXi = (\Sigma, w, \mathcal{H}, \delta, \alpha, C_\sigma = [(P_\sigma, w_\sigma, H_\sigma)])$, where $\mathcal{H}$ is a *ruleset*, $\delta \geq 1$ is a *delay*, and C_σ is an $\mathcal{H}$-valid initial *seed* conformation of arity at most α, upon which its *transcript* $w \in \Sigma^* \cup \Sigma^\omega$ is to be folded by stabilizing beads of w one at a time and minimize energy collaboratively with the succeeding $\delta - 1$ nascent beads. The energy of a conformation $C = [(P, w, H)]$ is $U(C) = -|H|$; namely, the more interactions a conformation has, the more stable it becomes. The set $\mathcal{F}(\Xi)$ of conformations *foldable* by this system is recursively defined as follows: The seed C_σ is in $\mathcal{F}(\Xi)$; and provided that an elongation C_i of C_σ by the prefix $w[1:i]$ be foldable (i.e., $C_0 = C_\sigma$), its further elongation C_{i+1} by the next bead $w[i+1]$ is foldable if

$$C_{i+1} \in \underset{\substack{C \in \mathcal{C}_{\leq \alpha} \text{s.t.} \\ C_i \xrightarrow{\mathcal{H}}_{w[i+1]} C}}{\text{argmin}} \min \left\{ U(C') \,\middle|\, C \xrightarrow{\mathcal{H}}^*_{w[i+2:i+k]} C', k \leq \delta, C' \in \mathcal{C}_{\leq \alpha} \right\}. \quad (1)$$

Once we have C_{i+1}, we say that the bead $w[i+1]$ and its interactions are *stabilized* according to C_{i+1}. A conformation foldable by Ξ is *terminal* if none of its elongations is foldable by Ξ. An OS is *deterministic* if, for all i, there exists at most one C_{i+1} that satisfies (1). Namely, a deterministic OS folds into a unique terminal conformation.

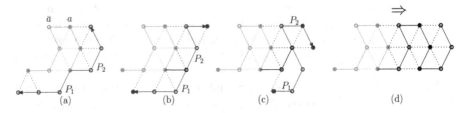

Fig. 2. An example OS with delay 3 and arity 4. Filled and unfilled circles represent bead types a and $\bar{a}$, respectively. The seed is colored in red, elongations are colored in blue, and the stabilized beads and interactions are colored in black. (Color figure online)

Figure 2 illustrates an example of an OS with delay 3, arity 4, complementary ruleset $\{(a, \bar{a})\}$ and transcript $w = \bar{a}\bar{a}\bar{a}aaa\bar{a}\bar{a}\bar{a}$; in (a), the system tries to stabilize the first bead $\bar{a}$ of the transcript, and the elongation P_1 gives 2 interactions, while the elongation P_2 gives 4 interactions, which is the most stable one. Thus, the first bead $\bar{a}$ is stabilized according to the location in P_2. In (b) and (c), P_2 is the most stable elongation and $\bar{a}$'s are stabilized according to P_2. As a result, the terminal conformation is given as in (d). Note that the system grows the terminal conformation straight without external interactions, and we can use an arbitrary prefix of $(\bar{a}\bar{a}\bar{a}aaa)^*$ to construct a conformation of an arbitrary length. This example is called a *glider* [4] and used in Sect. 3.1.

Conformations C_1 and C_2 are *isomorphic* if there exist an instance (P_1, w_1, H_1) of C_1 and an instance (P_2, w_2, H_2) of C_2 such that $P_1 = P_2$ and $H_1 = H_2$. For two sets $\mathcal{C}_1$ and $\mathcal{C}_2$ of conformations, we say that two sets are isomorphic if there exists a one-to-one mapping $C_1 \in \mathcal{C}_1 \to C_2 \in \mathcal{C}_2$ such that C_1 and C_2 are isomorphic. We say that two oritatami systems are isomorphic if they fold the isomorphic set of foldable terminal conformations.

We define the transcript design problem (TDP).

Problem 1 (Transcript Design Problem (TDP)). Given an alphabet Σ, a ruleset $\mathcal{H}$, a delay δ, an arity α, a seed $C_\sigma = [(P_\sigma, w_\sigma, H_\sigma)])$, a path P and a set H of interactions, find a transcript w such that an OS $\varXi = (\Sigma, w, \mathcal{H}, \delta, \alpha, C_\sigma)$ uniquely folds a terminal conformation $C = [(P, w, H)]$.[1]

The complementary transcript design problem (CTDP) is a subproblem of the TDP in which an input ruleset is required to be complementary.

3   Hardness of the TDP and the CTDP

We propose a generalized algorithm to solve the TDP, and prove hardness of CTDP. We first introduce the concept of the event horizon and its context, which will be used in the rest of the paper.

By definition, the stabilization of a bead $w[i]$ in a delay-δ OS is not affected by any bead whose distance from $w[i-1]$ is greater than $\delta + 1$. On the triangular lattice, we may draw a hexagonal border of radius $\delta+1$ from $w[i-1]$ to denote the set of points that may affect the stabilization, and we call the hexagon the *event horizon* of $w[i]$. Note that the event horizon can have at most $3(\delta+1)(\delta+2)$ beads within, aside from $w[i]$. We call the already stabilized beads within the event horizon, along with interactions, as the *event horizon context* to represent the context used to stabilize $w[i]$. Thus, if two beads $w[i]$ and $w[j]$ have the same event horizon context, then $w[i]$ and $w[j]$ will be stabilized at the same position with the same interactions, considering a translation, a reflection or a rotation (see Fig. 3.).

Now, we define the dependence distance of a TDP instance.

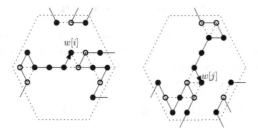

Fig. 3. Two same event horizon contexts when $\delta = 2$ and we have two bead types (black and white circles). The current bead, pointed by an arrow, is stabilized at the same position in both event horizon contexts.

---

[1] For the hardness proof, we use the decision variant of TDP, which determines whether or not such a transcript exists.

Definition 1. *Given a TDP instance* $(\Sigma, \mathcal{H}, \delta, \alpha, C_\sigma, P, H)$, *we define the dependence distance of the TDP instance as follows: Let* $w[i]$ *be the bead on the ith point of* P. *For each bead* $w[i]$, *let* r_i *be the smallest index such that while stabilizing* $w[i]$, $w[r_i]$ *is in the event horizon context of* $w[i]$. *We call* $\max(i+\delta-1-r_i)$ *the dependence distance.*

Namely, the dependence distance is the upper bound of the distance between a bead $w[i]$ and another bead $w[j]$ such that $w[j]$ affects the stabilization of $w[i]$. Note that the distance is independent from the delay of the system. Once the distance is bounded by a constant t, we can incrementally construct a transcript while having information of only t beads at a time, which results in the following theorem.

Theorem 1. *Given a TDP instance* $(\Sigma, \mathcal{H}, \delta, \alpha, C_\sigma, P, H)$, *we can solve the TDP in* $O(|\Sigma|^t \times |P|)$, *where* t *is the dependence distance of the TDP instance.*

Note that this general algorithm is fixed parameter linear. Next, we show that the CTDP is NP-hard in a general condition. We borrow the multi-chamber-gun construction from Ota and Seki [13] to reduce 1-IN-3-SAT to the CTDP at a long delay. The seed of multi-chamber-gun shape encodes the clauses of a given 1-IN-3-SAT instance. In order to go through the cannon tube as specified by the target conformation, the transcript must encode a satisfying assignment of truth values (T/F) to variables $v_1, v_2, \ldots, v_k$ for each of the m clauses in a uniform format like $(x_{1,1}x_{1,2}\ldots x_{1,k})(x_{2,1}\ldots x_{2,k})\ldots(x_{m,1}\ldots x_{m,k})$. For all $1 \leq i \leq k$, the assignments to v_i for every pair of the adjacent clauses are forced to be identical by chambers. The 1-IN-3-SAT instance is thus reduced to a TDP instance, and in fact, this reduction works with complementary ruleset.

Theorem 2. *For all* $\alpha \geq 1$, *the complementary transcript design problem (CTDP) at arity* α *is NP-hard. It remains NP-hard even if an input ruleset is restricted to be of size at most 2.*

3.1   Graph-Theoretic Approach to the CTDP

In the CTDP, since the ruleset is complementary, we may say that each bead type belongs to a rule in the ruleset. When the path P and the set H of interactions are given, we can retrieve necessary dependence conditions between two adjacent beads according to three different cases:

1. If two beads are connected with an interaction: Two beads should belong to the same rule.
2. If two beads are connected with a path: There is no necessary condition between two beads.
3. If there is no relationship between two beads: Two beads should not belong to the same rule, or two beads should have the same type.

We call these conditions static dependence (s-dependence in short), since these conditions are derived from the given path and the set of interactions, which do not include dynamics of stabilization of beads. From the first condition, if one of two beads is already stabilized or in the seed, we can find the bead type for the other bead. Moreover, if a set of beads are connected with interactions, one bead in the set determines bead types for the rest in the set. Therefore, we may regard this set of beads as a dependent set of beads. Each set should have one representative bead that represents the bead type assignment for all beads in the set, and additional information to find the transcript can be represented by the relationship between these representative beads. It takes $O(|w|)$ time to retrieve dependent sets from the given path and the set of interactions. When there exists a odd length cycle of interactions, we can immediately tell that the answer to the CTDP is no. Aside from this case, since each dependent set uses bead types that belong to one rule, we may represent each rule by a distinct color and regard the CTDP as a variant of the graph coloring problem (Fig. 4).

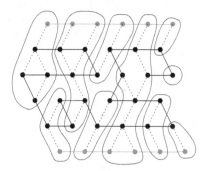

Fig. 4. Finding dependent sets. The seed is colored in red, and the dependent sets are colored in blue. (Color figure online)

There exists another category of conditions called dynamic dependence (d-dependence in short), which include dynamics of stabilization of beads. While stabilizing each bead of the transcript, there should exist one elongation of length δ that is used to stabilize the current bead at the designated point. Also, for all elongations that are not used to stabilize the current bead at the designated point, the number of interactions should be less than the number of interactions from the most stable elongation. For each possible bead type assignment for beads within the event horizon context, we can determine the possible bead type assignment for the current bead. According to dynamic dependence, there may exist some dependent sets that should have interactions with each other, and thus can be merged.

Now, we prove that the CTDP is NP-complete even for delay 3.

Theorem 3. *The CTDP is NP-complete when $\delta = 3$ and $|\mathcal{H}| = 3$.*

Proof. Once a proper transcript is given, we can check whether the given transcript successfully folds along the given path with the given set of interactions within $O(|w|)$ time. Thus, the problem is NP.

We prove that the problem is NP-hard, using the reduction from the planar 3-coloring problem [3]. Suppose that we are given a planar graph with n vertices. We can embed the graph on a square grid graph of size $O(n^2)$ [11]. An edge in the original planar graph is represented by a set of vertical and horizontal edges on the square grid graph.

The basic idea is to construct a path that spans the square grid graph horizontally using zigs and zags. We will represent a vertex from the original planar graph by a dependent set of beads connected with interactions, and an edge by a boundary between two dependent sets. We will force the adjacent dependent sets assign bead types from different rules.

We use the glider in Fig. 2 as a basic module, since it uses only 2 complementary bead types. We assume that we start to span the square grid graph from the northeast corner. We combine 24 beads in one zig and adjacent zag as one module to represent one vertex of the square grid as in Fig. 5. Note that all vertices are connected with interactions. The same paths are used to represent a horizontal edge of the square grid, and a vertical edge of the square grid is represented by interactions between two modules.

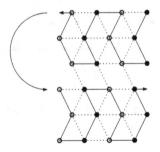

Fig. 5. A module that represent a vertex of the square grid

First, we present the module for a vertical edge of the square grid. If the edge does not represent an edge from the original graph, then the upper vertex module and the lower vertex module should be connected by interactions as in Fig. 6(a). If the edge represents an edge from the original graph, bead types from different rules should be assigned for the upper vertex module and the lower vertex module respectively. Thus, there should be no interaction between the upper vertex module and the lower vertex module, as in Fig. 6(b). In the red circle, a bead in the lower vertex module has no interaction with both complementary bead types in the upper vertex module, and they are not connected by the path either. This forces the assignment of bead types from different rules for the upper vertex module and the lower vertex module respectively.

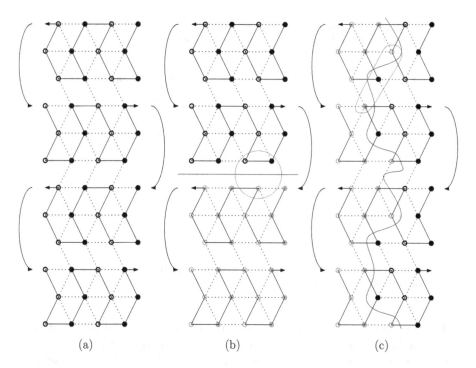

Fig. 6. (a) The module that represents the lack of a vertical edge. (b) The module representing the presence of a vertical edge. (c) The module representing the presence of a horizontal edge.

Next, we present the module for a horizontal edge of the square grid. If the edge does not represent an edge from the original graph, we can use the same module as the vertex module. If the edge represents an edge from the original graph, we need to embed two horizontally dependent sets in the module. Figure 6(c) shows the module for two horizontal edges of the square grid, where the blue line is the borderline between two dependent sets. While folding in a glider path, the module successfully embeds two dependent sets. In the red line, a bead in the right dependent set has no interaction with both complementary bead types in the left dependent set, and they are not connected by the path either. This forces the assignment of bead types from different rules for two dependent sets.

Lastly, we present the module for turns of zigs and zags, which should also represent a vertical edge of the square grid. If the edge does not represent an edge from the original graph, then the upper vertex module and the lower vertex module should be connected by interactions as in Fig. 7(a). If the edge represents an edge from the original graph, there should be no interaction between the upper vertex module and the lower vertex module, as in Fig. 7(b). In the red circle, a bead in the lower vertex module has no interaction with both complementary bead types in the upper vertex module, and they are not connected by the path either. This forces the assignment of bead types from different rules for the upper vertex module and the lower vertex module respectively.

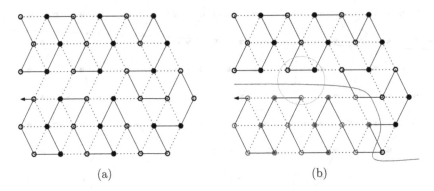

(a)   (b)

Fig. 7. The module for a turn. (a) The module does not represent a vertical edge. (b) The module represents a vertical edge.

We have successfully transformed a vertex in the original graph to a dependent set of beads, and an edge to a boundary between adjacent dependent sets, and forced that adjacent dependent sets should have bead types from different rules. Thus, we can color the original graph with three colors if and only if we can find a bead type assignment that satisfies s-dependence using three complementary rules. Moreover, for all cases, if s-dependence in a module is satisfied, so is d-dependence—regardless of the possible context, the module folds as a desired conformation. Thus, this bead type assignment implies a transcript that can be an answer for the reduced CTDP instance.   □

4   Delay-1 CTDP

Knowing that the TCP and the CTDP are NP-hard, we now try to find sufficient conditions that make the CTDP solvable in polynomial time. Here, we focus on the case where $\delta = 1$. Delay-1 CTDP is essentially different from the general CTDP. In the general CTDP, while stabilizing a bead, interactions in the most stable elongation may not appear in the terminal conformation if they are not from the current bead. Such interactions are called *phantom* interactions. However, when $\delta = 1$, there is no phantom interaction and we can explicitly count the number of interactions that are needed to stabilize each bead—the number of interactions that the current bead has in H. This explicit information helps us determine bead type relationships resulting from d-dependence, and design linear time algorithms to solve the CTDP under specific conditions.

Lemma 1. *We can solve the CTDP in $O(|w|)$ time when $\delta = 1$, $|\mathcal{H}| = 1$ and $\alpha \geq 4$.*

Proof. We start from writing s-dependence conditions between two adjacent beads in Sect. 3.1 when $|\mathcal{H}| = 1$.

1. If two beads are connected with an interaction: Two beads are of different types.
2. If two beads are connected with a path: There is no necessary condition between two beads.
3. If there is no relationship between two beads: Two beads have the same type.

Note that both the first and the third conditions uniquely determine the bead type of one based on the other.

   If the delay of the system is 1, for each bead b_1 to stabilize, there are two different cases (See Fig. 8):

1. Stabilization by interactions: The bead is stabilized deterministically by at least one interaction with neighbors on the conformation. In this case, the bead may be stabilized at another point without these interactions.
2. Stabilization by geometry: The bead is stabilized deterministically by geometric constraints. In this case, the possible interactions that the current bead may have do not change the stabilization point.

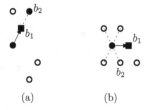

(a)   (b)

Fig. 8. Two cases when $\alpha \geq 4$. We assume that there are two types of beads: a black circle and a white circle. The current bead to stabilize is represented by a black square. (a) Stabilization by interactions (b) stabilization by geometry

   In both cases, while stabilizing the bead b_1, the bead should have at least one already stabilized bead b_2, where two beads are connected with an interaction (the first condition of s-dependence) or there is no relationship between them (the third condition of s-dependence). Otherwise, the system becomes nondeterministic or the bead cannot stabilize at the designated point. Since $\alpha \geq 4$, b_2 can have up to 4 interactions aside from two neighboring beads on the path, and if $(b_1, b_2) \in \mathcal{H}$, b_1 and b_2 always have an interaction.

   The first and the third conditions of s-dependence make the bead type assignment unique if the bead type of one of two beads is fixed. Therefore, for each bead, there exists unique bead type assignment resulting from the first or the third condition with an adjacent (already known) bead. Moreover, in both cases, since we are aware of all beads within the event horizon context, we can check that d-dependences are satisfied online: in other words, whether the current bead is stabilized as desired or not. Thus, the total runtime to find a transcript is $O(|w|)$.

Lemma 2. *We can solve the CTDP in $O(|w|)$ time when $\delta = 1$, $|\mathcal{H}| = 1$ and $\alpha = 1$.*

Proof. When $\alpha = 1$, once a bead forms an interaction with another, these two beads become inactive and cannot form an interaction anymore. We call beads that are not binded as active beads. For each bead b_1 to stabilize, there are three different cases (See Fig. 9.):

1. Stabilization by an interaction: The bead is stabilized deterministically by exactly one interaction with a neighbor on the conformation.
2. Stabilization by geometry, having an active neighbor: The bead is stabilized deterministically by geometric constraints. In addition, there exists at least one neighboring bead which did not have an interaction so far, which we call an active neighbor.
3. Stabilization by geometry, not having an active neighbor: The bead is stabilized deterministically by geometric constraints. In addition, all neighboring beads have interactions already.

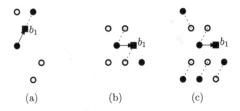

Fig. 9. Three cases when $\alpha = 1$. We assume that there are two types of beads: a black circle and a white circle. The current bead to stabilize is represented by a black square. (a) Stabilization by an interaction (b) stabilization by geometry, having an active neighbor (c) Stabilization by geometry, not having an active neighbor

We propose an algorithm to assign a bead type for these three cases.

1. Stabilization by geometry, not having an active neighbor: Since there is no active neighbor, we may assign an arbitrary bead type to the current bead at this timestamp. Thus, we introduce a new bead type variable v_{i+1}, given the most recent bead type variable v_i, and assign the bead type variable to the current bead.
2. Stabilization by geometry, having an active neighbor: Similar to the second case when $\alpha \geq 4$, we have a set of active neighbors whose bead types (or variables) are fixed. Based on the apparent interactions, we can assign the unique bead type (or variable) to the current bead, and may fix the bead type for a variable or merge two variables based on relationships within the event horizon context.

3. Stabilization by an interaction: Since the arity is 1, the current bead should have an active neighbor with the complementary bead type (or variable). Moreover, all active neighbors of neighbors of the previous bead except the stabilization point should have the same bead type as the current bead (or variable). Thus, we can assign the unique bead type (or variable) to the current bead, and may fix the bead type for a variable or merge two variables based on relationships within the event horizon context.

Note that for all cases, there exists an unique bead type (or variable) assignment for the current bead. Similar to the $\alpha \geq 4$ case in Lemma 1, we can check d-dependences are satisfied online. Moreover, possible changes on the variables (fixing the bead type or merging two variables) while stabilizing future beads do not change d-dependences and still result in the same isomorphic conformation. Thus, once we assign bead types (or variables) to the end of the transcript, we may assign arbitrary bead types for variables, and the resulting transcript always folds the conformation isomorphic to the original one. The total runtime to find a transcript is $O(|w|)$. □

Here, we relieve the CTDP by allowing isomorphism for the seed. Based on the relaxation, we claim that we may reduce the size of the ruleset without changing solvability, where the upper bound of the size of the ruleset is 27.

Lemma 3. *Let $P_1 = (\Sigma, \mathcal{H}, 1, 1, C_\sigma, P, H)$ be an instance of CTDP at delay 1 and arity 1. If $|\mathcal{H}| > 27$, one can construct a ruleset $\mathcal{H}' \subseteq \mathcal{H}$ of size 27 and the seed C'_σ over $\Sigma(\mathcal{H}')$ isomorphic to C_σ, such that if P_1 has a solution, then the instance of CTDP $P_2 = (\Sigma(\mathcal{H}'), \mathcal{H}', 1, 1, C'_\sigma, P, H)$ does.*

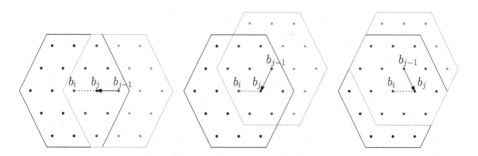

Fig. 10. The region of the influence of b_i at delay 1 and arity 1 in all the possible three cases modulo the reflectional symmetry along the line b_i–b_j. (Color figure online)

Proof. We claim that the bead type of a bead is dependent upon at most 26 other beads. Assume that the given seed C_σ consists of m beads and the path P consists of n beads. We index the beads of C_σ as $b_{-m+1}, b_{-m+2}, \ldots, b_{-1}, b_0$, where b_{-1} is connected to the first bead of P. For convenience, we also index the beads on P as $b_1, b_2, \ldots, b_n$, where $b_i = w[i]$.

We consider the relationship between two beads b_i and b_j, where $i < j$ and b_i and b_j have an interaction with each other. Since $\alpha = 1$, the preceding bead b_i must remain active when it is stabilized. For that, b_i may be a part of the seed C_σ, or there was only one empty neighbor of its predecessor b_{i-1} so that b_i was forced to be stabilized without interactions (Third case of the proof for Lemma 2). In the latter case, two of the neighboring beads of b_{i-1} can affect the stabilization of b_i. The bead b_i can affect the stabilization of another bead b_k for any $i + 1 \leq k < j$. In order for b_k to be affected by b_i, its predecessor b_{k-1} must have been stabilized in the event horizon context of b_{i+1} (The black hexagons in Fig. 10). The event horizon context has 19 points, 3 of which are to be stabilized by b_i, b_j, and b_{j-1}. Note that the two beads that can affect the stabilization of b_i are also in this event horizon context. Therefore, there can be at most 16 beads which can affect the stabilization of b_i or whose stabilization can be affected by b_i. The bead b_j is affected by at most 16 beads other than b_i, which are inside the event horizon context of b_j (The red hexagons in Fig. 10).

Now we have at most 32 beads that can be affected by b_i or affect b_j, but we may reduce the number by geometric constraints. Suppose we see all the neighbors of b_{j-1} except b_j. A bead at one of these neighbors, say p, if any, prevents a bead at the other side of p from b_{j-1} from affecting b_j. The number of beads that can affect b_j, denoted by $d(b_j)$, is thus at most 11. We can bound the number of beads that can affect b_i or be affected by b_i, which we denote by $d(b_i)$, by 15. The successor b_{i+1} of b_i is to be stabilized at one of the neighbors of b_i but the one for b_j. Being thus stabilized at a neighbor, say p', b_{i+1} geometrically prevents b_k from being affected by b_i if its predecessor b_{k-1} is stabilized at the other side of p from b_i. We call $d(b_i) + d(b_j)$ the *degree of dependence of the pair* (b_i, b_j). Then the *degree of dependence of* C_σ is the maximum of the degree of dependence of a pair (b_i, b_j) such that b_i is included in C_σ but b_j is not[2].

We have proved that the degree of dependence of C_σ is at most 26. It is well known that we can color a graph with $d + 1$ colors, where d is the maximum degree of a vertex. Here, we may regard each rule as a color. For each pair of beads, we may consider the degree of dependence and assign bead types from different rules for beads that are dependent to the pair. Thus, it is sufficient to have the ruleset of size 27 to color the transcript.   □

If a CTDP instance has no answer, we may increase the size of the ruleset and use additional bead types to find an answer. Note that there exists a CTDP instance without an answer, regardless of the size of the ruleset, as in Fig. 11. Aside from these apparent contradictory cases, we prove that there is no lower bound for the size of the ruleset where we can always find a transcript for the CTDP.

Lemma 4. *Given* $n \geq 1$, *there exists a CTDP instance* $P_1 = (\Sigma, \mathcal{H}, 1, 3, C_\sigma, P, H)$ *with* $|\mathcal{H}| = n$ *such that there is no answer for* P_1, *but*

---

[2] This definition does not consider any pair both of whose beads are included in C_σ because such a pair is already inert at the beginning of folding.

Fig. 11. One case where there is no answer for a CTDP instance, regardless of the size of the ruleset. The bead $w[1]$ both has and does not have an interaction with $\bar{a}$, which is a contradiction.

there exists a ruleset $\mathcal{H}' \supseteq \mathcal{H}$ of size $n + 1$ where the CTDP instance $P_2 = (\Sigma, \mathcal{H}', 1, 3, C_\sigma, P, H)$ has an answer.

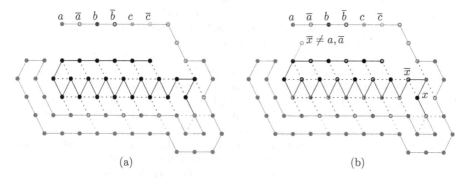

(a)   (b)

Fig. 12. (a) A CTDP instance with $n = 3$. (b) Bead type assignment and constraints for $\bar{x}$

Proof. Fig. 12 (a) shows a CTDP instance that satisfies the lemma when $n = 3$ and $\mathcal{H} = \{(a, \bar{a}), (b, \bar{b}), (c, \bar{c})\}$. The red line is a seed, bead types in different rules are colored differently, and complementary bead types are represented by full and empty circles.

The first bead of the system is stabilized by geometry, and since neighboring a and $\bar{a}$ are active, the first bead should have a different type from both a and $\bar{a}$. Let us use the variable x to represent that bead type. Following the s-dependences, we can assign bead types as in Fig. 12(b).

Now, we consider d-dependences for a straight line of beads at the last part of the transcript. While stabilizing the first $\bar{x}$ on the line, which is denoted by a black empty circle, the bead is stabilized by one interaction with x. However, it may stabilize upper left if it can interact with either a or $\bar{a}$. Thus, $\bar{x}$ cannot be neither a or $\bar{a}$. The same analysis holds for the following $\bar{x}$'s, which result in that $\bar{x}$ should be different with all beads in the alphabet. This contradiction can be solved if we add a new rule $(d, \bar{d})$ and assign $x = d$. This CTDP instance can be extended for arbitrary n, and the lemma holds.   □

Acknowledgements. Han was supported by NRF 2017K2A9A2A08000270 and NRF 2015R1D1A1A01060097, Kim was supported in part by the NIH grant R01 GM109459, and S. S. is supported in part by JST Program to Disseminate Tenure Tracking System, MEXT, Japan, No. 6F36, JSPS Grant-in-Aid for Young Scientists (A) No. 16H05854, and JSPS Bilateral Program No. YB29004.

References

1. Bonnet, É., Rzazewski, P., Sikora, F.: Designing RNA secondary structures is hard. In: Research in Computational Molecular Biology - 22nd Annual International Conference, RECOMB 2018 (2018, accepted)
2. Churkin, A., Retwitzer, M.D., Reinharz, V., Ponty, Y., Waldispühl, J., Barash, D.: Design of RNAs: comparing programs for inverse RNA folding. Brief. Bioinform. **19**, 350–358 (2017)
3. Garey, M.R., Johnson, D.S.: Computer and Intractability: A Guide to the Theory of NP-Completeness. W. H. Freeman, New York (1979)
4. Geary, C., Meunier, P., Schabanel, N., Seki, S.: Efficient universal computation by greedy molecular folding. CoRR, abs/1508.00510 (2015)
5. Geary, C., Meunier, P., Schabanel, N., Seki, S.: Programming biomolecules that fold greedily during transcription. In: Proceedings of the 41st International Symposium on Mathematical Foundations of Computer Science, pp. 43:1–43:14 (2016)
6. Geary, C., Rothemund, P.W.K., Andersen, E.S.: A single-stranded architecture for cotranscriptional folding of RNA nanostructures. Science **345**, 799–804 (2014)
7. Hales, J., Héliou, A., Manuch, J., Ponty, Y., Stacho, L.: Combinatorial RNA design: designability and structure-approximating algorithm in Watson-Crick and Nussinov-Jacobson energy models. Algorithmica **79**(3), 835–856 (2017)
8. Han, Y.-S., Kim, H.: Ruleset optimization on isomorphic oritatami systems. In: Brijder, R., Qian, L. (eds.) DNA 2017. LNCS, vol. 10467, pp. 33–45. Springer, Cham (2017). https://doi.org/10.1007/978-3-319-66799-7_3
9. Han, Y., Kim, H., Ota, M., Seki, S.: Nondeterministic seedless oritatami systems and hardness of testing their equivalence. Nat. Comput. **17**(1), 67–79 (2018)
10. Han, Y.-S., Kim, H., Rogers, T.A., Seki, S.: Self-attraction removal from oritatami systems. In: Pighizzini, G., Câmpeanu, C. (eds.) DCFS 2017. LNCS, vol. 10316, pp. 164–176. Springer, Cham (2017). https://doi.org/10.1007/978-3-319-60252-3_13
11. Harel, D., Sardas, M.: An algorithm for straight-line drawing of planar graphs. Algorithmica **20**(2), 119–135 (1998)
12. Hofacker, I.L., Fontana, W., Stadler, P.F., Bonhoeffer, L.S., Tacker, M., Schuster, P.: Fast folding and comparison of rna secondary structures. Monatshefte für Chemie / Chemical Monthly **125**(2), 167–188 (1994)
13. Ota, M., Seki, S.: Rule set design problems for oritatami system. Theor. Comput. Sci. **671**, 16–35 (2017)
14. Xayaphoummine, A., Viasnoff, V., Harlepp, S., Isambert, H.: Encoding folding paths of RNA switches. Nucleic Acids Res. **35**(2), 614–622 (2007)

Freezing Simulates Non-freezing Tile Automata

Cameron Chalk[1], Austin Luchsinger[2], Eric Martinez[2], Robert Schweller[2],
Andrew Winslow[2], and Tim Wylie[2(✉)]

[1] Department of Electrical and Computer Engineering,
University of Texas at Austin, Austin, USA
ctchalk@utexas.edu
[2] Department of Computer Science,
University of Texas Rio Grande Valley, Edinburg, USA
{austin.luchsinger01,robert.schweller,andrew.winslow,
timothy.wylie}@utrgv.edu

Abstract. Self-assembly is the process by which a system of particles randomly agitate and combine, through local interactions, to form larger complex structures. In this work, we fuse a particular well-studied generalization of tile assembly (the 2-*Handed* or *Hierarchical Tile Assembly Model*) with concepts from cellular automata such as states and state transitions characterized by neighboring states. This allows for a simplification of the concepts from active self-assembly, and gives us machinery to relate the disparate existing models. We show that this model, coined *Tile Automata*, is invariant with respect to *freezing* and *non-freezing* transition rules via a simulation theorem showing that any non-freezing tile automata system can be simulated by a freezing one. Freezing tile automata systems restrict state transitions such that each tile may visit a state only once, i.e., a tile may undergo only a finite number of transitions. We conjecture that this result can be used to show that the *Signal-passing Tile Assembly Model* is also invariant to this constraint via a series of simulation results between that model and the Tile Automata model. Further, we conjecture that this model can be used to consolidate the several oft-studied models of self-assembly wherein assemblies may break apart, such as the Signal-passing Tile Assembly Model, the *negative-glue* 2-Handed Tile Assembly Model, and the *Size-Dependent Tile Assembly Model*. Lastly, the Tile Automata model may prove useful in combining results in cellular automata with self-assembly.

1 Introduction

A diverse collection of different algorithmic self-assembly models have emerged in recent years to explore the theoretical power of self-assembling systems under a wide variety of experimentally motivated constraints. While many important

A. Luchsinger, R. Schweller and T. Wylie—This author's research is supported in part by National Science Foundation Grant CCF-1817602.

D. Doty and H. Dietz (Eds.): DNA 2018, LNCS 11145, pp. 155–172, 2018.
https://doi.org/10.1007/978-3-030-00030-1_10

results continue to develop within these models, relatively little is known about how models which allow active self assembly and/or disassembly relate to each other. In this paper we propose to develop a tool set for proving connections between a large set of diverse self-assembly models. Our approach is based on the proposal of a new mathematical abstraction we term *Tile Automata* (TA) which combines elements of passive tile self-assembly (such as the 2HAM [2]) with local state change rules similar to asynchronous cellular automata (see [9] for a survey on cellular automata). Our goal is to study fundamental properties of active self-assembly and connect the disparate models with this new abstract model and a powerful tool set.

Active Self-assembly. Self-assembly is the process by which a system of particles randomly agitate and combine through local interactions to form larger and more complex structures. Many forms of self-assembly are passive in nature, meaning the component system monomers are static with no internal changing of state, and simply interact based on a fixed surface chemistry. Newer models of self-assembly add an *active* component where system particles store an internal state that may adjust based on local interactions. These state changes affect how a particle interacts with others. Active self-assembly models may include substantial power (such as movement [4,12]) with an eye toward future technologies and swarm robotics. Other models focus on experimental techniques within emerging technologies such as DNA strand displacement cascades which permit a form of *signal passing* within tile systems [8,10,11].

Tile Automata. Tile Automata components are stateful square tiles living in a 2D grid. Pairs of states may be assigned an affinity value, allowing assembled collections of tiles to combine if a required threshold of affinity between the two assemblies is reached. In this way, Tile Automata incorporates 2-handed self-assembly. Similar to asynchronous cellular automata, a collection of transition rules dictate state changes based on local neighbor states. Thus, tiles within an assembly may undergo state changes, altering the internal affinities by which the assembly is bound. If new affinities are added, new combination events may occur. If affinities are removed, previously stable assemblies may become unstable and break apart.

The Tile Automata model is similar and partially inspired by the *nubots* model [12]. However, an important limitation with Tile Automata is the absence of a *movement* rule, which is a key feature prominent in nubot literature. Instead, Tile Automata is closely linked to models such as the signal tile model [10], and the active self-assembly model [8], in which tile self-assembly is augmented with a signal passing scheme permitting glues on tile edges to flip on and off dynamically. The Tile Automata model attempts to abstract away some of the specifics of these models to allow for a cleaner mathematical approach to understanding fundamental capabilities within this type of active self-assembly.

Our Contribution. Our primary result in this work is proving that *freezing*[1] Tile Automata systems, in which a tile must never revisit the same state twice, can simulate *non-freezing* systems, which have no such restriction. This shows that within self-assembly, freezing and non-freezing systems are equivalent up to constant scale simulation. This is in contrast to freezing within cellular automata [6,7], in which freezing systems are substantially weaker than non-freezing. The intuition for this contrast is that cellular automata cells are "stuck" in place, and thus "frozen" cells become useless, whereas "frozen" tiles may detach and be replaced by new ones. A freezing lemma such as this for TA has the potential to resolve open problems in established models. Consider the Signal Tile Assembly Model (STAM), where signals are "fire-once", i.e., not reusable. A generalized variant allowing perpetual reuse of signals would plausibly yield substantial power and ease system design. This freezing result in TA will give us the first tool needed in proving the conjecture that single-fire STAM is just as powerful as the perpetual-fire STAM.

2 Model and Definitions

A Tile Automata system is a marriage between cellular automata and 2-handed self-assembly. Systems consist of a set of monomer tile states, along with local affinities between states denoting the strength of attraction between adjacent monomer tiles in those states. A set of local state-change rules are included for pairs of adjacent states. Assemblies (collections of edge-connected tiles) in the model are created from an initial set of starting assemblies by combining previously built assemblies given sufficient binding strength from the affinity function. Further, existing assemblies may change states of internal monomer tiles according to any applicable state change rules. An example system is shown in Fig. 1.

2.1 States, Tiles, and Assemblies

Tiles and States. Consider an alphabet of *state types*[2] Σ. A tile t is an axis-aligned unit square centered at a point $L(t) \in \mathbb{Z}^2$. Further, tiles are assigned a state type from Σ, where $S(t)$ denotes the state type for a given tile t. We say two tiles t_1 and t_2 are of the same *tile type* if $S(t_1) = S(t_2)$.

---

[1] We borrow the notion of freezing from the cellular automata literature [1,6,7]. There are two informal perspectives towards freezing that are equivalent in CA but not equivalent in TA. One is that a cell (tile) must never revisit the same state twice. The other is that a position in $\mathbb{Z}^2$ must never revisit the same state twice. Intuitively, in TA, a position may see several tiles due to tiles attaching and detaching. Thus, the perspectives are different. We choose the first perspective, matching the notion that tiles themselves are stateful, and positions in space are not stateful.
[2] We note that Σ does not include an "empty" state. In tile self-assembly, unlike cellular automata, positions in $\mathbb{Z}^2$ may have no tile (and thus no state).

Affinity Function. An *affinity function* takes as input an element in $\Sigma^2 \times D$, where $D = \{\perp, \vdash\}$, and outputs an element in $\mathbb{N}$. This output is referred to as the *affinity strength* between two states, given direction $d \in D$. Directions $\perp$ and $\vdash$ indicate above-below and side-by-side orientations of states, respectively.

Transition Rules. Transition rules allow states to change based on their neighbors. Formally, a *transition rule* is a 5-tuple $(S_{1a}, S_{2a}, S_{1b}, S_{2b}, d)$ with each $S_{1a}, S_{2a}, S_{1b}, S_{2b} \in \Sigma$ and $d \in D = \{\perp, \vdash\}$. Essentially, a transition rule says that if states S_{1a} and S_{2a} are adjacent to each other, with a given orientation d, they can transition to states S_{1b} and S_{2b} respectively.

Assemblies. A *positioned shape* is any subset of $\mathbb{Z}^2$. A *positioned assembly* is a set of tiles at unique coordinates in $\mathbb{Z}^2$, and the positioned shape of a positioned assembly $\mathcal{A}$ is the set of coordinates of those tiles, denoted as $\mathsf{SHAPE}_\mathcal{A}$. For a positioned assembly $\mathcal{A}$, let $\mathcal{A}(x, y)$ denote the state type of the tile with location $(x, y) \in \mathbb{Z}^2$ in $\mathcal{A}$.

For a given positioned assembly $\mathcal{A}$ and affinity function Π, define the *bond graph* $G_\mathcal{A}$ to be the weighted grid graph in which:

- each tile of $\mathcal{A}$ is a vertex,
- no edge exists between non-adjacent tiles,
- the weight of an edge between adjacent tiles T_1 and T_2 with locations (x_1, y_1) and (x_2, y_2), respectively, is
  - $\Pi(S(T_1), S(T_2), \perp)$ if $y_1 > y_2$,
  - $\Pi(S(T_2), S(T_1), \perp)$ if $y_1 < y_2$,
  - $\Pi(S(T_1), S(T_2), \vdash)$ if $x_1 < x_2$,
  - $\Pi(S(T_2), S(T_1), \vdash)$ if $x_1 > x_2$.

A positioned assembly $\mathcal{A}$ is said to be τ-*stable* for positive integer τ provided the bond graph $G_\mathcal{A}$ has min-cut at least τ.

For a positioned assembly $\mathcal{A}$ and integer vector $\boldsymbol{v} = (v_1, v_2)$, let $\mathcal{A}_{\boldsymbol{v}}$ denote the positioned assembly obtained by translating each tile in $\mathcal{A}$ by vector $\boldsymbol{v}$. An *assembly* is a set of all translations $\mathcal{A}_{\boldsymbol{v}}$ of a positioned assembly $\mathcal{A}$. A *shape* is the set of all integer translations for some subset of $\mathbb{Z}^2$, and the shape of an assembly A is defined to be the set of the positioned shapes of all positioned assemblies in A. The *size* of either an assembly or shape X, denoted as $|X|$, refers to the number of elements of any positioned assembly of X.

Breakable Assemblies. An assembly is τ-*breakable* if it can be split into two assemblies along a cut whose total affinity strength sums to less than τ. Formally, an assembly C is *breakable* into assemblies A and B if the bond graph $G_\mathcal{C}$ for some positioned assembly $\mathcal{C} \in C$ has a cut $(\mathcal{A}, \mathcal{B})$ for positioned assemblies $\mathcal{A} \in A$ and $\mathcal{B} \in B$ of affinity strength less than τ. We call assemblies A and B *pieces* of the breakable assembly C.

Combinable Assemblies. Two assemblies are τ-*combinable* provided they may attach along a border whose strength sums to at least τ. Formally, two assemblies A and B are τ-*combinable* into an assembly C provided $G_\mathcal{C}$ for any $\mathcal{C} \in C$ has a cut $(\mathcal{A}, \mathcal{B})$ of strength at least τ for some positioned assemblies $\mathcal{A} \in A$ and $\mathcal{B} \in B$. We call C a *combination* of A and B.

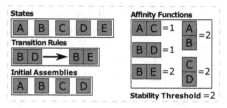 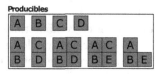

(a) Tile Automata System Γ.   (b) The producibles and terminals of Γ.

Fig. 1. An example of a tile automata system Γ. Recursively applying the transition rules and affinity functions to the initial assemblies of a system yields a set of producible assemblies. Any producibles that cannot combine with, break into, or transition to another assembly are considered to be terminal.

Transitionable Assemblies. Consider some set of transition rules Δ. An assembly A is *transitionable*, with respect to Δ, into assembly B if and only if there exist $\mathcal{A} \in A$ and $\mathcal{B} \in B$ such that for some pair of adjacent tiles $t_i, t_j \in \mathcal{A}$:

- $\exists$ a pair of adjacent tiles $t_h, t_k \in \mathcal{B}$ with $L(t_i) = L(t_h)$ and $L(t_j) = L(t_k)$
- $\exists$ a transition rule $\delta \in \Delta$ s.t. $\delta = (S(t_i), S(t_j), S(t_h), S(t_k), \bot)$ or
  $\delta = (S(t_i), S(t_j), S(t_h), S(t_k), \vdash)$
- $\mathcal{A} - \{t_i, t_j\} = \mathcal{B} - \{t_h, t_k\}$

2.2 Tile Automata Model (TA)

A *tile automata system* is a 5-tuple $(\Sigma, \Pi, \Lambda, \Delta, \tau)$ where Σ is an alphabet of state types, Π is an affinity function, Λ is a set of initial assemblies with each tile assigned a state from Σ, Δ is a set of transition rules for states in Σ, and $\tau \in \mathbb{N}$ is the *stability threshold*. When the affinity function and state types are implied, let (Λ, Δ, τ) denote a tile automata system. An example tile automata system can be seen in Fig. 1.

Definition 1 (Tile Automata Producibility). *For a given tile automata system $\Gamma = (\Sigma, \Lambda, \Pi, \Delta, \tau)$, the set of producible assemblies of Γ, denoted PROD$_\Gamma$, is defined recursively:*

- *(Base) $\Lambda \subseteq$ PROD$_\Gamma$*
- *(Recursion) Any of the following:*
  - *(Combinations) For any $A, B \in$ PROD$_\Gamma$ such that A and B are τ-combinable into C, then $C \in$ PROD$_\Gamma$.*
  - *(Breaks) For any $C \in$ PROD$_\Gamma$ such that C is τ-breakable into A and B, then $A, B \in$ PROD$_\Gamma$.*
  - *(Transitions) For any $A \in$ PROD$_\Gamma$ such that A is transitionable into B (with respect to Δ), then $B \in$ PROD$_\Gamma$.*

For a system $\Gamma = (\Sigma, \Lambda, \Pi, \Delta, \tau)$, we say $A \rightarrow_1^\Gamma B$ for assemblies A and B if A is τ-combinable with some producible assembly to form B, if A is transitionable into B (with respect to Δ), if A is τ-breakable into assembly B and some other assembly, or if $A = B$. Intuitively this means that A may grow into assembly B through one or fewer combinations, transitions, and breaks. We define the relation $\rightarrow^{\Gamma}$ to be the transitive closure of $\rightarrow_1^{\Gamma}$, i.e., $A \rightarrow^{\Gamma} B$ means that A may grow into B through a sequence of combinations, transitions, and/or breaks.

Definition 2 (Terminal Assemblies). *A producible assembly A of a tile automata system $\Gamma = (\Sigma, \Lambda, \Pi, \Delta, \tau)$ is terminal provided A is not τ-combinable with any producible assembly of Γ, A is not τ-breakable, and A is not transitionable to any producible assembly of Γ. Let TERM$_{\Gamma} \subseteq$ PROD$_{\Gamma}$ denote the set of producible assemblies of Γ which are terminal.*

Definition 3 (Unique Assembly). *A tile automata system Γ uniquely produces an assembly A if $A \in$ TERM$_{\Gamma}$ and for all $B \in$ PROD$_{\Gamma}$, $B \rightarrow^{\Gamma} A$.*

Definition 4 (Unique Shape Assembly). *A tile automata system Γ uniquely assembles a shape S provided that for all $A \in$ PROD$_{\Gamma}$, there exists some $B \in$ TERM$_{\Gamma}$ of shape S such that $A \rightarrow^{\Gamma} B$.*

Definition 5 (Freezing). *Consider a tile automata system $\Gamma = (\Sigma, \Lambda, \Pi, \Delta, \tau)$ and a directed graph G constructed as follows:*

- *each state type $\sigma \in \Sigma$ is a vertex*
- *for any two state types $\alpha, \beta \in \Sigma$, an edge from α to β exists if and only if there exists a transition rule in Δ s.t. α transitions to β*

   Γ is said to be freezing *if G is acyclic and* non-freezing *otherwise. Intuitively, a tile automata system is freezing if any one tile in the system can never return to a state which it held previously. This implies that any given tile in the system can only undergo a finite number of state transitions.*

2.3   Simulation Definitions

In this subsection we formally define what it means for one tile automata system to *simulate* another. We use a standard block-representation scheme, similar to what is done in [5], in which the simulating system maps $m \times m$ blocks of states (for a scale factor m simulation) to single states within the simulated system's state space. With this block mapping we can generate an *assembly* mapping as shown in Fig. 2. A system is said to *simulate* another system at scale factor m if such a block mapping exists such that it follows the rules laid out in this section. The purpose of these rules is to provide a reasonable definition for simulating the dynamics of a particular system. More exhaustive definitions for simulation have been considered before (see [3]); however, our intent is to provide relatively straightforward rules that allow for some flexibility while still capturing the essence of what it means for one system to simulate another.

   Consider two tile automata systems Γ and Γ'. Let Σ_{Γ} and $\Sigma_{\Gamma'}$ denote the set of state types used in Γ and Γ', respectively.

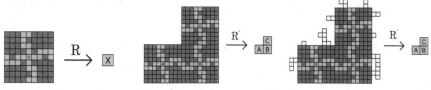

(a) An example entry in R: an m-block representation function with $m = 9$.

(b) An example entry in R': a positioned assembly replacement function.

(c) An example entry in R': the same replacement function with c-Fuzz.

Fig. 2. Examples of m-block representation and mapping. (a) Essentially, the partial function R, called an m-block representation function, takes a macro-block and maps it to a state in the state space of some other system. (b) The function R' takes a positioned assembly, containing m-blocks, and maps it to a positioned assembly over the state space of the other system using the m-block representation function to perform the mapping. (c) The lighter tiles represent c-fuzz which does not change the mapping of the macro-block.

Macro-blocks and Assemblies. An *m-block assembly*, or *macro-block*, is a partial function $\lambda : \mathbb{Z}_m \times \mathbb{Z}_m \to \Sigma_\Gamma$, where $\mathbb{Z}_m = \{0, 1, \ldots, m-1\}$. Let $B_m^{\Sigma_\Gamma}$ be the set of all m-block assemblies over Σ_Γ. The m-block with no domain of definition is said to be *empty*.

For an arbitrary positioned assembly $\mathcal{A}$ over state space Σ_Γ, define $\mathcal{A}_{x,y}^m$ to be the m-block defined by $\mathcal{A}_{x,y}^m(i, j) = \mathcal{A}(mx + i, my + j)$ for $0 \le i, j < m$.

Macro-block Representation and Mapping. As demonstrated in Fig. 2, our simulation definition uses a macro-block representation and mapping scheme. For a partial function $R : B_m^{\Sigma_\Gamma} \to \Sigma_{\Gamma'}$, known as an *m-block representation function*, define the partial function R' that takes as input a positioned assembly $\mathcal{A}$ over state space Σ_Γ and outputs a positioned assembly over state space $\Sigma_{\Gamma'}$. With T denoting a function whose input is an element in $\Sigma \times \mathbb{Z}^2$ and $T(\sigma, x, y)$ outputting a tile with state σ and location (x, y), define $R'(\mathcal{A}) = \{T(R(\mathcal{A}_{x,y}^m), x, y) \mid$ for all non-empty blocks $\mathcal{A}_{x,y}^m$ s.t. $\mathcal{A}_{x,y}^m \in dom(R)\}$.

c-Fuzz. The concept of c-fuzz is essentially the idea that a macro-block can have a bounded number of "extra" tiles attached to it without altering its mapping. This allows a simulating system to make minor intermediate attachments while enacting the simulation. Another way to think of c-fuzz is as a reasonable allowance for limited-size non-empty macro-blocks (that map to an empty tile in the simulated system) to be used in the simulation process. Formally, a mapping $R'(\mathcal{A}) = \mathcal{A}'$ is said to have *c-fuzz*, for some constant c, if and only if for all non-empty blocks $\mathcal{A}_{x,y}^m$, it is the case that $(x + u, y + v) \in dom(\mathcal{A}')$ for some $u, v \in [-c, c]$. R' is said to have c-fuzz if and only if every such mapping $R'(\mathcal{A}) = \mathcal{A}'$ has c-fuzz for all $\mathcal{A} \in dom(R')$. R has c-fuzz if R' has c-fuzz.

Assembly Replacement. For a c-fuzz R', define the *assembly replacement function* $R^* : \text{PROD}_\Gamma \to \text{PROD}_{\Gamma'}$ such that $R^*(A) = A'$ if and only if there exists a positioned assembly $\mathcal{A} \in A$ s.t. $R'(\mathcal{A}) \in A'$. When discussing the application of R^* to a set of assemblies Υ, we use the notation $R^*(\Upsilon)$, where $R^*(\Upsilon) = \{R^*(A)|A \in \Upsilon\}$.

Validity. A c-fuzz assembly replacement $R^*(A)$ is called *valid* if and only if: (1) $R'(\mathcal{A}) = \mathcal{A}'$, $\forall \mathcal{A} \in A$, or (2) $R'(\mathcal{A}) = \varnothing$ and the minimum-diameter bounding square of $\mathcal{A}$ is $\leq 2mc$, $\forall \mathcal{A} \in A$.

The assembly replacement function R^* is said to be Γ-*valid* if $R^*(A)$ is valid for all $A \in \Gamma$. The m-block representation function R is said to be Γ-valid if and only if R^* is Γ-valid.

Simulation. Given a tile automata system Γ, a tile automata system Γ', a constant c, and a Γ-valid c-fuzz m-block representation function $R : B_m^{\Sigma_\Gamma} \to \Sigma_{\Gamma'}$ we say Γ *simulates* tile automata system Γ' *under the c-fuzz rule* if and only if:

- $R^*(\text{PROD}_\Gamma) \supset \Lambda_{\Gamma'}$.
- For any two assemblies $A, B \in \text{PROD}_\Gamma$ s.t. $R^*(A) = \varnothing$ and $R^*(B) = \varnothing$, A and B can combine to form C only if the following is true:
  - $R^*(C) = \varnothing$
  - or, $R^*(C) \in \Lambda_{\Gamma'}$
- For any two assemblies $A', B' \in \text{PROD}_{\Gamma'}$, the following is true:
  - if $A' \to^{\Gamma'} B'$ then it must be that $\exists A, B \in \text{PROD}_\Gamma$ s.t. $R^*(A) = A'$, $R^*(B) = B'$, and $A \to^\Gamma B$.
  - if $A' \nrightarrow^{\Gamma'} B'$ then it must be that $\forall A, B \in \text{PROD}_\Gamma$ where $R^*(A) = A'$, and $R^*(B) = B'$, $A \nrightarrow^\Gamma B$.
- $\forall A \in \text{TERM}_\Gamma$: if $R^*(A) = A' \in \text{PROD}_{\Gamma'}$, then it must also be that $A' \in \text{TERM}_{\Gamma'}$.

Observation. It is important to note that with $R^*(\text{PROD}_\Gamma) \supset \Lambda_{\Gamma'}$, it follows directly from the application of our dynamics simulation definitions that $R^*(\text{PROD}_\Gamma) = \text{PROD}_{\Gamma'}$.

3   Simulating Non-freezing with Freezing Tile Automata

Here, we present the main result of the paper: for any non-freezing TA system, there is a freezing TA system that simulates it. Subsection 3.1 gives an overview of the construction. Subsection 3.2 presents some primitives for the construction. Section 4 gives a formal statement of the theorem and its proof.

3.1   Simulation Overview

At a high-level, the approach is to simulate state transitions between tiles with a process whereby a tile detaches from the assembly and is replaced by a new tile. In this way, any cyclic state transitions are simulated by instead detaching the tile whose state is to be transitioned and attaching a tile with the new state in its place. One immediate issue with a naïve, scale-1 version of this approach is connectivity—e.g., in a 1×3 assembly, replacing the middle tile while keeping the assembly connected is non-trivial.

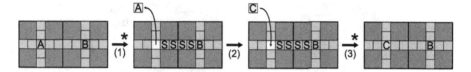

Fig. 3. A simplified overview of simulating the transition $AB \vdash CB$. $\xrightarrow{*}$ indicates a sequence of combination, breaking, and/or transition events occurring. The middle tile in the blocks are the clock tiles, and the rest are wires. Before (1) occurs, the blocks are attached at the adjacent wire tiles with affinity $\Pi(A, B, \vdash)$ from the original system. During (1), a signal proceeds down the wire from B to A. Once the signal reaches A, A detaches. (2) is the attachment event where C is placed within the formerly-A block. (3) indicates a signal returning down the wire after the C block has finished its transition. During (3), when the signal passes back through the boundary between the blocks, tiles are left where the wires meet with affinities matching $\Pi(A, B, \vdash)$, allowing combination/breaking events to follow matching the original system.

This issue motivates using a *block* scheme wherein each tile in the original system is simulated by a larger square block of tiles. The larger scale factor allows blocks to stay connected while some interior tiles detach and are replaced. In the center of the blocks is a *clock tile*, which determines which tile in the original system the block maps to in the m-block representation function. Extending from the clock tile to the four edges of the block are *wires*, a connected path of tiles which (1) send information via token-passing to adjacent blocks about initiating state transitions and (2) attach to wires on other blocks with affinities corresponding to the original system.

A high-level overview omitting some particular details follows. Attachment and detachment events are simulated by the wires exposing affinities matching that of the original system. To simulate state transitions, several steps occur. A simplified summary is in Fig. 3. It begins with a sequence of state transitions, called *signals*, beginning from a clock tile proceeding down a wire to an adjacent block's clock tile. Upon receiving signals from all neighbors, the clock tile detaches from the block, and a new clock tile representing the new state of the block takes its place. The wires are designed to be *replaceable*; in some cases, while sending a sequence of state transitions down the wire, the wire tiles detach (one-by-one) and are replaced with new tiles. This alleviates the issue of the wires themselves dissatisfying the freezing constraint. When a signal passes the boundary of one block and enters another, these tiles have full τ-strength affinity. This ensures the tiles may not detach while the transition occurs. After the clock tile is replaced and the signal passes back through this boundary, it leaves a tile with affinity matching the post-transition tile in the original system.

3.2 Simulation Primitives

Blocks. One block is constructed for each of the initial tile types in the original system. Each block consists of 3 portions; *filler* tiles, *wire* tiles, and a *clock* tile. The filler tiles are simply needed for the block to maintain connectivity when

(a) Primary components of a block.

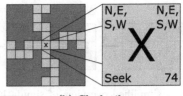

(b) Clock tile.

Fig. 4. Blocks and clock tiles. (a) The primary components of a block are the filler tiles (used for connectivity), the wire tiles (used for the passing of signals), and the clock tile (used to control signal flow). (b) The clock tile contains information about which of its tokens (N, E, S, W) it has, which of its neighbors tokens (N, E, S, W) it has, which mode it is in (seeking, sending, off), and how many of the constant number of transitions have occurred.

replacing the clock or portions of the wire. The filler tiles undergo no state transitions, save for one during the initial assembling of the block. The wires are responsible for propagating a block's incoming and outgoing signals to initiate transition rules between blocks' clocks. The wires in a block are used to maintain the affinities between blocks (all affinity between two blocks is between wire tiles) The clock tiles are the middle tile of each block, and send/receive signals to/from the wire tiles which can initiate a state transition of that clock or another clock. The clock tile is the main determinant used in the m-block replacement function (discussed in the simulation definition). A clock tile is designed to *represent* exactly one state x of the system to be simulated. We label the clock tiles' states according to the state they represent. We say a block *represents* exactly one state x if its clock tile represents x (Fig. 4).

Wires. Since each tile of the original system is replaced by a block, *wires* send transition rules from the middle of the block to the edges. Wires send a cascade of transition rules along a path of connected tiles. As an example (Fig. 5), given a path of horizontally connected w tiles and the transition rule $w_r w \vdash w_r w_r$, if the leftmost tile is transitioned to w_r (e.g. by a tile x to its left and the rule $xw \vdash xw_r$), the transition cascades down the path of w tiles (and, e.g., transitioning a tile y to z at the end of the wire by the rule $w_r y \vdash w_r z$. Then, the presence of the x tile has been detected by the non-adjacent y tile using a series of transitions along the wire.

In order to reuse the wires, the tiles must be replaced after at most a constant number of uses due to freezing transition rules; otherwise, the wire could be reset with transition rules alone. Figure 6 depicts this signal passing with the required tile replacements. Towards a wire with replaceable tiles, consider the following transition rules: $w_r w \vdash w_r w_r$ and $w_r w_r \vdash w_f w_r$. The first rule passes the transition along the wire. The second rule sets the previous tile to a "fall off" state which is not bound to the assembly which contains the wire. The w_f tile may detach from the assembly, and a new w tile may attach in its place.

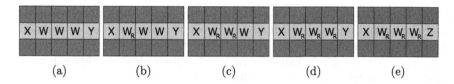

Fig. 5. A wire demonstrating its signal-passing ability. Given the rules $XW \vdash XW_R$, $W_RW \vdash W_RW_R$, and $W_RY \vdash W_RZ$ we can see the signal propogation from (a) to (e).

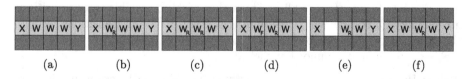

Fig. 6. A wire replacing tiles while passing a signal. Given the rules $W_RW \vdash W_RW_R$ and $W_RW_R \vdash W_FW_R$ we replace tiles once they transition. Once a signal has started propagating in (a) with the rule $XW \vdash XW_R$ yielding (b), any further transitions with allow (d) to occur. The tile with W_F has no affinity to its neighbors so it detaches (e) and a new tile with state W attaches (f).

State-State Wires. We augment the wire scheme with *state-state* information stored via the wire tiles' states. State-state refers to the two states represented by the clock tiles which the wire lies between. When a block representing x is first constructed, and when its wire is only touching one clock since the block has no neighbor in that direction, the wires' state-state is referred to as x-$\varnothing$. Without loss of generalization, x-$\varnothing$ is the information on the wire protruding east, and $\varnothing$-x is the information on the wire protruding west. If the wire is between two clocks, perhaps representing x and y, the state-state is then referred to as x-y (if the x block is to the west of the y block). When a block representing x has a new adjacent neighboring block representing y via an attachment to another assembly or via a block-state transition (Sect. 3.2), the state-state wire between the two blocks must be updated. For example, the result may be an x-z wire meeting a w-y wire. Via state transition, the wire information should then be updated to x-y. On a horizontal state-state wire (without loss of generalization), this updating is done by the following rules: if two state-state wires disagree, e.g. an x-z wire tile on the left meets a w-y wire tile on the right, the x-z wire changes the w-y wire tile to x-y. Similarly, the w-y wire tile can change the x-z tile to x-y. This works since the tile on the left-hand wire tile has the correct information about the left-hand block, and the right-hand wire tile has the right information about the right-hand block.

Seeking, Sending, and Off States. Clocks transition between *seeking, sending,* and *off* states depending on their adjacent state-state wire information. Transition of a clock tile representing x to the *seeking* state may occur if and only if an adjacent x-y wire is present such that a transition rule exists (w.r.t. the cardinal direction that the wire is coming from) between x and y that changes

x to another state. Transition of a clock tile representing x to the sending state may occur if and only if a neighbor block may transition to the seeking state. Explicitly, this transition can occur if and only if an adjacent x-y wire is present such that a transition rule exists (w.r.t. the cardinal direction that the wire is coming from) between x and y that changes y to another state. Transition of a clock tile to the off state may occur if and only if a clock holds all of its own *tokens* (tokens will be described in the next paragraph) and no others. The off state of the clock halts all token passing by the block. The purpose of these states is to simulate terminal assemblies. Assemblies with no possible state transitions are simulated by blocks which are all in the off state, halting transitions through the wires. If neighboring blocks have no applicable transition rules, then the seeking/sending state cannot be reached.

Token Passing. *Tokens* are passed between neighboring blocks using the wire signal passing scheme shown earlier. Clock tiles are responsible for sending and receiving tokens. A clock tile can have up to eight tokens: four of its own tokens (one for each cardinal direction) and up to four of its neighbor's tokens (one for each cardinal direction). If a clock is in the seeking or sending state, it may send its token through the wire to the clock on the other end. Token ownership is represented by the state of the clock tile. The following rules hold for token passing:

- With respect to one cardinal direction, tiles can have: their own token, their own token and their neighbor token, or no tokens, i.e., a clock cannot have its neighbor token but not its own. This is enforced via clock transition rules wherein clocks cannot send their token if they hold their neighbor's token.
- Tokens cannot pass through each other on the wire; if two tokens meet on the wire, one is (nondeterministically) forced back to its clock.
- Tiles in the off state cannot receive tokens.

Block-State Transitions. When a clock receives all eight possible tokens (its four own tokens and its four neighbor tokens), the clock may undergo a *block-state transition*: a series of transitions within the clock's block which changes the state in the simulated system which the block represents. The clock, upon receiving its eighth token, may go through the following sequence which simulates a state transition: First, the clock undergoes a transition due to one of its neighboring state-state wires (which inform the clock of what states his neighbor blocks represent). This way, the clock nondeterministically samples from the state transitions it may simulate based on the represented state of its neighbor blocks. Once selecting a state to transition to, the clock stores (in an adjacent wire tile) information about that state. Then, the clock tile transitions to a state in which it has no affinities and detaches from the block. A new tile attaches in its place whose state is designed to read from the adjacent wire which stored the information about which state it will become from the previous clock tile. Once the new clock tile's state is updated with the previous clock's information, the wire tile which stored the information then undergoes a state transition and detaches to be replaced with a new wire tile. Then, the clock tile updates its

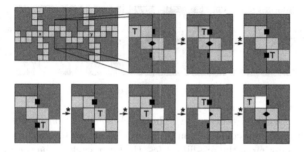

Fig. 7. Token passing between two blocks representing x and y. Squares on the edge of blocks signify τ-strength affinity. Rhombuses signify affinities equal to the affinity between x and y in the simulated system. As before, $\xrightarrow{*}$ indicates a sequence of attachment, detachment, and/or combination events have occurred. In the top sequence of transitions, the x block passes its token to y. As the token passes the border between the two blocks, the states in the wire bind with τ strength with the other block to ensure the blocks cannot detach until the token is returned. In the bottom sequence of transitions, the y block sends x's token back. In this case, the τ strength affinities with each block are removed, and only an affinity matching that of the state to be simulated remains. As the token returns, each wire tile is replaced with new tiles.

adjacent state-state wires to a new state-state wire effectively overwriting the old state from the wire and replacing with the new state (e.g., an x-y wire becomes a z-y wire as the block simulates a transition from x to z).

Clock Replacement. As the clocks send and receive tokens, they undergo state transitions. Therefore, the clock tiles must be replaced after a finite number of token passes. Each clock has a counter which increments each time it undergoes a state transition. Once the clock reaches an arbitrarily designated value, the clock will undergo a replacement. The clock first stores (in an adjacent wire tile) information about its possessed tokens and the state in the simulated system which it represents. Then, the clock tile transitions to a state in which it detaches from the block. A new tile attaches in its place whose state is designed to read from the adjacent wire which stored the information from the previous clock tile. Once the new clock tile's state is updated with the previous clock's information, the wire tile which stored the information then undergoes a state transition and detaches to be replaced with a new wire tile.

Dummy Blocks. To initiate a block-state transition (Sect. 3.2), a block requires four neighbors. Of course, in the simulated system, not all transitionable tiles will have neighboring tiles. To alleviate this, include a set of blocks called *dummy blocks*. Dummy blocks act as temporary neighbors to blocks which lack them. Dummy blocks may pass tokens to neighboring blocks, but cannot receive them. Include one set of dummy tiles for each cardinal direction. Dummy blocks have two states: attach and detach. Dummy blocks in the attach state may attach to any block in the system with τ strength from one direction, e.g., the north dummy block binds its south edge to the north edge of any block in the sys-

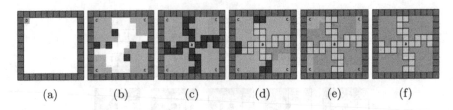

Fig. 8. Block construction process. (a) The block construction process begins with a pre-assembled frame. Four construction initiator tiles attach to the corners of the frame, initiating the assembling of the pre-filler tiles. (b) Once each of the pre-filler portions of the block are complete, blank wire tiles can begin attaching. (c) Upon completion of all four wire portions, a seed-clock tile can attach and (d) begin changing the blank wires into wires of the same type as the clock. (e) When a wire segment has been changed to a typed-wire, it begins transitioning the pre-filler tiles into filler tiles. (f) When all four filler sections have transitioned, the block no longer has any affinity with the frame, and detaches.

tem. Include a state transition between any block and the dummy block which transitions the dummy block from its attach state to its detach state.

The detach state has no affinity with any blocks in the system except in the case that a neighbor has received the dummy block's token, in which case a full τ strength bond is held. Then, dummy blocks may attach to unoccupied positions in the assembly, and subsequently transition and detach; however, they may first pass a token, in which case they are attached to the assembly until the token is removed from the neighbor. In this way, any block in the assembly with a missing neighbor has a chance at attaching a dummy block neighbor and grabbing its token. Dummy blocks cannot attach to blocks which are off.

3.3   Additional Simulation Primitives

Here we further detail a few of the primitives used in our construction with details that are not as important, but are useful nonetheless.

Wire Replacement. As discussed prior, wires may replace tiles as signals are passing through. Wires replace their tiles under the following circumstances: (1) if the block's neighbor's token is being sent back to its neighbor, and (2) if the block's own token is returning. Otherwise, signals may pass through the wires freely. These two conditions enforce that the wire is replaced after a finite number of signals are passed through.

Exposed Affinities on Blocks. The following rules are imposed on the affinities of the wire tiles of a block which are exposed to other blocks:

- If the block's token has not passed through the wire (the block still has its token), and the neighbor's token has not passed through the wire (the block does not have its neighbor's token), the affinity exposed matches the affinity exposed by the state in the to-be-simulated system that the block represents.

– Otherwise, as a token passes through the wire causing the above condition to fail, the wire attaches with full τ strength to the neighboring block.

These rules ensure that all detachment and attachment events of the to-be-simulated system may occur by the blocks, since the affinities exposed by blocks match those of the simulated states when the tokens meet the above requirements. Additionally, these rules ensure that when a block is undergoing a state transition, the block is attached with τ strength to his neighbors to ensure a detachment does not occur prior to the state change. The process whereby the affinity changes on the wire during token-passing is shown in Fig. 7.

Block Construction. The blocks must be constructed by a series of combination events beginning with single tiles. To imitate the tiles of the original system, the blocks must use one tile on each edge to expose the affinities of the original tile. Moreover, these edge affinities must be exposed "all at once" in order to simulate the behavior of the original tiles (i.e., incomplete blocks may expose only the northbound affinity of the original tile, whereas the original tiles expose all of their affinities from the get-go). To achieve this, the blocks are constructed inside a *frame*, inhibiting their affinities from being exposed. Then, a transition rule occurs between the block and the frame indicating that the block has completed construction, in which the frame detaches from the block. This process can be seen in Fig. 8.

4 Simulation Proof

Theorem 1. *Given a tile automata system Γ', there exists a freezing tile automata system Γ which simulates Γ' under the 2-fuzz rule via a 9-block replacement function.*

Proof. For a given tile automata system $\Gamma' = (\Sigma', \Lambda', \Pi', \Delta', \tau')$, we generate a tile automata system $\Gamma = (\Sigma, \Lambda, \Pi, \Delta, \tau)$. In Σ, include seed, clock, and wire tile types representing each state type in Σ'. Further, include the $\mathcal{O}(1)$ state types required for the block construction and dummy blocks (Sect. 3.2).

Stability Threshold. Γ requires $\tau \geq 2$ to use the wire technique Sect. 3.2. If Γ' has $\tau' = 1$, Γ must have $\tau = 2$. In this case, affinities of strength 1 in Γ' are simulated by affinities of strength 2 in Γ when blocks expose affinities on the wire designed to match the original system. Otherwise, to simulate a system with $\tau' \geq 2$, the simulating system uses $\tau = \tau'$.

State Complexity ($|\Sigma|$). Σ (the set of state types of Γ) includes state-state wires (Sect. 3.2) for each pair of states in Σ'. Due to this, $|\Sigma| = \mathcal{O}(|\Sigma'|^2)$. All other techniques require at most $c * \Sigma'$ state types for some constant c.

The Macro-block Representation and Mapping. The mapping of macro-blocks in Γ to states in Γ' is straightforward: for a state $s \in \Gamma'$, there exists a block in Γ whose clock represents s. Any block containing the clock representing s is mapped to s in the macro-block representation function R. When the clock is detached from the block, either through a block-state transition (Sect. 3.2) or a clock replacement (Sect. 3.2), the block is mapped according to the neighboring wire tile which is used to temporarily store the information of the clock tile.

2-*Fuzz Rule.* As the blocks of Γ' are being constructed via the block construction process, the clock tile does not represent any state in Γ. These blocks, along with the frame they are assembled within, still satisfy simulation under the 2-fuzz rule (diameter of the minimum-diameter bounding square of the blocks with frame is $<2mc$), and hence map to the empty assembly. Additionally, the attachment of dummy blocks (Sect. 3.2) which do not map to any states in Γ are also permissible under the 2-fuzz rule.

Initial Assemblies. Our construction is designed such that for every tile in each of the initial assemblies of Γ', there exists a block in Γ that was produced via the block construction process described above. Thus, we see that $R^*(\text{PROD}_\Gamma) \supset \Lambda_{\Gamma'}$.

Simulating Dynamics: Part 1. Consider the assemblies $A', B' \in \text{PROD}_{\Gamma'}$ s.t. $A' \to^{\Gamma'} B'$. Suppose that A' can transition into B' via an attachment using state s. Any assembly $A \in \text{PROD}_\Gamma$ where $R^*(A) = A'$ contains a 9×9 block which represents s. The A whose 9×9 "s"-block clock only has all four of its own tokens (and is not currently attached to a dummy block) is guaranteed to be able to make the same attachments via its 9×9 "s"-block as A' is via s. Now, suppose that A' can transition into B' via a state-transition of s into s'. Again, any assembly $A \in \text{PROD}_\Gamma$ where $R^*(A) = A'$ contains a 9×9 block which represents s. The A whose 9×9 "s"-block clock has collected all four of its own tokens, and all four of its neighbors' tokens is guaranteed to be able to make the same transitions via its 9×9 "s"-block as A' is via s.

Simulating Dynamics: Part 2. Consider the assemblies $C, D \in \text{PROD}_\Gamma$. Suppose that $C \to^\Gamma D$. There are only a few instances where $R^*(C) \neq R^*(D)$. First, note that none of the internal state-transitions of the 9×9 blocks that make up C, which are required for token-passing, alter the mapping of C. Nor do the attachment of dummy blocks to C alter its mapping. So for all of these transitions, $R^*(C) = R^*(D)$. So, the only instances $R^*(C) \neq R^*(D)$ would be due to a "block-sized" detachment event, an attachment event involving C and some other assembly, or a block-state transition within C. Since each 9×9 block in C inherits its affinity from the states in $R^*(C)$, any "block-sized" attachment/detachment events which involve C could only occur if their state-equivalent events were possible in $R^*(C)$. Furthermore, since block-state transitions are inherited the same way, the only block-state transitions that could occur in C must also be driven by equivalent events that could occur in $R^*(C)$.

Simulating Dynamics: Part 3. Consider an assembly $E \in \text{TERM}_\Gamma$. We know that every exposed wire on the perimeter of E must not have affinity towards any other 9×9 block in the system. This can only occur if $R^*(E)$ cannot attach to any other assembly in Γ'. Also, every clock in E must be stuck in the off state, meaning no transitions are possible. This can only occur if $R^*(E)$ cannot transition into any other assembly in Γ' via a state transition. It must also be the case that E is not breakable into any other assemblies. Since all of the clocks in A are off, we know that, internally, each 9×9 block is not breakable. Furthermore, we know that each 9×9 block in E is bound to its neighbors with a total strength of at least τ. This can only occur if $R^*(E)$ is not breakable. Therefore, by definition, $R^*(E) \in \text{TERM}_{\Gamma'}$.   □

5   Conclusion and Future Work

This work introduces Tile Automata as a hybrid between tile self-assembly and cellular automata. The model resembles other more complicated, well-studied forms of active self-assembly, and thus results about simulation between TA and other active self-assembly models should be pursued. We have shown in this work that freezing TA can simulate non-freezing TA, allowing future proofs about general TA to apply to freezing systems. Some optimizations are open: the simulation herein uses 9×9 macro-blocks and a quadratic state-complexity increase to achieve non-freezing behavior with a freezing system; a smaller macro-block size and smaller state-complexity increase are welcome.

References

1. Becker, F., Maldonado, D., Ollinger, N., Theyssier, G.: Universality in freezing cellular automata. CoRR, abs/1805.00059 (2018). http://arxiv.org/abs/1805.00059
2. Cannon, S., Demaine, E.D., et al.: Two hands are better than one (up to constant factors): self-assembly in the 2HAM vs. aTAM. In: STACS. LIPIcs, vol. 20, pp. 172–184 (2013)
3. Demaine, E.D., Patitz, M.J., Rogers, T.A., Schweller, R.T., Summers, S.M., Woods, D.: The two-handed tile assembly model is not intrinsically universal. Algorithmica **74**(2), 812–850 (2016)
4. Derakhshandeh, Z., Gmyr, R., Strothmann, T., Bazzi, R., Richa, A.W., Scheideler, C.: Leader election and shape formation with self-organizing programmable matter. In: Phillips, A., Yin, P. (eds.) DNA 2015. LNCS, vol. 9211, pp. 117–132. Springer, Cham (2015). https://doi.org/10.1007/978-3-319-21999-8_8
5. Doty, D., Lutz, J.H., Patitz, M.J., Schweller, R., Summers, S.M., Woods, D.: The tile assembly model is intrinsically universal. In: Proceedings of the 53rd Conference on Foundations of Computer Science, FOCS 2012 (2012)
6. Goles, E., Maldonado, D., Montealegre, P., Ollinger, N.: On the computational complexity of the freezing non-strict majority automata. In: Dennunzio, A., Formenti, E., Manzoni, L., Porreca, A.E. (eds.) AUTOMATA 2017. LNCS, vol. 10248, pp. 109–119. Springer, Cham (2017). https://doi.org/10.1007/978-3-319-58631-1_9
7. Goles, E., Ollinger, N., Theyssier, G.: Introducing freezing cellular automata. In: Cellular Automata and Discrete Complex Systems, AUTOMATA 2015, vol. 24, pp. 65–73 (2015)
8. Jonaska, N., Karpenko, D.: Active tile self-assembly, part 2: self-similar structures and structural recursion. Int. J. Found. Comput. Sci. **25**(02), 165–194 (2014)
9. Kari, J.: Theory of cellular automata: a survey. Theor. Comput. Sci. **334**(1), 3–33 (2005)

10. Padilla, J.E., et al.: Asynchronous signal passing for tile self-assembly: fuel efficient computation and efficient assembly of shapes. Int. J. Found. Comput. Sci. **25**, 459 (2014)
11. Padilla, J.E., Sha, R., Kristiansen, M., Chen, J., Jonoska, N., Seeman, N.C.: A signal-passing DNA-strand-exchange mechanism for active self-assembly of DNA nanostructures. Angew. Chem. Int. Ed. **54**(20), 5939–5942 (2015)
12. Woods, D., Chen, H.-L., Goodfriend, S., Dabby, N., Winfree, E., Yin, P.: Active self-assembly of algorithmic shapes and patterns in polylogarithmic time. In: Innovations in Theoretical Computer Science, ITCS 2013, pp. 353–354 (2013)

Construction of Geometric Structure
by Oritatami System

Yo-Sub Han[1] and Hwee Kim[2(✉)]

[1] Department of Computer Science, Yonsei University, 50 Yonsei-Ro, Seodaemun-Gu,
Seoul 03722, Republic of Korea
emmous@yonsei.ac.kr
[2] Department of Mathematics and Statistics, University of South Florida,
12010 USF Cherry Drive, Tampa, FL 33620, USA
hweekim@mail.usf.edu

Abstract. Self-assembly is the process where smaller components autonomously assemble to form a larger and more complex structure. One of the application areas of self-assembly is engineering and production of complicated nanostructures. Recently, researchers proposed a new folding model called the oritatami model (OM) that simulates the cotranscriptional self-assembly, based on the kinetics on the final shape of folded molecules. Nanostructures in oritatami system (OS) are represented by a sequence of beads and interactions on the lattice. We propose a method to design a general OS, which we call GEOS, that constructs a given geometric structure. The main idea is to design small modular OSs, which we call hinges, for every possible pair of adjacent points in the target structure. Once a shape filling curve for the target structure is ready, we construct an appropriate primary structure that follows the curve by a sequence of hinges. We establish generalized guidelines on designing a GEOS, and propose two GEOSs.

1 Introduction

Self-assembly is the process where smaller components—usually molecules—autonomously assemble to form a larger and more complex structure. Self-assembly plays an important role in constructing biological structures and high polymers [21]. Applications of self-assembly include nanostructured electric circuits [2,5] and smart drug delivery [13,20] (Fig. 1).

One well-known mathematical model of the self-assembly phenomenon is the abstract tile assembly model (aTAM) by Winfree [22]. Recently, Geary et al. [7] proposed a new folding model called the oritatami model (OM) that simulates the cotranscriptional self-assembly based on the experimental RNA transcription called RNA origami [8]. In general, OM assumes that a sequence of molecules is transcribed linearly, and predicts its geometric shape from the autonomous folding of the sequence based on the reaction rate of the folding. An oritatami system (OS) consists of a sequence of beads (which is the transcript) and a set of rules for possible intermolecular reactions between beads. For each bead

© Springer Nature Switzerland AG 2018
D. Doty and H. Dietz (Eds.): DNA 2018, LNCS 11145, pp. 173–188, 2018.
https://doi.org/10.1007/978-3-030-00030-1_11

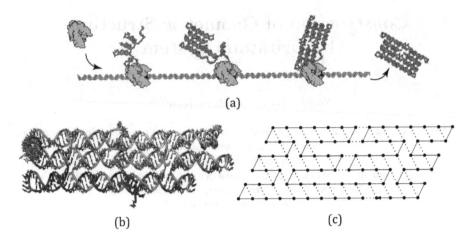

Fig. 1. The motivation of the oritatami model. (a) An illustration of an RNA Origami [7], which transcribes an RNA strand that self-assembles. (b) The product of an RNA Origami. (c) Abstraction of the product in oritatami system.

in the sequence, the system takes a lookahead of a few upcoming beads and determines the best location of the current bead that maximizes the number of possible interactions from the lookahead. Note that the lookahead represents the reaction rate of the cotranscriptional folding and the number of interactions represents the energy level (See Fig. 2 for the analogy between RNA origami and oritatami system.). Researchers designed various OSs including a binary counter [6] and a Boolean formula simulator [11]. It is known that OM is Turing complete [7] and there are several methods to optimize OSs [10,12,15]. There are also approaches to analyze construction of geometric structures [14,17].

RNA Origami	Oritatami System
Nucleotides	Beads
Transcript	Sequence of beads connected by a line
h-bonds between nucleotides	Interactions
Cotranscriptional folding rate	Delay
Resulting secondary structure	Conformation

(a)

$abbcbdbbe$

transcript

$(a, d), (c, e)$

interaction rules

$\Rightarrow$

interaction bead

conformation

(b)

Fig. 2. (a) Analogy between RNA origami and oritatami system. (b) Visualization of oritatami system and its terms.

There are many experimental researches on engineering nanostructures using self-assembly [16,18]. Since the trial-and-error approach in designing nanostructures is often costly, researchers instead rely on abstract models of self-assembly to engineer desired nanostructures. In aTAM, nanostructures are represented by shapes, and researchers focused on finding tile complexity of a target shape [1,19]. Because a nanostructure is represented by sequence of beads and bead interactions on the lattice in OS, one may ask; given a geometric structure on the lattice, how can we design an OS that constructs the given structure? A naive solution is to use unique bead types for all possible beads. However this approach is unrealistic in experiments and is not a desired solution. Instead, we want to use only a constant number of bead types and a fixed ruleset, and design a function that encodes a given geometric structure into a transcript such that the transcript folds as the given structure.

We propose a generalized method to design a geometric structure constructing OS (GEOS in short). The target structure is given as a set of points in an arbitrary lattice. We map each point in a target structure to a set of points in the triangular lattice for the OS. The main idea is to design small modular OSs, which we call hinges, for every possible pair of adjacent points in a target structure. These hinges use interactions of beads only within adjacent points instead of global interactions across many points. Moreover, the system constructs a complete structure for each point at a time instead of dividing a point into partial structures constructed at different times. This design policy yields robustness of the structure in realization. Once a shape filling curve—a skeleton sequence traversing the target structure—is given, we construct an appropriate transcript that follows the curve by a sequence of hinges (See Fig. 3). We establish generalized guidelines on designing a GEOS, and propose two GEOSs.

Recently, Demaine et al. [3] studied a similar problem of general geometric structure construction by OS. They considered a set of points on the triangular lattice, and mapped each point to an hexagon in the lattice for the OS. They filled the whole set of hexagons globally, without explicit point ordering. They proposed a basic module to fill the hexagon. They also suggested how to modify the module to be connected with neighboring modules, resulting in a target conformation spanning the whole set of hexagons. They used an OS of delay 1 and arity 4, and obtained the rigidity 1. Note that their scale is at least 19 according to our measure whereas our approach gives 25 in both designs.

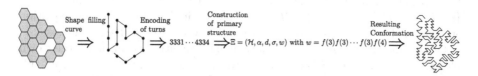

Fig. 3. An illustration of a geometric structure constructing OS. Once a shape filling curve for the given geometric structure is given, the curve is encoded as a sequence of numbers denoting consecutive turns. For each turn, we propose a partial primary structure called a hinge. The sequence of corresponding hinges forms the transcript of the geometric structure constructing OS, and the resulting conformation constructs the given structure.

2 Preliminaries

Let $w = a_1 a_2 \cdots a_n$ be a string over Σ of size n and bead types $a_1, \ldots, a_n \in \Sigma$. The *length* $|w|$ of w is n. For two indices i, j with $1 \leq i \leq j \leq n$, we let $w[i, j]$ be the substring $a_i a_{i+1} \cdots a_{j-1} a_j$; we use $w[i]$ to denote $w[i, i]$. We use w^n to denote the catenation of n copies of w.

Oritatami systems operate on the triangular lattice Λ_t with the vertex set V and the edge set E. For a point p and a bead type $a \in \Sigma$, we call the pair (p, a) an *annotated point*, or simply a *point* if being annotated is clear from context. Two points p, q (or annotated points $(p, a), (q, b)$) are *adjacent* if they are at unit distance. A *path* is a sequence $P = p_1 p_2 \cdots p_n$ of *pairwise-distinct* points $p_1, p_2, \ldots, p_n$ such that $p_i p_{i+1}$ is at unit distance for all $1 \leq i < n$. Given a string $w \in \Sigma^n$, a *path annotated by* w, or simply w-*path*, is a sequence P_w of annotated points $(p_1, w[1]), \ldots, (p_n, w[n])$, where $p_1 \cdots p_n$ is a path. We call points of the w-path beads, and we call the i-th point $(p_i, w[i])$ the i-th bead of the w-path. Let $\mathcal{H} \subseteq \Sigma \times \Sigma$ be a symmetric relation, specifying between which bead types can form a hydrogen-bond-based interaction (interaction for short). This relation $\mathcal{H}$ is called the *ruleset*.

A conformation instance, or *configuration*, is a triple (P, w, H) of a directed path P in Λ_t, $w \in \Sigma^* \cup \Sigma^\omega$, and a set $H \subseteq \{(i, j) \mid 1 \leq i, i + 2 \leq j, \{P[i], P[j]\} \in E\}$ of interactions. This is to be interpreted as the sequence w being folded while its i-th bead $w[i]$ is placed on the i-th point $P[i]$ along the path and there is an interaction between the i-th and j-th beads if and only if $(i, j) \in H$. Configurations (P_1, w_1, H_1) and (P_2, w_2, H_2) are *congruent* provided $w_1 = w_2$, $H_1 = H_2$, and P_1 can be transformed into P_2 by a combination of a translation, a reflection, and rotations by $60°$. The set of all configurations congruent to a configuration (P, w, H) is called the *conformation* of the configuration and denoted by $C = [(P, w, H)]$. We call w a *primary structure* of C. Let $\mathcal{H}$ be a ruleset. An interaction $(i, j) \in H$ is *valid with respect to* $\mathcal{H}$, or simply $\mathcal{H}$-*valid*, if $(w[i], w[j]) \in \mathcal{H}$. We say that a conformation C is $\mathcal{H}$-*valid* if all of its interactions are $\mathcal{H}$-valid. For an integer $\alpha \geq 1$, C is *of arity α* if the maximum number of interactions per bead is α, that is, if for any $k \geq 1$, $\left|\{i \mid (i, k) \in H\}\right| + \left|\{j \mid (k, j) \in H\}\right| \leq \alpha$ and this inequality holds as an equation for some k. By $\mathcal{C}_{\leq \alpha}$, we denote the set of all conformations of arity at most α.

Oritatami systems grow conformations by elongating them under their own ruleset. For a finite conformation C_1, we say that a finite conformation C_2 is an *elongation* of C_1 by a bead $b \in \Sigma$ under a ruleset $\mathcal{H}$, written as $C_1 \xrightarrow{\mathcal{H}}_b C_2$, if there exists a configuration (P, w, H) of C_1 such that C_2 includes a configuration $(P \cdot p, w \cdot b, H \cup H')$, where $p \in V$ is a point not in P and $H' \subseteq \{(i, |P|+1) \mid 1 \leq i \leq |P| - 1, \{P[i], p\} \in E, (w[i], b) \in \mathcal{H}\}$. This operation is recursively extended to the elongation by a finite sequence of beads as follows: For any conformation C, $C \xrightarrow{\mathcal{H}}{}^*_\lambda C$; and for a finite sequence of beads w and a bead b, a conformation C_1 is elongated to a conformation C_2 by $w \cdot b$, written as $C_1 \xrightarrow{\mathcal{H}}{}^*_{w \cdot b} C_2$, if there is a conformation C' that satisfies $C_1 \xrightarrow{\mathcal{H}}{}^*_w C'$ and $C' \xrightarrow{\mathcal{H}}_b C_2$.

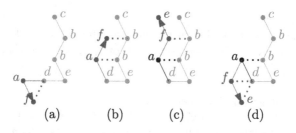

Fig. 4. An example OS with delay 2 and arity 2. The seed is colored in red, and the stabilized beads and interactions are colored in black. (Color figure online)

An *oritatami system (OS)* is a 6-tuple $\varXi = (\varSigma, w, \mathcal{H}, \delta, \alpha, C_\sigma = [(P_\sigma, w_\sigma, H_\sigma)])$, where $\mathcal{H}$ is a *ruleset*, $\delta \geq 1$ is a *delay*, and C_σ is an $\mathcal{H}$-valid initial *seed* conformation of arity at most α, upon which its *transcript* $w \in \varSigma^* \cup \varSigma^\mathbb{N}$ is to be folded by stabilizing beads of w one at a time and minimize energy collaboratively with the succeeding $\delta - 1$ nascent beads. The energy of a conformation $C = [(P, w, H)]$ is $U(C) = -|H|$; namely, the more interactions a conformation has, the more stable it becomes. The set $\mathcal{F}(\varXi)$ of conformations *foldable* by this system is recursively defined as follows: The seed C_σ is in $\mathcal{F}(\varXi)$; and provided that an elongation C_i of C_σ by the prefix $w[1:i]$ be foldable (i.e., $C_0 = C_\sigma$), its further elongation C_{i+1} by the next bead $w[i+1]$ is foldable if

$$C_{i+1} \in \underset{\substack{C \in \mathcal{C}_{\leq\alpha} \text{ s.t.} \\ C_i \xrightarrow{\mathcal{H}}_{w[i+1]} C}}{\operatorname{argmin}} \min\left\{ U(C') \,\Big|\, C \xrightarrow{\mathcal{H}}^*_{w[i+2:i+k]} C', k \leq \delta, C' \in \mathcal{C}_{\leq\alpha} \right\}. \quad (1)$$

Once we have C_{i+1}, we say that the bead $w[i+1]$ and its interactions are *stabilized* according to C_{i+1}. A conformation foldable by $\varXi$ is *terminal* if none of its elongations is foldable by $\varXi$.

Figure 4 illustrates an example of an OS with delay 2, arity 2 and the ruleset $\{(a, b), (b, f), (d, f), (d, e)\}$; in (a), the system tries to stabilize the first bead a of the transcript, and the elongation in (a) gives 1 interaction. However, it is not the most stable one since the elongation in (b) gives 2 interactions in total. Thus, the first bead a is stabilized according to the location in (b). In (c), the system tries to stabilize the second bead f, and the elongation in (c) gives 1 interaction for the primary structure fe. However, the elongation in (d) gives 2 interactions in total. Thus, the second bead f is stabilized according to the location in (d). Note that f is not stabilized according to the location in (b), although the elongation in (b) is used to stabilize the first bead a.

3   On the Generalized Design of GEOS

The input for the design of a geometric structure construction OS (GEOS) is as follows:

- A lattice Λ_0 on the plane.
- A shape that we want to fill on the lattice, which is given by the set $\mathbb{P}_0$ of points. It is necessary that the grid graph of $\mathbb{P}_0$ should be connected.

The output should include

- A triangular lattice Λ_t that spans Λ_0.
- An injective function $f_c : p \in \Lambda_0 \rightarrow p_c \in \Lambda_t$ that maps a point in Λ_0 to a point in Λ_t. For each point p in Λ, we call $f_c(p)$ the *core point*.
- A bijective mapping $f_u : p \in \Lambda_0 \rightarrow \mathbb{U}(p) \subset \Lambda_t$ that maps a point in Λ_0 to a set of points in Λ_t. For each point p in Λ, we call the induced graph of $f_u(p)$ the *unit shape*. The unit shape should be a solid grid graph, and the size of $f_u(p)$—which we call the *scale*—should be constant for all p's. Moreover, $f_u(\Lambda_0) = \Lambda_t$. The concept of the scale is introduced while proving intrinsic universality of aTAM [4] as the size of the metatile that can simulate one tile in the system. Here, the scale represents the size of the partial primary structure that can cover one point in $\mathbb{P}_0$.
- A deterministic OS $\varXi = (\Sigma, w, \mathcal{H}, \delta, \alpha, C_\sigma = [(P_\sigma, w_\sigma, H_\sigma)])$ on Λ_t, where the final conformation covers at least one point in $f_u(p)$ for each $p \in \mathbb{P}_0$.

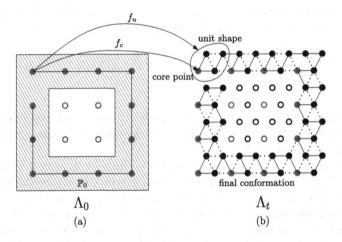

Fig. 5. An illustration of the input and the output for the GEOS. The figure in (a) shows the input and the figure in (b) shows the output. In figure (b), core points are colored in blue. The scale of the OS is 4. (Color figure online)

Figure 5 shows an example of the input and the output for the GEOS. Aside from the lattice, the mapping and OS, we establish desirable features that determine a good design of the geometric structure construction OS, motivated from the design of a shape-fitting aTAM by Soloveichik and Winfree [19].

- The scale should be as small as possible: Each point in $\mathbb{P}_0$ is mapped into a set of points in Λ_t, on which the conformation of the OS is stabilized. Thus, the smaller the size of $\mathbb{U}$, the shorter the length of the final conformation—which helps realization of the OS in experiments.

- The number of beads in Ξ should be as small as possible: This goal is motivated from minimizing the number of tiles in an aTAM, which also helps realization of the OS in experiments.
- The final conformation should fill as many points in $f(\mathbb{P}_0)$ as possible: We use *rigidity* to refer to the lower bound of the ratio of the number of filled points to the scale.

The basic idea of the GEOS is to design small OSs for all possible pairs of unit vectors in Λ_0. Namely, if we have a shape filling curve for $\mathbb{P}_0$ in Λ_0, the curve can be represented as a sequence of unit vectors. For each point, we have an in-vector and an out-vector that represent the curve. For each pair of vectors, we design a partial OS—which we call a *hinge*—that fills adjacent unit shapes in Λ_t. We propose design guidelines that are helpful in constructing a GEOS. Although there is no need to follow all of the guidelines, following each guideline provides a necessary condition for better features described above.

1. Unit shapes should be identical. Moreover, unit shapes considering core points should have reflection and rotational symmetry. Note that the number of beads we use depends on the number of possible pairs of adjacent unit shapes. Identical and symmetric unit shapes greatly reduce the number of possible cases, as shown in Fig. 6. The unit shape in (a) has partial rotational symmetry on the triangular lattice, and there are two different types of distinct unit vectors that we should consider (Namely, there are two distinct pairs of adjacent unit shapes.). Thus, we need to design 10 different hinges. On the other hand, the unit shape in (b) has full rotational symmetry on the triangular lattice, and all pairs of adjacent unit shapes are identical. Thus, we only need to design 5 different hinges.

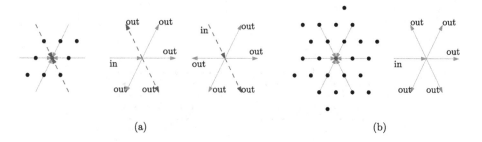

(a)   (b)

Fig. 6. Two possible unit shapes. We assume that Λ_0 is triangular.

2. We categorize beads into two categories: core beads and hinge beads. *Core beads* form a partial conformation (which we call a *core*) that covers the core point, and we use different *hinge beads* for different hinges to connect cores. We use distinct core for each pair $(\mathbb{U}(p), \overrightarrow{a})$ of an unit shape and an unit vector, which we call an *unit*. We establish two guideline for the core.

(a) Cores for different unit vectors should be rotationally symmetric. Like the guideline for the symmetry of unit shapes, this condition greatly reduces the number of hinges.

(b) For each point covered by the core, all neighbors of the point should be in the unit shape. Namely, core beads are not revealed on the surface of the unit shape, which prevents unintended interactions between core beads and hinge beads from another unit shape. Figure 7 shows two example cores, where only the example (a) follows the guideline.

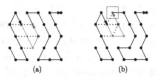

Fig. 7. Two possible cores, colored by red lines. While the core in (a) follows the guideline, the core in (b) does not, and reveals the purple core bead, which may cause unintended interactions with hinge beads from another unit shape. (Color figure online)

3. For each unit, we construct the core and the *context*—which points in the unit shape are filled before the core stabilizes. Namely, we divide $\mathbb{U}(p)$ except points occupied by core beads by two sets: preoccupied points $\mathbb{X}(p)$ and unoccupied points $\mathbb{O}(p)$. We have one more guideline for the context: For each possible pair $((\mathbb{U}(p_1), \vec{a_1}), (\mathbb{U}(p_2), \vec{a_2}))$ of adjacent units where $\vec{p_1} + \vec{a_2} = \vec{p_2}$, there should be a Hamiltonian path from the core of the first unit to the core of the second unit that covers $\mathbb{O}(p_1) \cup \mathbb{X}(p_2)$. This guideline ensures that the final conformation fills the maximum number of points in $f(\mathbb{P}_0)$. Figure 8 shows two example contexts, where only the example (a) follows the guideline.

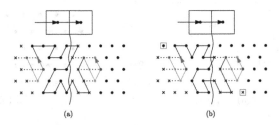

Fig. 8. Two possible contexts for units with the unit vector directing right. In each unit, preoccupied points are denoted by crosses. While the context in (a) allows maximum number of filled points, the context in (b) allows some points (in red boxes) that cannot be covered by the hinge. (Color figure online)

4. For each possible pair of adjacent units, we design a hinge that fits into the contexts. We establish one guideline for the hinge: Hinge beads interact only with hinge beads within the same hinge, or core beads. Namely, hinge beads in different types of hinges do not interact with each other. This guideline prevents unintended interactions between different types of hinges, and we only need to check interactions with the adjacent, same type of the hinge in the validation process. Figure 9 shows two example hinges, where only the example (a) follows the guideline.

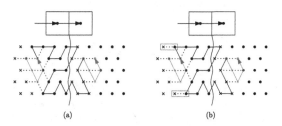

Fig. 9. Two possible hinges for the same pair of adjacent units. While the hinge in (a) has no interaction between current hinge beads and beads in preoccupied points, the hinge in (b) have some (in red boxes), which may cause unintended interaction when the neighboring units are filled with hinge beads in preoccupied points. (Color figure online)

Table 1. Summary of strengths of four guidelines on desirable features of GEOS.

Guidelines	Small $|\Sigma|$	High rigidity	Avoiding unintended interactions
(i)	✓		
(ii)(a)	✓		
(ii)(b)			✓
(iii)		✓	
(iv)			✓

We summarize the strengths of four guidelines on desirable features of GEOS in Table 1. Following the proposed design guidelines, we design two GEOSs in the following section.

4   Two GEOS Designs

4.1   A GEOS Oriented from a Triangular Lattice

In the first GEOS that we call $\Xi_\triangle$, we set Λ_0 as a triangular lattice. Note that we use a shape filling curve to encode the given geometric structure in the triangular lattice, and not all connected triangular grid graph is Hamiltonian. Thus, in general we assume that a shape filling curve instead of a geometric shape on the lattice is given as an input. However, when Λ_0 is a triangular lattice, we can construct a Hamiltonian path in return for tripling the scale. In the mapping of $\mathbb{P}_0$ to $\mathbb{U}(\mathbb{P}_0)$, we group and map three unit shapes and core points for one point in $\mathbb{P}_0$ to use the algorithm proposed by Gordon et al. [9], who proved that there exists a polynomial algorithm to find a Hamiltonian path in a connected, locally connected triangular grid graph. We can successfully make the grid graph of $\mathbb{U}(\mathbb{P}_0)$ locally connected by mapping multiple core points and adding additional filling points to $\mathbb{U}(\mathbb{P}_0)$ as shown in Fig. 10.

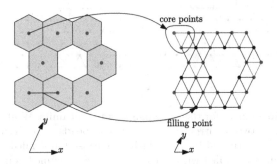

Fig. 10. Construction of a locally connected grid graph from $\mathbb{P}_0$. We map three core points from a point in $\mathbb{P}_0$. In addition, we add a filling point between two sets of core points for each edge in the grid graph of $\mathbb{P}_0$. The resulting grid graph is always locally connected.

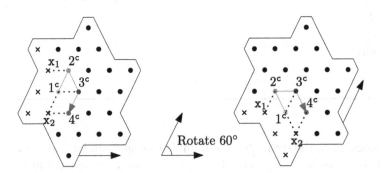

Fig. 11. Two of six units including cores. Cores are represented with colored beads, dotted lines and red arrowed lines. Crosses represent preoccupied points. All units and cores are rotationally symmetric according to unit vectors. (Color figure online)

Formally, the set $\mathbb{P}_0$ of points on the lattice Λ_0 is encoded to the set $\mathbb{C}_t$ of core points on the triangular lattice Λ_t as follows:

- For each point $(x, y) \in \mathbb{P}_0$, we add three points $(2x, 2y), (2x - 1, 2y + 1), (2x, 2y + 1)$ to $\mathbb{C}_t$.
- If two points $(x, y), (x + 1, y)$ are in $\mathbb{P}_0$, we add $(2x + 1, 2y)$ to $\mathbb{C}_t$.
- If two points $(x, y), (x, y + 1)$ are in $\mathbb{P}_0$, we add $(2x - 1, 2y + 2)$ to $\mathbb{C}_t$.
- If two points $(x, y), (x - 1, y + 1)$ are in $\mathbb{P}_0$, we add $(2x + 1, 2y + 2)$ to $\mathbb{C}_t$.

Note that the grid graph of $\mathbb{C}_t$ is always locally connected.

In $\Xi_\triangle$, we use one unit shape and six unit vectors (from Λ_0). A part of the units including cores is shown in Fig. 11. We use integers to represent bead types and superscripts to represent different sets of bead types. We observe that all units and cores are rotationally symmetric according to unit vectors, following design guidelines (i) and (ii)(a). Thus, we need to consider only 5 hinges. We can observe that cores are not revealed on the surface of unit shapes, following design guideline (ii)(b). Note that we use distinct sets of beads for different hinges, and there is no interaction between hinge beads from different hinges, following design guideline (iv). Also note that for each hinge, there exists one point that cannot be filled. Thus, the rigidity of this OS is 24/25.

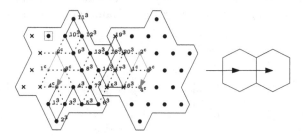

Fig. 12. An illustration of the hinge h_1. Core beads are represented with superscript c, and hinge beads are represented with superscript 1.

Figure 12 shows one of the five hinges, representing that the shape filling curve proceeds straight. We use 20 distinct hinge beads for this hinge. The delay is 4, and each bead in the hinge is stabilized by at least 4 interactions. Note that once all hinges are given, it is straightforward to design sequences of beads for borderlines of the shape filling curve, where the starting sequence becomes a seed and the ending sequence becomes a suffix of the primary structure.

An example of $\Xi_\triangle$ is shown in Fig. 13. Once the set $\mathbb{P}$ of points is given as in (a), we construct the set of core points as in (b) and find a Hamiltonian path for the grid graph. Then we connect hinges according to the triples of consecutive points in the path as in (c). Red lines represent core beads.

4.2   A GEOS Oriented from a Square Lattice

Note that the rigidity of $\Xi_\triangle$ is not 1. We design the second GEOS called $\Xi_\square$ that uses Λ_0 as a square lattice, whose rigidity is 1. Since not all connected grid

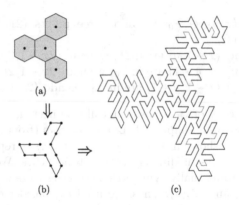

Fig. 13. An example of $\varXi_\triangle$

graph of $\varLambda_0$ is Hamiltonian, we first transform a square lattice into an affine triangular lattice, as in Fig. 14(b). Then, we can transform the grid graph into a locally connected grid graph by quadrupling the scale as in Fig. 14(c). From the locally connected grid graph, we can extract a Hamiltonian path as in Fig. 14(d).

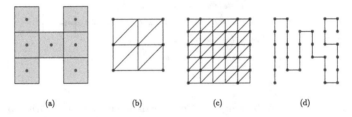

Fig. 14. (a) The input shape (b) the input shape on the affine triangular lattice (c) construction of a locally connected graph (d) a retrieved Hamiltonian path

We use two unit shapes and four unit vectors (from $\varSigma_0$). Figure 15 shows the mapping of core points and unit shapes from $\varLambda_0$. Two types α, β of unit shapes of size 25 appear in Fig. 15, where one is rotationally symmetric to the other.

Units including cores are shown in Fig. 16. We refer to a hinge as a pair of an unit shape type and an unit vector, i.e. (α, up). Considering symmetry of units, we need to design 11 hinges. The delay of the system is 5, and each bead in the hinge is stabilized by at least 5 interactions. We can observe the following properties of the design of hinges.

- All neighbors of the core points are in the unit shape, following design guideline (ii)(b).
- Hinge beads in different types of hinges do not interact with each other, following design guideline (iv).

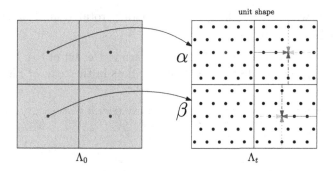

Fig. 15. The mapping of core points and unit shapes from Λ_0. Arrows on the right unit shapes represent unit vectors

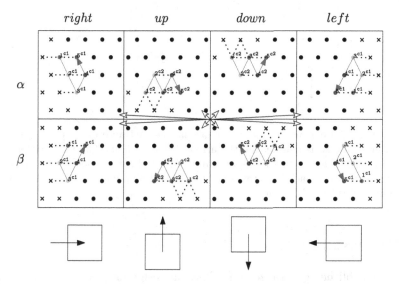

Fig. 16. Eight units including cores. Cores are represented with colored beads, dotted lines and red arrowed lines. Crosses represent preoccupied points. Rotationally symmetric units are paired by white arrows. (Color figure online)

- In all hinges that connect two points p_1 and p_2, the grid graph of $\mathbb{O}(p_1) \cup \mathbb{X}(p_2)$ is Hamiltonian, following design guideline (iii). Moreover, every hinge fills $\mathbb{O}(p_1) \cup \mathbb{X}(p_2)$. Thus, $\Xi_\square$ covers all points in $f(\mathbb{P}_0)$.
- There are hinges covering at least 2 pairs of units due to the rotational symmetry of units.
- When the filling curve goes upward, we consider only one hinge due to the reflection symmetry of cores in units (α, up) and (β, up).
- In the hinge connecting two units (β, up) and $(\beta, right)$, the core for $(\beta, right)$ is horizontally rotated. From the point in the shape filling curve that maps

to the unit, we regard all hinges as horizontally rotated until we use another hinge for (β, up) and $(\beta, right)$.

An example of $\mathbb{P}_0$ in a square lattice is shown in the left of Fig. 17. Given the set of points $\mathbb{P}_0$, the GEOS fills points in $f(\mathbb{P}_0)$ as in the right of Fig. 17.

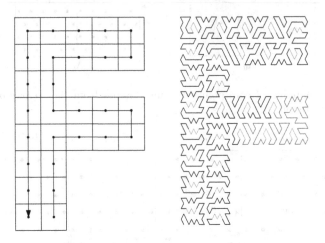

Fig. 17. (Left) An example of $\mathbb{P}_0$ in a square lattice. A Hamiltonian path that covers the grid graph of $\mathbb{P}_0$ is denoted by the arrowed line. (Right) The final conformation that fills $f(\mathbb{P}_0)$. The conformation starts and ends at the downmost unit shapes. Red lines represent cores, black lines represent hinges and blue lines represent horizontally rotated hinges. (Color figure online)

5   Conclusions

We have established generalized guidelines on designing a GEOS, and proposed two GEOSs summarized in Fig. 18. Although we can construct an arbitrary shape out of a GEOS, there are optimization problems. In general, reducing the scale also reduces the number of hinge beads we use, but also makes it harder to design symmetric unit shapes for the tessellation and may increase the number of units to consider. Reducing the scale may also increase the possibility of unintended interaction between different hinges. Thus, it is a challenging question to find a GEOS that uses the minimum number of bead types while achieving maximum rigidity.

GEOS	Scale	Rigidity	# of Hinges	# of Bead Types
$\Xi_\triangle$	25 (75 when group core points)	24/25	5	104
$\Xi_\square$	25 (100 when group core points)	1	11	223

Fig. 18. Summary of two proposed GEOSs

Our two GEOS designs have approached the objective by setting up four design guidelines. It turns out that the first $\Xi_\triangle$ cannot achieve rigidity 1, while the second $\Xi_\square$ achieves rigidity 1 using more bead types. Our future work includes finding bead complexity–the lower bound of the number of beads–for a given lattice Λ_0 and optimization of GEOSs.

Acknowledgements. This work has been supported in part by the NIH grant R01 GM109459.

References

1. Adleman, L., Cheng, Q., Goel, A., Huang, M.-D., Wasserman, H.: Linear self-assemblies: equilibria, entropy, and convergence rates. In: Proceedings of the 6th International Conference on Difference Equations and Applications, pp. 51–60 (2001)
2. Bhuvana, T., Smith, K.C., Fisher, T.S., Kulkarni, G.U.: Self-assembled CNT circuits with ohmic contacts using Pd hexadecanethiolate as in situ solder. Nanoscale **1**(2), 271–275 (2009)
3. Demaine, E.D., et al.: Know when to fold 'em: self-assembly of shapes by folding in oritatami. In: Doty, D., Dietz, H. (eds.): DNA 2018. LNCS, vol. 11145, pp. 19–36. Springer, Cham (2018)
4. Doty, D., Lutz, J.H., Patitz, M.J., Schweller, R.T., Summers, S.M., Woods, D.: The tile assembly model is intrinsically universal. In: Proceedings of the IEEE 53rd Annual Symposium on Foundations of Computer Science, pp. 302–310 (2012)
5. Eichen, Y., Braun, E., Sivan, U., Ben-Yoseph, G.: Self-assembly of nanoelectronic components and circuits using biological templates. Acta Polym. **49**(10–11), 663–670 (1998)
6. Geary, C., Meunier, P., Schabanel, N., Seki, S.: Efficient universal computation by greedy molecular folding. CoRR, abs/1508.00510 (2015)
7. Geary, C., Meunier, P., Schabanel, N., Seki, S.: Programming biomolecules that fold greedily during transcription. In: Proceedings of the 41st International Symposium on Mathematical Foundations of Computer Science, pp. 43:1–43:14 (2016)
8. Geary, C., Rothemund, P.W.K., Andersen, E.S.: A single-stranded architecture for cotranscriptional folding of RNA nanostructures. Science **345**, 799–804 (2014)
9. Gordon, V.S., Orlovich, Y.L., Werner, F.: Hamiltonian properties of triangular grid graphs. Discret. Math. **308**(24), 6166–6188 (2008)
10. Han, Y.-S., Kim, H.: Ruleset optimization on isomorphic oritatami systems. In: Brijder, R., Qian, L. (eds.) DNA 2017. LNCS, vol. 10467, pp. 33–45. Springer, Cham (2017). https://doi.org/10.1007/978-3-319-66799-7_3
11. Han, Y., Kim, H., Ota, M., Seki, S.: Nondeterministic seedless oritatami systems and hardness of testing their equivalence. Nat. Comput. **17**(1), 67–79 (2018)
12. Han, Y.-S., Kim, H., Rogers, T.A., Seki, S.: Self-attraction removal from oritatami systems. In: Pighizzini, G., Câmpeanu, C. (eds.) DCFS 2017. LNCS, vol. 10316, pp. 164–176. Springer, Cham (2017). https://doi.org/10.1007/978-3-319-60252-3_13
13. Li, J., Fan, C., Pei, H., Shi, J., Huang, Q.: Smart drug delivery nanocarriers with self-assembled DNA nanostructures. Adv. Mater. **25**(32), 4386–4396 (2013)
14. Masuda, Y., Seki, S., Ubukata, Y.: Towards the algorithmic molecular self-assembly of fractals by cotranscriptional folding. In: Câmpeanu, C. (ed.) CIAA 2018. LNCS, vol. 10977, pp. 261–273. Springer, Cham (2018). https://doi.org/10.1007/978-3-319-94812-6_22

15. Ota, M., Seki, S.: Rule set design problems for oritatami systems. Theor. Comput. Sci. **671**, 26–35 (2017)
16. Pistol, C., Lebeck, A.R., Dwyer, C.: Design automation for DNA self-assembled nanostructures. In: Proceedings of the 43rd ACM/IEEE Design Automation Conference, pp. 919–924 (2006)
17. Rogers, T.A., Seki, S.: Oritatami system; a survey and the impossibility of simple simulation at small delays. Fundamenta Informaticae **154**(1–4), 359–372 (2017)
18. Santis, E.D., Ryadnov, M.G.: Self-assembling peptide motifs for nanostructure design and applications. Amino Acids Peptides Proteins **40**, 199–238 (2016)
19. Soloveichik, D., Winfree, E.: Complexity of self-assembled shapes. SIAM J. Comput. **36**(6), 1544–1569 (2007)
20. Verma, G., Hassan, P.A.: Self assembled materials: design strategies and drug delivery perspectives. Phys. Chem. Chem. Phys. **15**(40), 17016–17028 (2013)
21. Whitesides, G.M., Boncheva, M.: Beyond molecules: self-assembly of mesoscopic and macroscopic components. Proc. Natl. Acad. Sci. U.S.A. **99**(8), 4769–4774 (2002)
22. Winfree, E.: Algorithmic self-assembly of DNA. Ph.D. thesis, California Institute of Technology (1998)

A Reaction Network Scheme Which Implements the EM Algorithm

Muppirala Viswa Virinchi, Abhishek Behera, and Manoj Gopalkrishnan$^{(\boxtimes)}$

India Institute of Technology Bombay, Mumbai, India
axlevisu@gmail.com, abhishek.enlightened@gmail.com,
manoj.gopalkrishnan@gmail.com

Abstract. A detailed algorithmic explanation is required for how a network of chemical reactions can generate the sophisticated behavior displayed by living cells. Though several previous works have shown that reaction networks are computationally universal and can in principle implement any algorithm, there is scope for constructions that map well onto biological reality, make efficient use of the computational potential of the native dynamics of reaction networks, and make contact with statistical mechanics. We describe a new reaction network scheme for solving a large class of statistical problems. Specifically we show how reaction networks can implement information projection, and consequently a generalized Expectation-Maximization algorithm, to solve maximum likelihood estimation problems in partially-observed exponential families on categorical data. Our scheme can be thought of as an algorithmic interpretation of E. T. Jaynes's vision of statistical mechanics as statistical inference.

1 Introduction

Many statistical problems involve fitting an exponential family of probability distributions to some data [2]. Fisher's method of Maximum Likelihood gives a prescription for the best fit: pick that parameter θ that maximizes the likelihood $\Pr[x \mid \theta]$ of generating the data x. In problems of practical interest, the data x is rarely available in full. It is more common to want to maximize a likelihood $\Pr[s \mid \theta]$ where $s = Sx$ is a low-dimensional linear projection of the data x.[1] The EM algorithm [14] is one way to solve this class of problems. We describe a reaction network scheme that implements a geometric version of the EM algorithm [1] for exponential families, and linear projections. To fix ideas, consider this example.

---

[1] This situation can arise because only a linear projection is observable. It can also happen because we require a rich family of probability distributions on the space of s points, but don't want to give away the nice properties of exponential families. We can achieve both by imagining that our observation s comes from projection from a data vector x living in a higher-dimensional space, and then employ an exponential family of probability distributions on this higher-dimensional space.

© Springer Nature Switzerland AG 2018
D. Doty and H. Dietz (Eds.): DNA 2018, LNCS 11145, pp. 189–207, 2018.
https://doi.org/10.1007/978-3-030-00030-1_12

Example 1. Consider a three-sided die with the three sides labeled X_1, X_2, X_3 respectively. Suppose the probabilities of the three outcomes depend on two hidden parameters θ_1, θ_2 according to $\Pr[X_1 \mid \theta_1, \theta_2] \propto \theta_1^2$, $\Pr[X_2 \mid \theta_1, \theta_2] \propto \theta_1\theta_2$, $\Pr[X_3 \mid \theta_1, \theta_2] \propto \theta_2^2$. Further suppose that the die is rolled many times by a referee who records the frequences n_1, n_2, n_3 of the three outcomes. The outcomes are not visible directly to us. The referee tells us some linear combinations of n_1, n_2, n_3, and this is the only information available to us. For example, suppose the referee tells us $s_1 = n_1 + n_2 + n_3$, the total number of die rolls, and also $s_2 = n_1 + n_2$, the total number of times the die outcome was either X_1 or X_2. We may be interested in the maximum likelihood estimator (MLE)

$$\theta^* = \arg \sup_{\substack{\theta: \\ x_1+x_2+x_3=s_1 \\ x_1+x_2=s_2}} \Pr[x_1, x_2, x_3 \mid \theta_1, \theta_2].$$

Let $y(\theta_1, \theta_2) := (\theta_1^2, \theta_1\theta_2, \theta_2^2)$. The EM algorithm finds a local minimum of $D((x_1, x_2, x_3)\|y(\theta_1, \theta_2)) := x_1 \log(x_1/\theta_1^2) - x_1 + \theta_1^2 + x_2 \log(x_2/\theta_1\theta_2) - x_2 + \theta_1\theta_2 + x_3 \log(x_3/\theta_2^2) - x_3 + \theta_2^2$ where $x_1 + x_2 + x_3 = s_1$, $x_1 + x_2 = s_2$, and $x_1, x_2, x_3, \theta_1, \theta_2 > 0$. We minimize D because its global minimum is related to the maximum likelihood estimator. The EM algorithm proceeds by alternately minimizing D over the space of points x that are consistent with the observations while keeping θ fixed (called E-projection), then minimizing D with respect to θ keeping x fixed (called M-projection), and so on iteratively. It halts when we encounter a pair (x^*, θ^*) which is a fixed point of the iteration.

Our main contribution in this paper is to describe and analyze a novel reaction network scheme that implements the EM algorithm, and computes the MLE from partial observations. This builds on our previous works [19] where we describe a reaction network scheme that performs the M-projection and computes the MLE from full observations, and [40] where we describe a reaction network scheme that performs the E-projection and computes full observations from partial observations. Simply combining the schemes in [19,40] does not yield a correct scheme for computing MLE from partial observations. Our chief innovation is to come up with a new M-projection scheme which combines well with the E-projection scheme from [40], allowing the joint system to perform a generalized EM algorithm in the sense of [28]. This new M-projection scheme requires a proper subset of the reactions described in [19], and the proof of its correctness is novel and unexpected.

Below is a reaction network obtained by our scheme for the die example. The dynamics of this network implements a generalized EM algorithm and finds a local minimum of D.

$$X_1 \xrightarrow{k_1} X_1 + 2\theta_1 \quad 2\theta_1 \xrightarrow{k_2} 0 \quad\quad X_2 \xrightarrow{k_3} X_2 + \theta_1 + \theta_2 \quad \theta_1 + \theta_2 \xrightarrow{k_4} 0$$

$$X_3 \xrightarrow{k_5} X_3 + 2\theta_2 \quad 2\theta_2 \xrightarrow{k_6} 0 \quad X_1 + \theta_2 \xrightarrow{k_7} X_2 + \theta_2 \quad\quad X_2 + \theta_1 \xrightarrow{k_8} X_1 + \theta_1$$

where the rates are chosen such that $\frac{k_1}{k_2} = \frac{k_3}{k_4} = \frac{k_5}{k_6}$ and $k_7 = k_8$. If $(x(t), \theta(t)) := (x_1(t), x_2(t), x_3(t), \theta_1(t), \theta_2(t))$ are solutions to the mass-action ODEs for this system then we show in Theorem 6 that $\frac{dD(x(t)\|y(\theta(t)))}{dt} \leq 0$ for all $t \geq 0$. Further if the initial concentrations are chosen so that $\frac{x_1(0)+x_2(0)}{x_1(0)+x_2(0)+x_3(0)} = \frac{s_1}{s_2}$ then $\lim_{t\to\infty} \theta(t)$ is a critical point of D. In particular, if the optimization succeeds in finding the global minimum, then this limit will be the MLE θ^*.

Notice that the first six reactions change the numbers of the θ_1, θ_2 species while the X_1, X_2, X_3 species do not change in number. The last two reactions change the numbers of the X_1, X_2, X_3 species while the species θ_1, θ_2 do not change in number. This is a general feature of our reaction scheme. There are two subnetworks, one which changes only the θ species and in which the X species appear only catalytically, and the other which changes only the X species and in which the θ species appear only catalytically. The first subnetwork computes an **M-Projection**, and the second computes an **E-Projection** (Definition 1).

The last two reactions in our example compute an E-Projection, i.e., if $x(t)$ is a solution trajectory to the last two reactions when θ_1, θ_2 are held fixed, then $\frac{dD(x(t)\|y(\theta))}{dt} \leq 0$. We have described this scheme to compute the E-Projection previously in [40]. Subsection 3.1 summarizes this previous work, showing that the subreaction network of our scheme that changes only the X species always has this property, and will find a global minimum over all x compatible with the observations for the function $D(x\|y(\theta))$ when keeping θ fixed (Theorem 4).

Theorem 4 can be thought of as exploiting a formal similarity between free energy in physics and relative entropy in information theory. We encode the dynamics of the system so that its free energy corresponds to the function that we want to minimize, while the system explores the same space as allowed by the optimization constraints. In this way, we design our chemical system to solve the desired optimization problem.

Though an M-projection scheme was described before in [19], it is not satisfactory for our current purposes since combining it with the E-projection scheme does not yield a correct EM algorithm. So we have come up with a new M-projection scheme in this paper, which incidentally also employs fewer reactions. The first six reactions in our example compute the M-Projection in this new way, i.e., if $\theta(t) = (\theta_1(t), \theta_2(t))$ is a solution trajectory to the first six reactions when x_1, x_2, x_3 are held fixed, then $\frac{dD(x\|y(\theta(t)))}{dt} \leq 0$. The dynamics of this system will find a global minimum for $D(x\|y(\theta))$ over all θ while keeping x fixed. We present the new M-projection scheme in Subsect. 3.2, along with a completely novel proof of correctness (Theorem 5).

Functions of the form $D(x(t)\|x'(t))$ are known to be Lyapunov functions for Markov chains when $x(t)$ and $x'(t)$ are solutions to the Markov chain's Master equation [39]. For nonlinear reaction networks, in contrast, prior to this work, only functions of the form $D(x(t)\|q)$ have been known to be Lyapunov functions, where q is a point of detailed balance for the reaction network. Our M-projection systems are the first class of examples of nonlinear reaction networks with Lyapunov functions of the form $D(x\|x'(t))$ with time dependence on the second argument. The discovery of such a class of reaction networks and Lyapunov functions is a key and novel contribution in this paper.

When the E-Projection reaction network and the new M-Projection reaction network evolve simultaneously, we get a continuous-time generalized EM algorithm, where both the x coordinates and the θ coordinates are being updated continuously. We show in Subsect. 3.3 that if $(x(t), \theta(t))$ is a solution trajectory to the reaction network then $\frac{dD(x(t)\|y(\theta(t)))}{dt} \leq 0$, so that for a generic initial point the system eventually settles into a local minimum $(\hat{x}, \hat{\theta})$ of $D(x\|y(\theta))$ with x constrained to values consistent with the observations.

2   Preliminaries

Notation: For $u = (u_1, u_2, \ldots, u_n) \in \mathbb{R}^n$, define $e^u := (e^{u_1}, e^{u_2}, \ldots, e^{u_n}) \in \mathbb{R}^n_{>0}$. For $x = (x_1, x_2, \ldots, x_n) \in \mathbb{R}^n_{>0}$, define $\log x := (\log x_1, \log x_2, \ldots, \log x_n)$. Define $x^u = \prod_{i=1}^n x_i^{u_i}$. For $S \subseteq \mathbb{R}^n$ and $\beta \in \mathbb{R}^n$, define $\beta + S := \{\beta + x \mid x \in S\}$ and $e^S := \{e^x \mid x \in S\} \subseteq \mathbb{R}^n_{>0}$. For a matrix $(a_{ij})_{m \times n}$, its i'th row will be denoted by $a_{i.}$ and its j'th column will be denoted by $a_{.j}$.

Fix a countable set I. The **extended relative entropy** $D : \mathbb{R}^I_{\geq 0} \times \mathbb{R}^I_{\geq 0} \to [-\infty, \infty]$ is $D(x\|y) := \sum_{i \in I} x_i \log \left(\frac{x_i}{y_i} \right) - x_i + y_i$ with the convention $0 \log 0 = 0$ and $x \log 0 = -\infty$ when $x \neq 0$.

Note 1. $D(x\|y) = \sum_{i \in I} y_i h(x_i/y_i)$ where $h(x) = x \log x - x + 1$. Since $h(x)$ is nonnegative for all $x \in \mathbb{R}_{\geq 0}$, it follows that $D(x\|y) \geq 0$ with equality iff $x = y$.

Note 2. If $\sum_{i \in I} x_i = \sum_{i \in I} y_i$, in particular if x, y are probability distributions on I, then $D(x\|y) = \sum_{i \in I} x_i \log \left(\frac{x_i}{y_i} \right)$.

Note 3. If x, y are Poisson distributions, i.e., $x_i = e^{-\lambda} \frac{\lambda^i}{i!}$ and $y_i = e^{-\mu} \frac{\mu^i}{i!}$ for $i \in \mathbb{Z}_{\geq 0}$ then $\sum_{i \in \mathbb{Z}_{\geq 0}} x_i \log \frac{x_i}{y_i} = D(\lambda\|\mu) = \lambda \log \frac{\lambda}{\mu} - \lambda + \mu$. More generally, the relative entropy between two distributions, each of which is a product of Poisson distributions, equals the extended relative entropy between their rate vectors.

We state the Pythagorean Theorem of Information Geometry [1, Theorem 1.2] for our special case, and give the short proof for completeness.

Theorem 1 (Pythagorean Theorem). *For all $P, Q, R \in \mathbb{R}^n_{>0}$, we have $(P - Q) \cdot (\log Q - \log R) = 0$ iff $D(P\|Q) + D(Q\|R) = D(P\|R)$.*

Proof. $D(P\|Q) + D(Q\|R) - D(P\|R) = \sum_{i=1}^n P_i \log \frac{P_i}{Q_i} - P_i + Q_i + Q_i \log \frac{Q_i}{R_i} - Q_i + R_i - P_i \log \frac{P_i}{R_i} + P_i - R_i = \sum_{i=1}^n (P_i - Q_i)(\log R_i - \log Q_i)$.

Definition 1. *An Exponential Projection or **E-Projection** [1] (also called Information Projection or I-Projection [13]) of a point $y \in \mathbb{R}^n_{\geq 0}$ to a set $X \subset \mathbb{R}^n_{\geq 0}$ is a point $x^* = \arg\min_{x \in X} D(x\|y)$. A Mixture Projection or **M-Projection** (or reverse I-projection) of a point $x \in \mathbb{R}^n_{\geq 0}$ to a set $Y \subseteq \mathbb{R}^n_{>0}$ is a point $y^* = \arg\min_{y \in Y} D(x\|y)$.*

If X is convex then the E-Projection x^* is unique [12]. If Y is log-convex (i.e., $\log Y$ is convex) then the M-Projection y^* is unique [12]. We will be interested in E-Projections when X is an affine subspace (and hence convex), and M-projections when Y is an exponential family (and hence log-convex). Various problems in probability and statistics can be reduced to computing such projections [12]. Amari [1] has shown that an alternation of these two projections corresponds to the usual EM algorithm [14], and has further argued that various other algorithms in Machine Learning such as k-means clustering, belief propagation, boosting, etc. can be understood as EM.

Birch's theorem is a well-known theorem in the statistics and reaction networks communities [7,32, Theorem 1.10]. Below we state an extension of Birch's theorem which applies to the extended KL-divergence function, and show the connection to Information Projection. Our contribution is to present the results in a form that brings out the geometry of the situation.

Theorem 2 (Birch's theorem and Information Projection). *Fix a positive integer n. Let $V \subseteq \mathbb{R}^n$ be an affine subspace and let $V^{\perp} = \{w \mid v \cdot w = 0 \text{ for all } v \in V\}$ be the orthogonal complement of V in $\mathbb{R}^n$. Then*

1. *For all $\alpha \in \mathbb{R}^n_{>0}$, the intersection of the polytope $(\alpha + V^{\perp}) \cap \mathbb{R}^n_{\geq 0}$ with the hypersurface e^V consists of precisely one point α^* called the Birch point of α relative to V.*
2. *For every $\beta \in e^V$, the E-Projection of β to the polytope $(\alpha + V^{\perp}) \cap \mathbb{R}^n_{\geq 0}$ is α^*. In particular, this E-Projection is unique.*
3. *The M-projection of α to e^V is α^*. In particular, this M-projection is unique.*

See Appendix A for the proof.

2.1 Reaction Network Theory

We recall some concepts from reaction network theory [3,16–18,22,40].

Fix a finite set S of species. An S-reaction, or simply a **reaction** when S is understood from context, is a formal chemical equation

$$\sum_{X \in S} y_X X \to \sum_{X \in S} y'_X X$$

where the numbers $y_X, y'_X \in \mathbb{Z}_{\geq 0}$ are the **stoichiometric coefficients** of species X on the **reactant** side and **product** side respectively. We write this reaction more pithily as $y \to y'$ where $y, y' \in \mathbb{Z}^S_{\geq 0}$. A **reaction network** is a pair (S, R) where R is a finite set of S-reactions. It is **reversible** iff $y \to y' \in R$ implies $y' \to y \in R$.

Fix $n, n' \in \mathbb{Z}^S_{\geq 0}$. We say that $n \mapsto_R n'$ iff there exists a reaction $y \to y' \in R$ with $n - y \in \mathbb{Z}^S_{\geq 0}$ and $n' = n + y' - y$. The **reachability** relation $n \Rightarrow_R n'$ is the transitive and reflexive closure of $\mapsto_R$. The **forward reachability class** of $n_0 \in \mathbb{Z}^S_{\geq 0}$ is the set $\text{post}(n_0) = \{n \mid n_0 \Rightarrow_R n\}$. The **stoichiometric subspace** H_R is the real span of the vectors $\{y' - y \mid y \to y' \in R\}$. The **conservation**

class containing $x_0 \in \mathbb{R}^S_{\geq 0}$ is the set $C(x_0) = (x_0 + H_R) \cap \mathbb{R}^S_{\geq 0}$. A reaction network (S, R) is **weakly reversible** iff for every reaction $y \rightarrow y' \in R$, we have $y' \Rightarrow_R y$.

Fix a weakly reversible reaction network (S, R). The **associated ideal** $I_{(S,R)} \subseteq \mathbb{C}[S]$ is the ideal generated by the binomials $\{x^y - x^{y'} \mid y \rightarrow y' \in R\}$ where x denotes the formal tuple of elements in S. A reaction network is **prime** iff its associated ideal is a prime ideal, i.e., for all $f, g \in \mathbb{C}[S]$, if $fg \in I$ then either $f \in I$ or $g \in I$.

Example 2. The reaction network given by the reactions $2X \rightleftharpoons 2Y$ is not prime, as the associated ideal I_1 is generated by the binomial $x^2 - y^2 = (x+y)(x-y) \in I_1$ but $(x + y) \notin I_1$ and $(x - y) \notin I_1$. The reaction network given by the reactions $2X \rightleftharpoons Y$ is prime since the associated ideal I_2 is generated by the irreducible binomial $x^2 - y$, and if $fg \in I_2$ then either $x^2 - y$ divides f or $x^2 - y$ divides g, that is either $f \in I_2$ or $g \in I_2$.

A **reaction system** is a triple (S, R, k) where (S, R) is a reaction network and $k : R \rightarrow \mathbb{R}_{>0}$ is called the **rate function**. We denote $k(y \rightarrow y')$ by $k_{y \rightarrow y'}$. It is **detailed balanced** iff it is reversible and there exists a point $q \in \mathbb{R}^S_{>0}$ such that $k_{y \rightarrow y'} q^y = k_{y' \rightarrow y} q^{y'}$ for every reaction $y \rightarrow y' \in R$. A point $q \in \mathbb{R}^S_{>0}$ that satisfies the above condition is called a **point of detailed balance**.

Note 4. The set $\{\log q \mid q$ is a point of detailed balance for $(S, R, k)\}$ is the simultaneous solution set to the affine system of equations $(y - y') \cdot \log q = \log \frac{k_{y' \rightarrow y}}{k_{y \rightarrow y'}}$ for all $y \rightarrow y' \in R$, and hence constitutes an affine space.

3   Main

Definition 2. *Let S be a finite set, and let $\mathcal{B} = \{b_1, b_2, \ldots, b_r\} \subseteq \mathbb{Z}^S$ be a finite set of integer vectors. For $l = 1$ to r, let $b_l^+, b_l^- \in \mathbb{Z}^S_{\geq 0}$ be the positive part and negative part of b_l, i.e.,*

$$b_{lj}^+ = \begin{cases} b_{lj} \text{ if } b_{lj} > 0 \\ 0 \text{ otherwise} \end{cases} \quad \text{and } b_{lj}^- = \begin{cases} -b_{lj} \text{ if } b_{lj} < 0 \\ 0 \text{ otherwise} \end{cases} \quad \text{for all } j \in S.$$

*Then the reaction network $(S, \mathcal{R}_\mathcal{B})$ **generated by** $\mathcal{B}$ is given by the reactions: $b_l^+ \rightleftharpoons b_l^-$ for $l \in \{1, \ldots, r\}$.*

Example 3. If $S = \{X_1, X_2, X_3\}$ and $\mathcal{B} = \{(1, 0, 1), (-2, 1, 1), (1, 1, -3)\}$ then $(S, \mathcal{R}_\mathcal{B})$ is given by: $X_1 + X_3 \rightleftharpoons 0$, $X_2 + X_3 \rightleftharpoons 2X_1$, $X_1 + X_2 \rightleftharpoons 3X_3$.

3.1   Reaction Networks Compute E-Projections

The following theorem shows that points of detailed balance correspond to E-Projections. Further, if a detailed balanced reaction network has no critical siphons then solutions to mass-action kinetics converge to the E-Projections.

We recall the notion of critical siphon [5,18]. A **siphon** in a reaction network (S, R) is a set $T \subseteq S$ of species such that for every reaction $y \to y' \in R$, if there exists $i \in T$ such that $y'_i > 0$ then there exists $j \in T$ such that $y_j > 0$. Equivalently, if all siphon species are absent, then they remain absent in future. A siphon T is **critical** iff there exist $x \in \mathbb{R}^S_{\geq 0}$ and $y \in \mathbb{R}^S_{>0}$ such that $x - y \in H_R$ and $\{i \mid x_i = 0\} = T$.

The significance of critical siphons is that their absence allows easy demonstration of a detailed balanced reaction network version of the Markov Chain Ergodic Theorem, which is known as the Global Attractor Conjecture [20,23]. We take care to construct reaction network schemes that avoid critical siphons, thus ensuring that our reaction network dynamics provably converges to the right answer. It appears that avoiding critical siphons also confers advantages in terms of rate of convergence. We discuss this further in Subsect. 5.1.

Theorem 3. *Fix a detailed balanced reaction system (S, R, k) with point of detailed balance $y \in \mathbb{R}^S_{>0}$. Let $x(t)$ be a solution to the mass-action equations for (S, R, k) with $x(0) \in \mathbb{R}^S_{\geq 0}$. Then*

1. *There exists a unique point of detailed balance $x^* \in (x(0) + H_R) \cap \mathbb{R}^S_{>0}$.*
2. $\frac{dD(x(t)\|y)}{dt} \leq 0$ *with equality iff $x(t)$ is a point of detailed balance.*
3. *If (S, R) has no critical siphons then $\lim_{t \to \infty} x(t) = x^*$.*
4. *The point x^* is the E-Projection of y to the polytope $(x(0) + H_R) \cap \mathbb{R}^S_{\geq 0}$.*

Parts (1), (2), (3) are well-known in the theory of chemical reaction networks. We include the proofs of (1) and (2) for completeness.

Proof. (1) follows from Note 4 and Theorem 2.2. For (2) by explicit calculation note that

$$\frac{dD(x(t)\|y)}{dt} = \sum_{r \rightleftharpoons r' \in R} (k_{r \to r'} x(t)^r - k_{r' \to r} x(t)^{r'}) \log \frac{k_{r' \to r} x(t)^{r'}}{k_{r \to r'} x(t)^r}$$

where each summand is ≤ 0, hence $dD/dt \leq 0$ with equality iff $x(t)$ is a point of detailed balance. (3) follows from [4, Theorem 2]. (4) follows from Theorem 2.2.

We are now going to describe a reaction network scheme to compute the E-Projection of an arbitrary point in $\mathbb{R}^n_{>0}$ to an arbitrary polytope in $\mathbb{R}^n_{\geq 0}$. Significantly our scheme will only create detailed balanced reaction networks without critical siphons, allowing the use of Theorem 3. To show that the reation networks described by this scheme have no critical siphons, we will need a definition and two lemmas which employ concepts from the theory of binomial ideals, and will not be used elsewhere in the paper. A reader who is not particularly concerned about critical siphons can omit these lemmas and jump to Theorem 4.

Fix a positive integer n. A **sublattice** of $\mathbb{Z}^n$ is a subgroup of the additive group $\mathbb{Z}^n$. It is necessarily a free and finitely generated abelian group, and hence isomorphic to an integer lattice. A sublattice $L \subseteq \mathbb{Z}^n$ is **saturated** iff for all $k \in \mathbb{Z} \setminus \{0\}$ and $v \in \mathbb{Z}^n$, if $kv \in L$ then $v \in L$.

Example 4. The sublattice $L_1 = \{(x_1, 3x_2) \mid x_1, x_2 \in \mathbb{Z}\}$ of $\mathbb{Z}^2$ is unsaturated since $(0,3) \in L_1$ but $(0,1) \notin L_1$, whereas $L_2 = \{(x, 3x) \mid x \in \mathbb{Z}\}$ is saturated.

Lemma 1. *Let S be a finite set, and let $\mathcal{B} \subseteq \mathbb{Z}^S$ be a finite set of integer vectors. Then the reaction network $(S, \mathcal{R}_\mathcal{B})$ generated by $\mathcal{B}$ is prime iff the sublattice $L_\mathcal{B} \subseteq \mathbb{Z}^S$ is saturated.*

Proof. This follows from [29, Corollary 2.15], taking for A the matrix whose rows form a basis for the sublattice perpendicular to $L_\mathcal{B}$, so that I_A becomes the associated ideal $I_{(S,R)}$. The assumption of saturation is used in identifying the perpendicular to the perpendicular with the original lattice.

Lemma 2. *A prime weakly-reversible reaction network has no critical siphons.*

Proof. Follows from [18, Theorems 4.1, 5.2].

E-Projection Reaction Network Scheme: Fix a positive integer $n \in \mathbb{Z}_{>0}$. Consider $x_0, y \in \mathbb{R}^n_{\geq 0}$ and an n-column **sensitivity matrix** S of integers. Let $H_{x_0} = \{x \in \mathbb{R}^n_{\geq 0} \mid Sx = Sx_0\}$. To compute the E-Projection $\hat{x}$ of y to H_{x_0}, we first compute a basis $\mathcal{B} = \{b_1, b_2, \ldots, b_r\}$ to the sublattice $(\ker S) \cap \mathbb{Z}^n$. Using this, we describe a reaction system as follows:

1. The set of species is $\mathfrak{X} = \{X_1, X_2, \ldots, X_n\}$,
2. The set of reactions is $R_\mathcal{B}$,
3. The reaction rates are chosen so that y is a point of detailed balance, i.e.,
$$\frac{k_{b_l^- \to b_l^+}}{k_{b_l^+ \to b_l^-}} = y^{b_l} \text{ for } l = 1 \text{ to } r, \text{ where } b_l^-, b_l^+ \text{ are as in Definition 2}$$

We obtain the main theorem of this paper.

Theorem 4. *Let $x(t)$ be a solution to the mass-action equations for the reaction system $(\mathfrak{X}, R_\mathcal{B}, k)$ described above with $x(0) = x_0$. Then $\hat{x} = \lim_{t \to \infty} x(t)$ exists and equals the E-Projection of y to H_{x_0}.*

Proof. From Lemmas 1 and 2, the reaction network $(S, R_\mathcal{B})$ has no critical siphons. From Theorem 3.3 and 3.4, the result follows.

Example 5 (contd. from Example 1). For the three sided die, $S = \begin{pmatrix} 1 & 1 & 1 \\ 1 & 1 & 0 \end{pmatrix}$ where the first row represents s_1, the total number of times the die is rolled by the referee, and the second row represents s_2, the total number of times the die comes up either X_1 or X_2. The vector $\begin{pmatrix} 1 \\ -1 \\ 0 \end{pmatrix}$ is a basis for $\ker S$. The corresponding E-Projection reaction network is $X_1 \rightleftharpoons X_2$. If $y = (1/3, 1/3, 1/3)$ represents our prior belief about the die, i.e., that it is a fair die and all three outcomes are equally likely, then we can set all reaction rates to 1, and concentrations evolve according to the differential equations $\dot{x}_1 = -\dot{x}_2 = x_2 - x_1, \dot{x}_3 = 0$.

The derivative $dD(x(t)\|y)/dt = (x_1 - x_2)\log(x_2/x_1) \leq 0$, showing that the dynamics is moving the system towards the E-Projection. If $x(0) = (2, 20, 27)$ then the system reaches equilibrium at $x_1 = 11$, $x_2 = 11$, and $x_3 = 27$ which is the E-Projection of $(1/3, 1/3, 1/3)$ to $H_{x_0} = \{x \mid Sx = Sx_0\}$. This is also the most likely outcome corresponding to the observations $s_1 = 49$, $s_2 = 22$.

3.2   Reaction Networks Compute M-Projections

M-Projection Reaction Network Scheme: Fix positive integers $m, n \in \mathbb{Z}_{>0}$. Consider $x \in \mathbb{R}^n_{>0}$, and a matrix $A = (a_{ij})_{m \times n}$ of *nonnegative* integers. Let $\mathrm{Col}(A) = \{a_{.1}, a_{.2}, \ldots, a_{.n}\}$ denote the columns of A. Fix a map $y_A : \mathbb{R}^m \to \mathbb{R}^n_{>0}$ sending $\theta \longmapsto (c_1\theta^{a_{.1}}, c_2\theta^{a_{.2}}, \ldots, c_n\theta^{a_{.n}})$ where $c_1, c_2, \ldots, c_n \in \mathbb{R}_{>0}$. To compute the M-Projection $\hat{y}$ of x to $y_A(\mathbb{R}^m)$, we describe a reaction system as follows:

1. The set of species is $\Theta = \{\theta_1, \theta_2, \ldots, \theta_m\}$,
2. The set of reactions is $R_{\mathrm{Col}(A)} = \{0 \rightleftharpoons a_{.1}, 0 \rightleftharpoons a_{.2}, \ldots, 0 \rightleftharpoons a_{.n}\}$,
3. The reaction rates are chosen so that $\frac{k_{0 \to a_{.j}}}{k_{a_{.j} \to 0}} = \frac{x_j}{c_j}$ for $j = 1$ to n.

We obtain the following theorem.

Theorem 5. *Let $\theta(t)$ be a solution to the mass-action equations for the reaction system $(\Theta, R_\mathcal{B}, k)$ described above. Then*

1. $\dot{\theta} = A(x - y_A \circ \theta(t))$.
2. $\frac{\dot{\theta}_i}{\theta_i(t)} = -\frac{\partial D(x\|y_A(\theta))}{\partial \theta_i}\big|_{\theta=\theta(t)}$.
3. $\frac{dD(x\|y_A\circ\theta(t))}{dt} \leq 0$ *with equality iff* $A(x - y_A \circ \theta(t)) = 0$.
4. *The limit* $\hat{\theta} = \lim_{t\to\infty}\theta(t) \in \mathbb{R}^m_{\geq 0}$ *exists and* $y_A(\hat{\theta}) = \hat{y}$ *is the M-projection of* x *to* $y_A(\mathbb{R}^m)$.

Proof. (1) and (2) are easily verified by explicit calculation. (3) follows from (2) by the chain rule, since $\frac{dD(x\|y_A\circ\theta(t))}{dt} = \sum_{i=1}^{m} \frac{\partial D(x\|y_A(\theta))}{\partial \theta_i}\big|_{\theta(t)} \cdot \dot{\theta}_i$

$= -\sum_{i=1}^{m} \frac{1}{\theta_i(t)} \left(\frac{\partial D(x\|y_A(\theta))}{\partial \theta_i}\big|_{\theta(t)} \right)^2 \leq 0$. Equality implies $\frac{\dot{\theta}_i}{\theta_i(t)} = 0$ for all i, hence by (1) we have $\dot{\theta} = A(x - y_A \circ \theta(t)) = 0$. To see (4), note that the limit exists because D is decreasing in time, and bounded from below, and $\dot{D} = 0$ implies $\dot{\theta} = 0$. The limit point $\hat{\theta}$ is the M-projection because $A(x - y_A(\hat{\theta})) = 0$ implies $\hat{\theta}$ is the Birch point of x relative to $\log(y_A(\mathbb{R}^m))$, from Theorem 2.

Example 6 (contd. from Example 5). For the three sided die, the design matrix is $A = \begin{pmatrix} 2 & 1 & 0 \\ 0 & 1 & 2 \end{pmatrix}$, and $y_A(\theta_1, \theta_2) = (\theta_1^2, \theta_1\theta_2, \theta_2^2)$. The corresponding network is:

$$0 \underset{1}{\overset{x_1}{\rightleftharpoons}} 2\theta_1 \qquad\qquad 0 \underset{1}{\overset{x_2}{\rightleftharpoons}} \theta_1 + \theta_2 \qquad\qquad 0 \underset{1}{\overset{x_3}{\rightleftharpoons}} 2\theta_2$$

Suppose the die was rolled 49 times and the outcomes were $x_1 = 11$, $x_2 = 11$ and $x_3 = 27$ respectively. We get the differential equations $\dot{\theta}_1 = 2(11 - \theta_1^2) + (11 - \theta_1\theta_2)$, $\dot{\theta}_2 = 2(27 - \theta_2^2) + (11 - \theta_1\theta_2)$ The derivative $dD(x(t)\|y)/dt = -\left(\dot{\theta}_1^2/\theta_1 + \dot{\theta}_2^2/\theta_2 \right) \leq 0$ The system is stationary (but not detailed balanced) at $\hat{\theta}_1 = 3$ and $\hat{\theta}_2 = 5$. The E-Projection point is $(9, 15, 25)$, and $Ay_A(\hat{\theta}) = Ax$.

3.3   Reaction Networks Implement a Generalized EM Algorithm

EM Reaction Network Scheme: Fix positive integers $m, n \in \mathbb{Z}_{>0}$. Consider $x_0 \in \mathbb{R}^n_{>0}$ and an n-column matrix $\mathcal{S} = (s_{ij})$ of integers. Let $H_{x_0} = \{x \in \mathbb{R}^n_{\geq 0} \mid \mathcal{S}x = \mathcal{S}x_0\}$.

Fix a matrix $A = (a_{ij})_{m \times n}$ of *nonnegative* integers. Let $\mathrm{Col}(A) = \{a_{.1}, a_{.2}, \ldots, a_{.n}\}$ denote the columns of A. Fix a map $y_A : \mathbb{R}^m \to \mathbb{R}^n_{>0}$ sending $\theta \longmapsto (c_1\theta^{a_{.1}}, c_2\theta^{a_{.2}}, \ldots, c_n\theta^{a_{.n}})$ where $c_1, c_2, \ldots, c_n \in \mathbb{R}_{>0}$.

To compute $(\hat{x}, \hat{\theta})$ which is a local minimum of $D(x \| y_A(\theta))$ when $x \in H_{x_0}$, we first compute a basis $\mathcal{B} = \{b_1, b_2, \ldots, b_r\}$ to the sublattice $(\ker \mathcal{S}) \cap \mathbb{Z}^n$. Using this, we describe a reaction system $\mathrm{EM}(A, \mathcal{B})$:

1. The set of species is $S = \mathfrak{X} \cup \Theta$ where $\mathfrak{X} = \{X_1, X_2, \ldots, X_n\}$ and $\Theta = \{\theta_1, \theta_2, \ldots, \theta_m\}$,
2. The reactions with rates are

$$X_j \xrightarrow{k^+_{a_{.j}}} X_j + \sum_{i=1}^m a_{ij}\theta_i \text{ and } \sum_{i=1}^m a_{ij}\theta_i \xrightarrow{k^-_{a_{.j}}} 0 \qquad \text{for } j = 1 \text{ to } n$$

$$\left.\begin{array}{l} \displaystyle\sum_{j:b_{lj}>0} b_{lj}X_j + \sum_{i=1}^m d_{il}\theta_i \xrightarrow{k^+_l} \sum_{j:b_{lj}<0} -b_{lj}X_j + \sum_{i=1}^m d_{il}\theta_i \\[2em] \displaystyle\sum_{j:b_{lj}<0} -b_{lj}X_j + \sum_{i=1}^m e_{il}\theta_i \xrightarrow{k^-_l} \sum_{j:b_{lj}>0} b_{lj}X_j + \sum_{i=1}^m e_{il}\theta_i \end{array}\right\} \quad \text{for } l = 1 \text{ to } r$$

3. The reaction rates $k^+_{a_{.j}}$ and $k^-_{a_{.j}}$ are chosen so that $k^-_{a_{.j}} = c_j k^+_{a_{.j}}$ for $j = 1$ to n. A special choice is $k^+_{a_{.j}} = 1$ and $k^-_{a_{.j}} = c_j$. The reaction rates k^+_l, k^-_l and the stoichiometric coefficients d_{il}, e_{il} for the reactions are chosen so that

$$\frac{k^-_l}{k^+_l} \prod_{i=1}^m \theta_i^{e_{il}-d_{il}} = y(\theta)^{b_l} \text{ for } l = 1 \text{ to } r. \text{ A special choice is } k^-_l = y(1)^{b_l}, k^+_l =$$

$$1, e_{il} = \begin{cases} a_{i.} \cdot b_l \text{ if } a_{i.} \cdot b_l > 0 \\ 0 \text{ otherwise,} \end{cases} \text{ and } d_{il} = \begin{cases} -a_{i.} \cdot b_l \text{ if } a_{i.} \cdot b_l < 0 \\ 0 \text{ otherwise,} \end{cases} \text{ for } i = 1$$

to m, where $a_{i.} = (a_{i1}, a_{i2}, \ldots, a_{in})$ is the i'th row of A.

We obtain the following theorem.

Theorem 6. *Let $(x(t), \theta(t))$ be a solution to the mass-action equations for the reaction system $\mathrm{EM}(A, \mathcal{B})$ described above with initial condition $(x(0), \theta(0)) \in \mathbb{R}^{\mathfrak{X}}_{>0} \times \mathbb{R}^{\Theta}_{>0}$. Then*

1. $\frac{dD(x(t) \| y_A \circ \theta(t))}{dt} \leq 0$ *with equality iff both $x(t)$ is the E-Projection of $y_A \circ \theta(t)$ to H_{x_0} and $y_A \circ \theta(t)$ is the M-Projection of $x(t)$ to $y_A(\mathbb{R}^m)$.*
2. *The limit $(\hat{x}, \hat{\theta}) = \lim_{t \to \infty}(x(t), \theta(t))$ exists.*
3. $\nabla_\theta D(x \| y_A(\theta))|_{\hat{x}, \hat{\theta}} = 0$ *if $\hat{\theta} \in \mathbb{R}^{\Theta}_{>0}$.*
4. $\nabla_x D(x \| y_A(\theta))|_{\hat{x}, \hat{\theta}}$ *is perpendicular to the stoichiometric subspace $H_{R_\mathcal{B}}$.*

For the proof see Appendix A.

Example 7 (contd. from Example 6). For the three sided die, the design matrix is $A = \begin{pmatrix} 2 & 1 & 0 \\ 0 & 1 & 2 \end{pmatrix}$, $y_A(\theta_1, \theta_2) = (\theta_1^2, \theta_1\theta_2, \theta_2^2)$, $\mathcal{S} = \begin{pmatrix} 1 & 1 & 1 \\ 1 & 1 & 0 \end{pmatrix}$ with basis $\begin{pmatrix} 1 \\ -1 \\ 0 \end{pmatrix}$ for ker $\mathcal{S}$. The corresponding EM reaction network is:

$$X_1 \to X_1 + 2\theta_1 \quad 2\theta_1 \to 0 \qquad X_2 \to X_2 + \theta_1 + \theta_2 \quad \theta_1 + \theta_2 \to 0$$
$$X_3 \to X_3 + 2\theta_2 \quad 2\theta_2 \to 0 \quad X_1 + \theta_2 \to X_2 + \theta_2 \qquad X_2 + \theta_1 \to X_1 + \theta_1$$

With all reaction rates set to 1, the concentrations evolve according to:

$$\dot{\theta}_1 = 2(x_1 - \theta_1^2) + (x_2 - \theta_1\theta_2) \qquad \dot{\theta}_2 = 2(x_3 - \theta_2^2) + (x_2 - \theta_1\theta_2)$$
$$\dot{x}_1 = -\dot{x}_2 = \theta_1 x_2 - \theta_2 x_1 \qquad \dot{x}_3 = 0$$

The derivative $dD(x(t)\|y_A \circ \theta(t))/dt = (x_1 - x_2)\log(x_2/x_1) - \dot{\theta}_1^2/\theta_1 - \dot{\theta}_2^2/\theta_2 \leq 0$.

If $x(0) = (1, 23, 25)$ then irrespective of $\theta(0)$, the system reaches equilibrium at $\hat{\theta}_1 = 3$, $\hat{\theta}_2 = 5$, $\hat{x}_1 = 9$, $\hat{x}_2 = 15$, $\hat{x}_3 = 25$. The MLE $\hat{\theta} = \arg\sup_\theta \Pr[s_1, s_2 \mid \theta] = \arg\sup_\theta \sum_{i=0}^{24} \binom{49}{i,24-i,25}\theta_1^{24+i}\theta_2^{74-i}$ when maximized analytically through gradient descent converges to $\theta_1 = 0.42007781$ and $\theta_2 = 0.70013016$, which is proportional to $(3, 5)$ upto numerical error. Since the likelihood doesn't change when the parameters are multiplied by the same factor, in this example the EM CRN has indeed found the MLE. The following graph shows how concentrations change through time to approach the steady state.

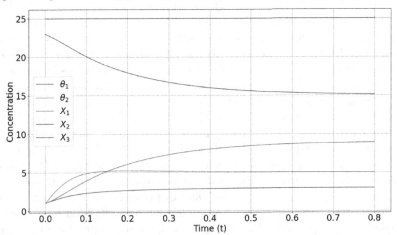

In the appendix, we present a few more examples that show the working of EM reaction networks. Example 8 shows that there can be multiple steady states. Example 9 shows that concentrations can tend to 0 asymptotically. Example 10 shows that our scheme can implement Boltzmann machine learning.

4   Related Work

There is a rich history of theoretical and empirical results showing that reaction networks can perform computations [8, 9, 11, 21, 30, 31, 34–37]. Typically these results take a known algorithm, and show how to implement it with chemical reaction networks. In contrast, we have obtained what appears to be a new algorithm within the broad class of generalized EM algorithms. Our algorithm is *natural* in the sense that it was suggested by the mathematical structure of reaction network dynamics itself, so that analysis of our scheme proceeds from insights about reaction network kinetics rather than from insights about the behavior of some existing classical algorithm.

Similarities in the mathematical structure of statistics, statistical mechanics, and information theory have been noticed and remarked upon several times [13, 38, 41, 44], and have led to multiple contributions [1, 6, 10, 26, 27, 42] with the goal of presenting some or all of these topics from "the point of view from which the subject appears in the greatest simplicity," to borrow a prescient quote from J. W. Gibbs. Our EM reaction network scheme employs a statistical mechanical system to minimize an information theoretic quantity in the service of solving a statistical problem. It is a concrete illustration of the connections between these three disciplines, and of the opportunities that lie at their intersection.

We now compare our scheme with three other schemes that show how to implement machine learning algorithms with reaction networks.

The belief propagation scheme of Napp and Adams [30] shows how reaction networks can implement sum-product algorithms from probabilistic graphical models to compute marginals of joint distributions. There is some formal similarity between the reaction networks of Napp and Adams, and our EM reaction network. In particular, their scheme also has two sets of species, "sum" and "product" species, and two subnetworks. In each subnetwork, one set of species changes in number, and the other set appears catalytically. We speculate that this may be because message passing algorithms are themselves a special case of the EM algorithm [24, 25], in which case possibly the Napp-Adams scheme may be related in some as-yet-undiscovered way to our EM scheme.

In a brilliant paper, Zechner et al. [43] show how to implement a Kalman filter with reaction networks, and implement this scheme *in vivo* in E. Coli. Their approach is to write down a dynamical system describing the filter, then change variables if required so the dynamical system falls within the class of systems that are implementable with CRNs, and finally obtain a DNA strand displacement implementation for the dynamical system. Their work shows that filters, being self-correcting, are robust, and can tolerate some amount of model mismatch. Further, such systems when implemented *in vitro* and *in vivo* work as advertised. This is very encouraging for the empirical prospects of our schemes.

There appears to be a certain degree of art involved in Zechner et al.'s setting to get the right change of variables which makes the dynamical system implementable by CRNs. In comparison, the information processing task directly informs our CRN architecture. Since Hidden Markov Models (HMMs) are special cases of exponential families as well, our EM reaction network can in principle be extended to implementations of the forward-backward algorithm for HMMs, which is closely related to the Kalman filter.

In [33], Poole et al. have shown how to implement a Boltzmann machine with reaction networks. The reaction network is able to do inference, but the Boltzmann machine training to learn weights has to be done *in silico*. In Example 10, we have shown how the EM algorithm can also be used to implement Boltzmann machines. There are pros and cons to our EM approach for this problem. The advantage is that Boltzmann machine training also happens *in vitro* and in an online manner. The disadvantage is that as described the EM implementation has not exploited the graphical structure of Boltzmann machines, and hence requires an exponentially large number of species for implementation. In contrast, the Poole et al. construction requires a linear number of species.

5 Discussion

5.1 Rate of Convergence

Speed is a key aspect of the analysis of any algorithm. We would like to be able to say that every mass-action trajectory $x(t)$ to a reaction network described by our scheme converges exponentially fast to the stationary state x^*, i.e. there exists $T > 0$ such that for all $\epsilon > 0$, for all $x(0) \in \mathbb{R}_{\geq 0}^S$, for all $\tau \geq T \log \frac{d(x(0), x^*)}{\epsilon}$ the distance $d(x(\tau), x^*) \leq \epsilon$. We would like to say this for the E-projection system, the M-projection system, and the EM system. The E-projection system has the nicest structure, being detailed balanced, and hence is the first candidate for showing such a result. Even here, the best available result appears to be slightly weaker: Desvillettes et al. [15] have shown that if a detailed balanced system has no boundary equilibria then for all $x(0) \in \mathbb{R}_{\geq 0}^S$, there exists $T > 0$ such that for all $\epsilon > 0$, for all $\tau \geq T \log \frac{d(x(0), x^*)}{\epsilon}$ the distance $d(x(\tau), x^*) \leq \epsilon$. The gap is that here T may depend on $x(0)$. We conjecture that exponential convergence should be true for the E-projection and M-projection systems. One could try to prove this via an entropy production inequality: there exists $\lambda > 0$ such that $-\dot{D}(t) \geq \lambda D(t) - D^*$ where D^* is the value of D at the stationary point.

5.2 A Proposal for How a Biological Cell Infers Its Environment

Biological cells are capable of identifying and responding to the environment from the information provided to them by transmembrane receptors. Given partial observations, biochemical reaction networks have to identify the most likely environment that could have caused these observations.

In this setting, the EM reaction network can behave like an online algorithm. As new information streams into the cell, the reaction network dynamics tracks the current state of the environment, making the necessary modifications to the concentrations of the θ and X species. In the biological context, the concentrations of the θ species may represent underlying environmental variables like threat level and food level that are not directly observable but whose estimation is key to survival, whereas the X species might represent the cell's "imagination" of the state of the outside world obtained by combining partial observations with the priors based on previously inferred θ values.

Perhaps our scheme can serve as a point of departure for the study of the actual schemes that cells employ. The schemes nature employs are likely to be far more sophisticated than our first attempts, having had the advantage of several billion years of evolution.

Appendix A

Proof (Proof of Theorem 2). (1) Fix $\alpha \in \mathbb{R}^n_{>0}$. We first prove uniqueness: suppose for contradiction that there are at least two points of intersection α_1^*, α_2^* of the polytope $(\alpha + V^\perp) \cap \mathbb{R}^n_{\geq 0}$ with the hypersurface e^V. Since $\alpha_1^*, \alpha_2^* \in e^V$, we have $\log \alpha_1^* - \log \alpha_2^* \in V$. Since $\alpha - \alpha_1^* \in V^\perp$, we have $(\alpha - \alpha_1^*) \cdot (\log \alpha_1^* - \log \alpha_2^*) = 0$. Then by the Pythagorean theorem, $D(\alpha \| \alpha_1^*) = D(\alpha \| \alpha_2^*) + D(\alpha_2^* \| \alpha_1^*)$ which implies $D(\alpha \| \alpha_1^*) \geq D(\alpha \| \alpha_2^*)$. By a symmetric argument, $D(\alpha \| \alpha_2^*) \geq D(\alpha \| \alpha_1^*)$ and we conclude $D(\alpha \| \alpha_2^*) = D(\alpha \| \alpha_1^*)$. In particular, $D(\alpha_2^* \| \alpha_1^*) = 0$ which implies $\alpha_1^* = \alpha_2^*$ by Note 1.

To prove that there exists at least one point of intersection, and to show (2), fix $\beta \in e^V$. We will show that the E-Projection α^* of β to $(\alpha + V^\perp) \cap \mathbb{R}^n_{\geq 0}$ belongs to e^V. This point α^* exists since $D(x \| \beta)$ is continuous, and hence attains its minimum over the compact set $(\alpha + V^\perp) \cap \mathbb{R}^n_{\geq 0}$. Further, because α^* is an infimum, we need that $\lim_{\lambda \to 0} \frac{df((1-\lambda)\alpha^* + \lambda\alpha)}{d\lambda} = 0$. That is, $(\alpha - \alpha^*) \log \frac{\alpha^*}{\beta} = 0$, which implies that $\alpha^* \in e^V$ since α could have been replaced by any other arbitrary point of $(\alpha + V^\perp) \cap \mathbb{R}^n_{>0}$.

(3) now follows because $\alpha^* \in e^V$ implies $D(\alpha \| \alpha^*) + D(\alpha^* \| \beta) = D(\alpha \| \beta)$ for all $\beta \in e^V$, hence α^* is the M-Projection of α to e^V.

Proof (Proof of Theorem 6).

(1) From the chain rule, $\dot{D}(x(t) \| y_A \circ \theta(t)) = (\nabla_x D \cdot \dot{x} + \nabla_\theta D \cdot \dot{\theta})|_{(x(t), \theta(t))}$. From Theorem 4, the first term is nonpositive with equality iff $x(t)$ is the E-Projection of $y(\theta(t))$ onto H_{x_0}. From Theorem 5, the second term is nonpositive with equality iff $y(\theta(t))$ is the M-Projection of $x(t)$ onto $y_A(\mathbb{R}^m)$. Hence $dD(x(t) \| y_A \circ \theta(t))/dt \leq 0$ with equality iff both $x(t)$ is the E-Projection of $y_A \circ \theta(t)$ to H_{x_0} and $y_A \circ \theta(t)$ is the M-Projection of $x(t)$ to $y_A(\mathbb{R}^m)$.
(2) Since $D(x(t) \| y_A \circ \theta(t))$ has a lower bound and $dD(x(t) \| y_A \circ \theta(t))/dt \leq 0$, eventually $dD(x(t) \| y_A \circ \theta(t))/dt = 0$ at which point, by the above argument, both the E-Projection and M-Projection subnetworks are stationary, so that $\dot{x} = 0$ and $\dot{\theta} = 0$. Hence the limit $(\hat{x}, \hat{\theta}) = \lim_{t \to \infty}(x(t), \theta(t))$ exists.
(3) follows since $\nabla_\theta D(x \| y_A(\theta))|_{\hat{x}, \hat{\theta}} = \dot{\theta}(t)/\theta(t)|_{\hat{x}, \hat{\theta}} = 0$ when $\hat{\theta} \in \mathbb{R}^\Theta_{>0}$.
(4) $\nabla_x D(x \| y_A(\theta))|_{\hat{x}, \hat{\theta}} = \log\left(\frac{\hat{x}}{y_A(\hat{\theta})}\right)$. By (1), the point $\hat{x}$ is the E-Projection of $y_A(\hat{\theta})$ to H_{x_0}. Hence by Theorem 2, the point $\hat{x}$ is the Birch point of x_0 relative to the affine space $\log y_A(\mathbb{R}^m)$, so that $(x - \hat{x}) \log\left(\frac{\hat{x}}{y_A(\hat{\theta})}\right) = 0$ for all $x \in H_{x_0}$. Hence the gradient $\nabla_x D(x \| y_A(\theta))|_{\hat{x}, \hat{\theta}}$ is perpendicular to H_{R_B}.

Example 8. Consider $A = \begin{pmatrix} 2 & 1 & 0 \\ 0 & 1 & 2 \end{pmatrix}$ and $\mathcal{S} = \begin{pmatrix} 1 & 0 & 1 \\ 1 & 1 & 1 \end{pmatrix}$. The vector $\begin{pmatrix} 1 \\ 0 \\ -1 \end{pmatrix}$ spans

$\ker \mathcal{S}$. The corresponding reaction network is

$$X_1 \to X_1 + 2\theta_1 \quad 2\theta_1 \to 0 \quad X_2 \to X_2 + \theta_1 + \theta_2 \qquad \theta_1 + \theta_2 \to 0$$
$$X_3 \to X_3 + 2\theta_2 \quad 2\theta_2 \to 0 \quad X_1 + 2\theta_2 \to X_3 + 2\theta_2 \quad X_3 + 2\theta_1 \to X_1 + 2\theta_1$$

Here the concentration of X_2 remains invariant with time. Let c be the initial concentration of X_2. If $c < 1/3$ then the system admits two stable equilibria and one unstable equilibrium. The points $(y_1, c, y_2, \sqrt{y_1}, \sqrt{y_2})$ and $(y_2, c, y_1, \sqrt{y_2}, \sqrt{y_1})$ are the stable equilibria where $y_1 = \frac{1-c}{2} + \frac{\sqrt{(1-3c)(1+c)}}{2}$ and $y_2 = \frac{1-c}{2} - \frac{\sqrt{(1-3c)(1+c)}}{2}$, and $\left(\frac{1-c}{2}, c, \frac{1-c}{2}, \sqrt{\frac{1}{3}}, \sqrt{\frac{1}{3}}\right)$ is the unstable equilibrium. On the other hand, if $c \geq 1/3$ then there is only one equilibrium point at $\left(\frac{1-c}{2}, c, \frac{1-c}{2}, \sqrt{\frac{1}{3}}, \sqrt{\frac{1}{3}}\right)$, and this point is stable.

Example 9. Consider $A = \begin{pmatrix} 2 & 1 & 0 \\ 0 & 1 & 2 \end{pmatrix}$ and $\mathcal{S} = \begin{pmatrix} 1 & -1 & 0 \\ 1 & 1 & 1 \end{pmatrix}$. The vector $\begin{pmatrix} 1 \\ 1 \\ -2 \end{pmatrix}$

spans $\ker \mathcal{S}$. The corresponding reaction network is

$$X_1 \to X_1 + 2\theta_1, \quad 2\theta_1 \to 0, \quad X_2 \to X_2 + \theta_1 + \theta_2, \quad X_1 + X_2 + 3\theta_2 \to 2X_3 + 3\theta_2$$
$$X_3 \to X_3 + 2\theta_2, \quad 2\theta_2 \to 0, \quad \theta_1 + \theta_2 \to 0, \qquad 2X_3 + 3\theta_1 \to X_1 + X_2 + 3\theta_1$$

Here the set $\{X_1, X_2, \theta_1\}$ is a critical siphon. If we start at the initial concentrations $x_1 = 0.05, x_2 = 0.05, x_3 = 0.9, \theta_1 = 0.1, \theta_2 = 1.0$, then the system converges to $x_1 = 0, x_2 = 0, x_3 = 1, \theta_1 = 0, \theta_2 = 1$, hence this system is not persistent. This provides one explanation for this data: all the outcomes were of type X_3. If instead we start at $\theta_1 = 0.5, \theta_2 = 1.0$ and the same x concentrations, then the system converges to $x_1 = x_2 = x_3 = 1/3, \theta_1 = \theta_2 = 1/\sqrt{c}$. This provides a different explanation for the same data: all three outcomes have occurred equally frequently.

Example 10. Boltzmann machines are a popular model in machine learning. Formally a Boltzmann machine is a graph $G = (V, E)$, each of whose nodes can be either 1 or 0. One associates to every configuration $s \in \{0,1\}^V$ of the Boltzmann machine an energy $E(s) = -\sum_i b_i s_i - \sum_{ij} w_{ij} s_i s_j$. The probability of the Boltzmann machine being in configuration s is given by the exponential family $P(s; b, w) \propto \exp(-E(s))$. Boltzmann machines can be used to do inference conditioned on partial observations, and learning of the maximum likelihood values of the parameters b_i, w_{ij} can be done by a stochastic gradient descent.

Our EM scheme can be used to implement the learning rule of arbitrary Boltzmann machines in chemistry. We illustrate the construction on the 3-node Boltzmann machine with $V = \{x_1, x_2, x_3\}$:

with biases b_1, b_2, b_3 and weights w_{12} and w_{23}. We will work with parameters $\theta_i = \exp(b_i)$ and $\theta_{ij} = \exp(w_{ij})$. The design matrix $A = (a_{ij})_{5 \times 8}$ is

$$
A = \begin{array}{c} \\ \theta_1 \\ \theta_2 \\ \theta_3 \\ \theta_{12} \\ \theta_{23} \end{array}
\begin{array}{c} X_{000}\ X_{001}\ X_{010}\ X_{011}\ X_{100}\ X_{101}\ X_{110}\ X_{111} \\
\left[\begin{array}{cccccccc}
0 & 0 & 0 & 0 & 1 & 1 & 1 & 1 \\
0 & 0 & 1 & 1 & 0 & 0 & 1 & 1 \\
0 & 1 & 0 & 1 & 0 & 1 & 0 & 1 \\
0 & 0 & 0 & 0 & 0 & 0 & 1 & 1 \\
0 & 0 & 0 & 1 & 0 & 0 & 0 & 1
\end{array} \right]
\end{array}
$$

and the corresponding exponential model $y_A : \mathbb{R}^5 \to \mathbb{R}^8_{>0}$ sends $\theta = (\theta_1, \theta_2, \theta_3, \theta_{12}, \theta_{23}) \longmapsto (\theta^{a_{.1}}, \theta^{a_{.2}}, \dots, \theta^{a_{.8}})$. If the node x_2 is hidden then the observation matrix S is

$$
S = \begin{array}{c} X_{000}\ X_{001}\ X_{010}\ X_{011}\ X_{100}\ X_{101}\ X_{110}\ X_{111} \\
\left[\begin{array}{cccccccc}
1 & 0 & 1 & 0 & 0 & 0 & 0 & 0 \\
0 & 1 & 0 & 1 & 0 & 0 & 0 & 0 \\
0 & 0 & 0 & 0 & 1 & 0 & 1 & 0 \\
0 & 0 & 0 & 0 & 0 & 1 & 0 & 1
\end{array} \right]
\end{array}
$$

Our EM scheme yields the reaction network

$$
\left. \begin{array}{l}
X_{ijk} \to X_{ijk} + i\theta_1 + j\theta_2 + k\theta_3 + ij\theta_{12} + jk\theta_{23}, \\
i\theta_1 + j\theta_2 + k\theta_3 + ij\theta_{12} + jk\theta_{23} \to 0
\end{array} \right\} \text{ for } i, j, k = 0, 1
$$

$$
\left. \begin{array}{l}
X_{i1k} \to X_{i0k} \\
X_{i0k} + \theta_2 + i\theta_{12} + k\theta_{23} \to X_{i1k} + \theta_2 + i\theta_{12} + k\theta_{23}
\end{array} \right\} \text{ for } i, k = 0, 1
$$

Suppose we observe a marginal distribution $(0.24, 0.04, 0.17, 0.55)$ on the visible nodes x_1, x_3. To solve for the maximum likelihood $\hat{\theta}$, we can initialize the system with $X_{000} = 0.24, X_{001} = 0.04, X_{010} = 0, X_{011} = 0, X_{100} = 0.17, X_{101} = 0.55, X_{110} = 0, X_{111} = 0$ and all θ's initialized to 1, the system reaches steady state at $\hat{\theta}_1 = 0.5176, \hat{\theta}_2 = 0.0018, \hat{\theta}_3 = 0.3881, \hat{\theta}_{12} = 0.8246, \hat{\theta}_{23} = 0.7969, \hat{X}_{000} = 0.2391, \hat{X}_{001} = 0.0389, \hat{X}_{010} = 0.0009, \hat{X}_{011} = 0.011, \hat{X}_{100} = 0.1695, \hat{X}_{101} = 0.5487, \hat{X}_{110} = 0.0005, \hat{X}_{111} = 0.0013$.

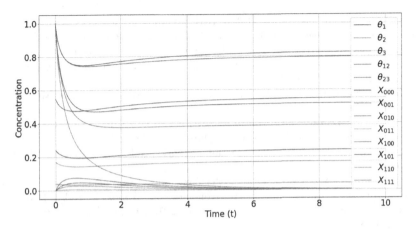

References

1. Amari, S.: Information Geometry and Its Applications. AMS, vol. 194. Springer, Tokyo (2016). https://doi.org/10.1007/978-4-431-55978-8
2. Andersen, E.B.: Sufficiency and exponential families for discrete sample spaces. J. Am. Stat. Assoc. **65**(331), 1248–1255 (1970)
3. Anderson, D.F., Craciun, G., Kurtz, T.G.: Product-form stationary distributions for deficiency zero chemical reaction networks. Bull. Math. Biol. **72**(8), 1947–1970 (2010)
4. Angeli, D., De Leenheer, P., Sontag, E.: A Petri net approach to persistence analysis in chemical reaction networks. In: Queinnec, I., Tarbouriech, S., Garcia, G., Niculescu, S.-I. (eds.) Biology and Control Theory: Current Challenges. LNCIS, vol. 357, pp. 181–216. Springer, Berlin / Heidelberg (2007). https://doi.org/10.1007/978-3-540-71988-5_9
5. Angeli, D., De Leenheer, P., Sontag, E.D.: A Petri net approach to the study of persistence in chemical reaction networks. Math. Biosci. **210**(2), 598–618 (2007)
6. Baez, J., Stay, M.: Algorithmic thermodynamics. Math. Struct. Comput. Sci. **22**(5), 771–787 (2012)
7. Birch, M.W.: Maximum likelihood in three-way contingency tables. J. R. Stat. Soc. Ser. B **25**, 220–233 (1963)
8. Buisman, H.J., ten Eikelder, H.M.M., Hilbers, P.A.J., Liekens, A.M.L., Liekens, A.M.L.: Computing algebraic functions with biochemical reaction networks. Artif. Life **15**(1), 5–19 (2009)
9. Cardelli, L., Kwiatkowska, M., Whitby, M.: Chemical reaction network designs for asynchronous logic circuits. Nat. Comput. **17**(1), 109–130 (2018)
10. Cencov, N.N.: Statistical Decision Rules and Optimal Inference. Translation of Mathematical Monographs, vol. 53. American Mathematical Society, Providence (2000)
11. Chen, H.-L., Doty, D., Soloveichik, D.: Deterministic function computation with chemical reaction networks. Nat. Comput. **13**(4), 517–534 (2014)
12. Csiszár, I., Matus, F.: Information projections revisited. IEEE Trans. Inf. Theory **49**(6), 1474–1490 (2003)
13. Csiszár, I., Shields, P.C.: Information theory and statistics: a tutorial. Found. Trends Commun. Inf. Theory **1**(4), 417–528 (2004)

14. Dempster, A.P., Laird, N.M., Rubin, D.B.: Maximum likelihood from incomplete data via the EM algorithm. J. R. Stat. Soc. Ser. B (Methodol.), 1–38 (1977)
15. Desvillettes, L., Fellner, K., Tang, B.Q.: Trend to equilibrium for reaction-diffusion systems arising from complex balanced chemical reaction networks. SIAM J. Math. Anal. **49**(4), 2666–2709 (2017)
16. Feinberg, M.: On chemical kinetics of a certain class. Arch. Ration. Mech. Anal. **46**, 1–41 (1972)
17. Feinberg, M.: Lectures on chemical reaction networks (1979). http://www.che.eng. ohio-state.edu/~FEINBERG/LecturesOnReactionNetworks/
18. Gopalkrishnan, M.: Catalysis in reaction networks. Bull. Math. Biol. **73**(12), 2962–2982 (2011)
19. Gopalkrishnan, M.: A scheme for molecular computation of maximum likelihood estimators for log-linear models. In: Rondelez, Y., Woods, D. (eds.) DNA 2016. LNCS, vol. 9818, pp. 3–18. Springer, Cham (2016). https://doi.org/10.1007/978-3-319-43994-5_1
20. Gopalkrishnan, M., Miller, E., Shiu, A.: A geometric approach to the global attractor conjecture. SIAM J. Appl. Dyn. Syst. **13**(2), 758–797 (2014)
21. Hjelmfelt, A., Weinberger, E.D., Ross, J.: Chemical implementation of neural networks and turing machines. Proc. Natl. Acad. Sci. **88**(24), 10983–10987 (1991)
22. Horn, F.J.M.: Necessary and sufficient conditions for complex balancing in chemical kinetics. Arch. Ration. Mech. Anal. **49**, 172–186 (1972)
23. Horn, F.J.M.: The dynamics of open reaction systems. In: Mathematical Aspects of Chemical and Biochemical Problems and Quantum Chemistry. Proceedings of Symposia in Applied Mathematics, vol. VIII, New York (1974)
24. Ikeda, S., Tanaka, T., Amari, S.: Information geometry of turbo and low-density parity-check codes. IEEE Trans. Inf. Theory **50**(6), 1097–1114 (2004)
25. Ikeda, S., Tanaka, T., Amari, S.: Stochastic reasoning, free energy, and information geometry. Neural Comput. **16**(9), 1779–1810 (2004)
26. Jaynes, E.T.: Information theory and statistical mechanics. Phys. Rev. **106**(4), 620 (1957)
27. MacKay, D.J.C.: Information Theory, Inference and Learning Algorithms. Cambridge University Press, Cambridge (2003)
28. McLachlan, G., Krishnan, T.: The EM Algorithm and Extensions, vol. 382. Wiley, Hoboken (2007)
29. Miller, E.: Theory and applications of lattice point methods for binomial ideals. In: Fløystad, G., Johnsen, T., Knutsen, A. (eds.) Combinatorial Aspects of Commutative Algebra and Algebraic Geometry, pp. 99–154. Springer, Heidelberg (2011). https://doi.org/10.1007/978-3-642-19492-4_8
30. Napp, N.E., Adams, R.P.: Message passing inference with chemical reaction networks. In: Advances in Neural Information Processing Systems, pp. 2247–2255 (2013)
31. Oishi, K., Klavins, E.: Biomolecular implementation of linear I/O systems. Syst. Biol. IET **5**(4), 252–260 (2011)
32. Pachter, L., Sturmfels, B.: Algebraic Statistics for Computational Biology, vol. 13. Cambridge University Press, Cambridge (2005)
33. Poole, W., et al.: Chemical Boltzmann machines. In: Brijder, R., Qian, L. (eds.) DNA 2017. LNCS, vol. 10467, pp. 210–231. Springer, Cham (2017). https://doi.org/10.1007/978-3-319-66799-7_14
34. Qian, L., Winfree, E.: Scaling up digital circuit computation with DNA strand displacement cascades. Science **332**(6034), 1196–1201 (2011)

35. Qian, L., Winfree, E., Bruck, J.: Neural network computation with DNA strand displacement cascades. Nature **475**(7356), 368–372 (2011)
36. Sarpeshkar, R.: Analog synthetic biology. Philos. Trans. R. Soc. A: Math. Phys. Eng. Sci. **372**(2012), 20130110 (2014)
37. Soloveichik, D., Cook, M., Winfree, E., Bruck, J.: Computation with finite stochastic chemical reaction networks. Nat. Comput. **7**(4), 615–633 (2008)
38. Tribus, M., McIrvine, E.C.: Energy and information. Sci. Am. **225**(3), 179–190 (1971)
39. Van Kampen, N.G.: Stochastic Processes in Physics and Chemistry, vol. 1. Elsevier, New York (1992)
40. Virinchi, M.V., Behera, A., Gopalkrishnan, M.: A stochastic molecular scheme for an artificial cell to infer its environment from partial observations. In: Brijder, R., Qian, L. (eds.) DNA 2017. LNCS, vol. 10467, pp. 82–97. Springer, Cham (2017). https://doi.org/10.1007/978-3-319-66799-7_6
41. Wainwright, M.J., Jordan, M.I.: Graphical models, exponential families, and variational inference. Found. Trends Mach. Learn. **1**(1–2), 1–305 (2008)
42. Wiener, N.: Cybernetics or Control and Communication in the Animal and the Machine, vol. 25. MIT Press, Cambridge (1961)
43. Zechner, C., Seelig, G., Rullan, M., Khammash, M.: Molecular circuits for dynamic noise filtering. Proc. Natl. Acad. Sci. **113**(17), 4729–4734 (2016)
44. Zellner, A.: Optimal information processing and Bayes's theorem. Am. Stat. **42**(4), 278–280 (1988)

Author Index

Printed in the United States
By Bookmasters